Kerala Christian Sainthood

Kerala Christian Sainthood

Collisions of Culture and Worldview in South India

CORINNE G. DEMPSEY

OXFORD
UNIVERSITY PRESS
2001

OXFORD
UNIVERSITY PRESS

Oxford   New York
Athens   Auckland   Bangkok   Bogotá   Buenos Aires   Calcutta
Cape Town   Chennai   Dar es Salaam   Delhi   Florence   Hong Kong   Istanbul
Karachi   Kuala Lumpur   Madrid   Melbourne   Mexico City   Mumbai
Nairobi   Paris   São Paulo   Shanghai   Singapore   Taipei   Tokyo   Toronto   Warsaw
and associated companies in
Berlin   Ibadan

Copyright © 2001 by Corinne G. Dempsey

Published by Oxford University Press, Inc.
198 Madison Avenue, New York, New York 10016

Oxford is a registered trademark of Oxford University Press

Library of Congress Cataloging-in-Publication Data

Dempsey, Corinne G.
Kerala Christian sainthood: collisions of culture and worldview in South India/
Corinne G. Dempsey.
p. cm.
Includes bibliographical references and index.
ISBN 0-19-513028-6
1. Christians—India—Kerala. 2. Christian saints—Cult—India—Kerala.
3. Alphonsa, Sister, 1910–1946—Cult—India—Kerala.
4. Christianity and other religions—Hinduism. 5. Hinduism—Relations—Christianity.
6. Kerala (India)—Religious life and customs. I. Title.
BR1156.K47D45   2000
275.4'83—dc21   99–15339

Portions of chapter 1 first appeared as "St. George the Indigenous Foreigner," *Religion* (1998) 28, 171–183.
Portions of chapter 3 appeared as "Rivalry, Reliance, and Resemblance: Siblings as Metaphor for
Hindu-Christian Relations in Kerala State," *Asian Folklore Studies* (1998) 57, 51–70.
Both are reprinted with permission.

1 3 5 7 9 8 6 4 2
Printed in the United States of America
on acid-free paper

Dedicated to the memory of
Sumathy "Amma" Menon
and
to my favorite superheroes,
Nick, Jack, and Sam

Acknowledgments

The following is a tribute to saints, yet it is testimony to the fact that they cannot exist without devotees. Pierre Delooz observes that "one is never a saint except *for other people*" (1983: 194), implying that perceptions of sainthood cannot be viewed simply as unfettered portrayals of lives lived but rather as mirrored reflections of a devotional community.[1] This book is thus indebted to the generous reflections of many, of countless pilgrims and ardent devotees of all ages and backgrounds, who shared with me their portraits of Kerala's saintly heroes and heroines.

Just as culturally and personally tailored omissions and emphases contribute to hagiography's "making" of a saint, an ethnographer's academically and individually molded perceptions are instrumental to the creation of her own product—which is, most classically and elusively speaking, "culture" (Wagner 1981).[2] I thus imagine my writing to be something like an ethnographer's "hagiography" (or, rather, a hagiography of hagiographies) of Kerala Christian saints and, by association, their devotees.[3]

In spite of this acknowledgment of the liberties ethnographers and hagiographers unavoidably take in conveying others' lives, I must also insist upon the possibility that the people about whom they write will get to have their "say" as well.[4] I agree with Sherry Ortner when she argues against recent claims that colonial or academic texts irretrievably erase or distort the images of those whom they claim to portray. Such assertions, according to Ortner, ultimately give these texts "far greater power than they have" (1995: 188). Her description of the text as existing somewhere between representation and fiction is particularly helpful:

> The anthropologist and the historian are charged with representing the lives of people who are living or once lived, and as we attempt to push these people into the molds of our texts, they push back. The final text is a product of our pushing and their pushing back, and no text, however dominant, lacks the traces of this counterforce. (189)

This book thus represents a textual tussle with Kerala Christian saints and with those who give life to their devotional cults. Although I do not pretend that this "hagiography" is immune from the inescapable entanglements of such a text, I do assume that some of the strands running through it—not necessarily in an identifiable or even systematic manner—will indeed belong to Kerala Christian saints and their devotees. It is my hope that, in spite of its many theoretical and interpretive meanderings, the following does justice, at some level, to the saints and those whose rich relationships with them have taught me so much.

This book would not exist if it were not for the generosity of the many stranger-devotees with whom I had fleeting encounters at shrines and temples or on buses and trains; yet neither would it have come about if it were not for the many people who were a steady and welcome part of our lives while in Kerala. Among the many friends who offered regular assistance to my work, I want to especially acknowledge the following: Dr. Alexander Raju kindly and abundantly gave of his time and expertise to offer in-depth histories and explanations of a variety of Kerala's saints. Many priests and seminarians at the St. Thomas Apostolic Seminary, particularly Bruno Golfier, Fr. Jacob Kattackal, Fr. Mathew Kizhakarunjanayil, and Br. (now Fr.) Thomas Njalliyil, enthusiastically shared their thoughts and experiences and welcomed me into their fine library. Fr. Kurian, the librarian at the Orthodox Syrian Seminary in Chungam, always gentle and intelligent in his suggestions, was indispensable in helping me dig up obscure and priceless pieces of information. Ann and Ancy were both wonderfully insightful and engaging when accompanying me to a long list of churches and temples and displayed poetic grace when helping me transcribe and translate after the fact. Fr. Abraham Vellamthadathil, a healthy skeptic, skillful debater, and loyal friend, was generously instrumental in keeping me well informed and on my toes at all times. To all the affectionate and endlessly supportive Sisters at the Bharananganam Clarist Convent, particularly Srs. Florence, Christie, and Thomasina, along with the Mother Superior and the Vice Postulator, I owe so very much.

My family and I are also grateful to the many whose friendships nurtured us as we worked to make a home for ourselves in Kerala. Among them I thank the Vellamthadathil family for opening their home and their hearts to us, Jyothi Mathew for her raucous sense of humor and keen sense of spirit, Thankamma and Babuji and family for being vigilant to our every need, and the rest of the wonderful and welcoming neighbors in our Vadavathur community on the hill (among them, James and Molly and family, Anish and family, Asha and family, and the Kurians). Thanks to Fr. Abraham CMI for kindly paving the way for our arrival, Prabha Rajan for being my singing friend and for her gourmet cooking, and Beena Xavier whose daily gentle presence added so much richness to our lives. The loving support and camaraderie of the extended Menon family including General P.M., Mrs. Sumathy, Sujata, Sharat, Anu, Govind, Latika, and Kutoos were no less than a godsend for us. We will never be able to thank them enough.

I am particularly indebted to two Keralite women, Sr. Florence OFC and Mrs. Sumathy "Amma" Menon, both of whom supported me intellectually as well as personally throughout my stay. They were, in essence, like mothers to me. For Sr. Florence, my hope is that this product will do some justice to the countless hours of lively conversation, sound advice, and fastidious networking she tirelessly generated on my behalf. For those who knew and loved Amma, her recent death (June 1999) leaves a considerable void. Her miraculous ability to ensure a smooth existence for us in Kerala was indeed astounding and will remain with us always. Because she made such an enormous impact on our lives, Nick and I used to "joke" that we would dedicate a temple to her when we returned to the United States. Since we are having difficulty with the temple, I dedicate, instead, this book to her memory.

Back in the United States, I thank my friends and Malayalam tutors Suneetha Menon, Krishna Kumar, and Shanti Menon for their jovial patience with my efforts to learn their language. I also extend my appreciation to The American Institute of Indian Studies for supporting our existence and my research while in India and to the NDEA Title VI Fellowship for South Asian Studies for funding after I returned home. Anitha Chrisanthus, Tom and Fran Dempsey, Wendy Doniger, Pat Garigliano, Krishna and Hari Kumar, Bill Preston, Fr. Thomas Mundukuzhy of the Syrian Orthodox church in Syracuse, and Whitney Sanford kindly pored over the manuscript at different points in its development, offering important editorial and interpretive insights. I also benefited from a good many conversations with friends and colleagues—more than I can recount. Most particularly I wish to thank Craig Burgdoff, Joyce Flueckiger, Bill Harman, Dennis Hudson, Patty Ingham, Barbara Johnson, Mary Keller, Vasudha Narayanan, Susan Nowak, Selva Raj, Paula Richman, and Paul Younger. To the editors at Oxford University Press, especially Cynthia Read and MaryBeth Branigan, I offer my appreciation for their expertise, diligence, and encouragement. Thanks also to the outside readers for their insightful suggestions for improving the manuscript and to Margaret Case, the copyeditor, for her superhuman attention to detail.

Most intimately involved in this project's earliest stages were Ann Grodzins Gold, Susan Snow Wadley, H. Daniel Smith, and Dianne Bazelle, each of whom has been indispensable to its outcome. Dianne Bazelle's vast store of knowledge of the Christian tradition and of female asceticism and her careful consideration of my writing have been invaluable. Dan Smith's long-term dedication to and keen appreciation for South Indian religious traditions as well as his meticulous eye for detail have supported me on numerous levels. Ann Gold's generous and poetic vision and style of ethnography have been an inspiration to me for a long time. Having her join the religion faculty at Syracuse University as I embarked on this project was far better than a dream come true. Sue Wadley's wise counsel, extraordinary support, and unflappable faith in my ability to pursue this eclectic project in spite of the obstacles are, in my eyes, legendary and will not be forgotten. Responsibility for the book's shortcomings, whether due to oversight or overuse of "hagiographic" license, is, of course, mine alone.

Finally, I wish to extend my heartfelt appreciation for my family's consistent good humor and support. I am indebted to my parents, Tom and Fran Dempsey, for continuously sustaining me with their love and an unlimited faith in what girls (and women) can achieve. As for my *sattvic* husband Nick D. Garigliano and sons Jack and Sam Dempsey Garigliano, I could not ask for better traveling companions, whether at home or across the world. Their grounded wisdom and playfulness are among my life's greatest gifts. This book is dedicated to them as well.

Contents

Note on Transliteration

All italicized Malayalam and Sanskrit terms have been transliterated according to the 1991 Library of Congress system for non-Roman scripts. Malayalam words in the plural form are given appropriate Malayalam endings (normally "*kaḷ*" for words not describing [male] people—in which case it is "*mar*") rather than an anglicized "s" ending. Exceptions to this apply to the pluralization of more commonly used Sanskrit words such as sannyasini or *bhakta* in which case I use the "s" ending. In cases where well-known Indian words and names are given slightly different pronunciations when spoken in Malayalam (e.g., *dharma* becomes *dharmma*, *karma* becomes *karmma*, Kālī becomes Kāḷi, yakṣī becomes yakṣī, etc.). I keep to the more conventionally used spelling and transliteration to avoid confusion. Quite commonly, as is sometimes reflected in the following, Malayalam usage changes words more significantly from their better-known forms, almost always by adding an "m" or an "am" to the end (for example, *āśram* or *āśrama* become *āśramam*, *prasād* or *prasāda* become *prasādam*, *śrāddha* becomes *śrāddham*, etc.).

Proper place names follow recent attempts to deanglicize (for example, Trivandrum is now Thiravananthapuram, Cochin is Kochi, and so on) when applicable. For consistency I have used place names as designated by a road map of Kerala designed and published by T. T. Maps and Publications, Ltd. in Madras, 1991. I have chosen to use this particular map because of its detail and because it honors the process of deanglicization. Names of villages too small to locate on the map are spelled following the same rules of transliteration used by the map publishers.

Kerala Christian Sainthood

Introduction

Kerala, God's Own Country

"Kerala, God's own country," a pithy promotion commonly invoked (and perhaps even invented) by the tourist industry, has become a kind of state motto, familiar to visitors and locals alike.[1] Although the saying is rendered for the most part in English to coax outsiders to the region, a sliver of tropical abundance in India's southwest, Malayalis also use it among themselves, thereby reflecting a shared pride in their unique corner of India and, often, distinguishing themselves from the rest of the subcontinent. Postcards that depict lush tropical greenery, inviting sandy beaches, breathtaking mountain vistas, and markets overflowing with local produce are often designed with these words emblazoned across their glossy fronts. The images demonstrate the many blessings showered upon a chosen people or, perhaps, a chosen visitor: "God's own." Whether local motto or touristic jingle, the saying points to what seems obvious to most—the undeniable richness, beauty, and bounty of Kerala.

Yet in the context of another kind of bounty found throughout Kerala, readily acknowledged by both inhabitants and casual visitors, the expression "God's own country" (or, perhaps, "the gods' own country"), opens up a completely different set of images. This other conspicuous abundance is Kerala's religious pluralism, marked by the variety of churches, temples, and mosques nestled throughout its tropical landscape. Moreover, beyond the many impressive Christian and Muslim edifices standing alongside those of the Hindu majority, we can see other reflections of this plurality. These take shape in the ecumenical—although mainly Christian and Hindu—heavenly characters who populate Kerala's terrain.[2] In fact, one need not even enter a church or temple to find them. Saints and deities, colorfully painted on trucks and auto-rickshaws, regularly vie for space on busy streets; others, encased in roadside shrines, receive visits from devotees who light candles or lamps, offer flowers, or slip coins into metal offering boxes. It is from this "other" abundance in Kerala that the seemingly self-evident (yet still applicable) motto "God's own country" raises more questions than answers: Whose God? Which God? And because many of the Christian figures appear to hail from foreign shores, one might even ask, which country?

3

Although images of tropical splendor do not disappear from the following pages, this book focuses on issues raised by this latter type of affluence—that of religious pluralities and associated worldviews and cultures. It is, as its title promises, a study of Christian sainthood in India's southwest; but a study of Kerala's saints raises questions no less unwieldy than those raised about the motto. The following account thus regularly winds its way far afield from the shrine itself, beyond dynamics between devotee and sacred figure, and finds that perceptions of and devotion to these saints implicate a larger, unavoidable world of "colliding" perspectives intrinsic to Kerala's pluralistic milieu.

The presupposition that saints—whether in Kerala or elsewhere—have much to tell us about their devotees and the society in which they live is not unlike the Malayalam proverb, *Kūṭṭāli nannengil kaṇṇāṭi vēṇḍa* (Whoever has a good companion does not need a mirror).[3] People with whom we choose to surround ourselves—heavenly or mundane—have a propensity for casting back to us aspects of our personalities, our views, and our lives. Yet the cults of saints do more than simply mirror devotees' lifestyles and beliefs; they provide forums whereby devotees potentially carve for themselves a place within their many worlds: religious, communal, and global. For those of us who look for insights into the complex weave of identities that make up Kerala Christian society, Kerala Christian sainthood providentially offers a kind of multidimensional looking glass as a guide.[4]

Beyond simply noting and analyzing the pluralisms that are reflected by Kerala Christian sainthood, the following discussion also addresses tensions if not exploitations (implied by sometimes violent "collisions") intrinsic to competing cultures and worldviews. To begin untangling and analyzing such complex and often troubled dynamics of power, I have found postcolonial theories of hybridization and ambivalence to be helpful.[5] Such theories are useful in that they complicate perceptions of absolute domination/subordination between groups while, at the same time, they avoid romantic Utopian notions of religious and cultural syncretism.[6] The idea that separate religious, political, or supernatural contingents can be at odds but interdependently bound is a theme that emerges repeatedly in the following chapters. The book, by unfolding various examples of ambivalent reciprocity, ultimately aims at discouraging the tendency to draw absolute contrasts or stark oppositions between coexisting groups and ideologies, and furthermore to question the extent to which dominance is as total as the dominant group would like us to believe.

A logical extension of these efforts to highlight hybrid traditions and question claims for absolute power is the suspicion that the following chapters will reveal concerning ideologies that promote rigid understandings of "authentic" religious, national, or communal identity. Such prescriptions for pure identities and origins, seen from the context of this book's view of Kerala Christian saints and their devotees, tend to emerge in the form of abstracted ideologies and from places of actual or desired power. Less absolutized, more earth-bound, and therefore more complicated constructions of identities and relations, on the other hand, often stem from shrine practice and locally based traditions.[7] Although the following discussion attempts to locate exceptions to this pattern, the bulk of my observations are consistent with those of theorists of religion who find that institutional religious prescriptions are of limited use for understanding complicated local categories and perceptions.[8] As such, this study represents a shift away from a more traditional emphasis on belief as a means of constructing the category "religion"—a scholarly perspective that, according to Asad (1993), is rife with post-Enlightenment bias.[9] By framing religion in terms of practice rather than precept, reflected identities and delineations can at times appear more "hybrid" and fluid, particularly in contrast to power-charged claims for purity and authenticity.

The ethnographic lens through which this book views saints—allowing this shift in emphasis from official to localized manifestations of religion—furthermore requires a nuanced reading of (and likewise brings down to earth) postcolonial theories arguing for the hybridity of colonial traditions and the disruption of absolute authority. Particularly in the first chapter, while discussing colonial and postcolonial dynamics of "foreign" saint cults, I argue that the ambivalent "hybrid" authority of these imports cannot be taken for granted when we consider different vantage points. Although they appear as an outside "imposition" to the untrained eye, a European saint or tradition may in fact act to bolster indigenous agendas to an extent that its foreignness is all but forgotten or becomes, for many people, irrelevant. I thus emphasize that the perception of the degree to which an imported saint cult (or ideology or piece of clothing) represents domestic and/or foreign agendas cannot be an abstracted "given" but is a matter of one's point of view and place in history.[10]

Kerala Christianity: A Brief Overview

As I discuss Kerala Christian sainthood, I commonly label churches, saints, and people according to denominational affiliation. These include Jacobite, Orthodox Syrian, Latin Catholic, Syrian Catholic (including Syro-Malabar and Syro-Malankara rites), and Mar Thomite. Because Kerala's jumble of Christian traditions reflects an intricate mix of internal and international schisms and alliances that have taken place over many centuries, an historical overview seems the most useful form of explanation. Historical details of Kerala's Christianities are not only irrepressible in their complexity but also form the basis for heated disputes, and so the following brief sketch attempts only to keep to the largely agreed-upon basics.[11]

According to a widely held Keralite tradition, the beginning of Christianity on the Malabar coast was marked by the arrival of St. Thomas the apostle in Kodungalur (Anglicized as Cranganore) in or around 52 C.E. After he carried out his mission of evangelization and church building, St. Thomas purportedly traveled east to Mylapore in Tamil Nadu, where he died a martyr's death in the year 72. Although there is no way to prove or disprove St. Thomas's mission to Kerala, there is ample historical evidence of an East Syrian Chaldean Christian community by at least the fourth century, which was reinforced by continuous waves of Syrian immigrants involved in Kerala's thriving spice trade. Few details are known about this early community except that it had become, by the time of the Portuguese arrival in the late fifteenth century, highly integrated into Hindu society. Through their practice of local customs, including a variety of ritual observances for upholding "caste" purity, it seems these early Christians enjoyed a high social status similar to that of the well-to-do Hindu Nair caste. Although these Kerala Christians kept their use of east Syrian liturgical language and canon law, they tended to model their churches after south Indian temples, and their priests bore a marked resemblance to Hindu sannyasis.

Roman Catholicism in Kerala, introduced by Portuguese missionaries, officially arrived in 1503 with the completion of the first Catholic church in Kochi, five years after the Portuguese explorer Vasco de Gama landed on the shores of northern Kerala. The Portuguese, like the Syrians before them, busied themselves in establishing trade routes between Kerala and their home country. But unlike their predecessors, they were fervently bent upon converting the masses to their (Roman Catholic) Christian tradition. As a result of their zealous mercantile and missionary efforts, the Portuguese eventually succeeded not only in blocking competing Arab trade routes but in cutting off Syrian Christian ecclesial ties to east Syria, as well. The flow of foreign bishops upon which Kerala's Syrian Christian community depended thus slowed to a standstill during much of the sixteenth century.

Animosity between Portuguese missionaries and Syrian Christians built up during the sixteenth century and came to a head during the latter part of the same century, after the deportation of Syrian bishop Mar Joseph and the death of the last remaining foreign bishop in Kerala, Mar Abraham. To add fuel to existing tensions, Alexis de Menezes—the Portuguese archbishop of Goa who was instrumental in cutting all ties with the Chaldean Church—was spurred on by the pope to investigate and punish doctrinal disobediences of the Kerala Christian community. Menezes thus put into motion a campaign to purge from the Malabar Church—once and for all—its troublesome Nestorian heresies and "Hindu" superstitions.[12] These efforts culminated in the 1599 Synod of Udiyamperur (known also as Diamper), which officially placed the Malabar Christians under the jurisdiction of the Portuguese Jesuits. The Goan Inquisition, begun in 1560, had also become a showcase of Portuguese muscle and cause for Indian (mainly Hindu and Muslim) anxiety up through the seventeenth century. Rather than securing a strengthened position, the Portuguese eventually shattered any possibility for cordial (or even functional) relations between themselves and the powerful Hindu courts and, as a result, their stronghold began to slip away by the seventeenth century.

In 1653, during a time when Portuguese power was at a particularly low ebb, roughly one-third of the St. Thomas Christian population, frustrated by increasingly harsh Portuguese impositions—as well as the continued lack of Syrian leadership—gathered in Mattanssery. Here they crowded around a large crucifix outside the main church, lit candles, and took an oath swearing that they would never again be under the sway of the foreign Jesuits.[13] Five months later, twelve priests ritually laid their hands on a Malayali archdeacon, Mar Thomas, installing him as the archbishop of the community. From this "Coonan Cross Oath" and appointment of indigenous leadership emerged a separate Christian community which, in 1665, recognized ecclesial leadership in Antioch, west Syria, upon the arrival of an Antiochan Jacobite bishop, Mar Gregorius, from Jerusalem.[14] As a result, Syrian Christians who currently claim an allegiance to the patriarch of Antioch refer to themselves as Jacobites ("Yakoba" in Syrian).

In 1911 a schism emerged within the Jacobite Church upon the dismissal of

Malayali bishop Vattasserril Mar Dionisius by the Antioch patriarch, Mar Abdulla. This was in answer to the Malayali bishop's insistence that the patriarch, while having the power to consecrate domestic bishops, need not have jurisdiction over Church properties in Kerala, as well. Roughly half of the dioceses eventually sided with the indigenous bishop, and formed the denomination presently known as Orthodox Syrian with its ecclesial head, the Katholicos, stationed permanently in Kerala.[15] In 1958, the Jacobites and Orthodox Syrians reunited under the Keralite Katholicos, only to go their separate ways once again shortly thereafter.

The Syrian Christians who maintained their allegiance to Rome (that is, descendants of those not present at the Coonan Cross event) are known as Syrian Catholics of the Syro-Malabar rite and constitute the largest contingent of Christians in Kerala today. The smallest rite within Kerala Catholicism, Syro-Malankara, presently numbers around 300,000 members. This latter group was formed when a portion of the Orthodox Syrian community united with the Roman Catholic Church in 1932 under the leadership of a Malayali bishop, Mar Ivanios. Both the Syro-Malabar and the Syro-Malankara communities are generically referred to as Syrian Catholic.

Latin-rite Catholics, comprising about 32 percent of the Kerala Catholic population, are largely made up of Hindu communities who were converted in the sixteenth and seventeenth centuries by Portuguese missionaries. Although a number of high-caste Hindus also converted to Catholicism, most Latin Catholics are from low-caste fishing communities. Syrian Christians, long established as a high-ranking "caste" within Kerala society by the time of the Portuguese arrival, did not normally intermarry with members of the Latin Catholic community. Similarly, because of their interest in upholding high social status, it made little sense to recruit new members into their tradition, particularly from the lower castes. As a result, a significant divide continues to lie between Latin- and Syrian-rite Catholics in terms of social and economic status as well as political clout.[16]

Aside from the Jacobites, Orthodox Syrians, and Roman Catholics, Kerala Christianity also includes a variety of Protestant traditions. Although the North American-inspired Pentecostal movement appears to be the fastest growing among them to date, the largest Protestant denominations currently in operation are of British origin. The two major branches of Anglican-influenced traditions include the Mar Thomites and the Church of South India (C.S.I.), which make up approximately 7 and 5 percent of the Kerala Christian population, respectively. The Mar Thomite tradition, established in 1889, is a result of an Anglican-influenced reform of the Jacobite tradition. Largely Protestant in their teaching and theology, Mar Thomites have maintained much of their Jacobite heritage, as is reflected in their liturgical practices and their self-proclaimed Syrian Christian identity.[17] C.S.I. stems from the unification of the Anglican dioceses in south India, the South India United Church (based on a 1908 coalition of Congregational and Presbyterian Churches), and the south Indian districts of the Methodist Church (of British origin). Although a large portion of C.S.I. members include low-caste converts, charter affiliates included approximately 6,000 parishioners from Jacobite and, later, Orthodox Syrian communities. Many who converted from the higher social classes (and lower classes as well) did so as a

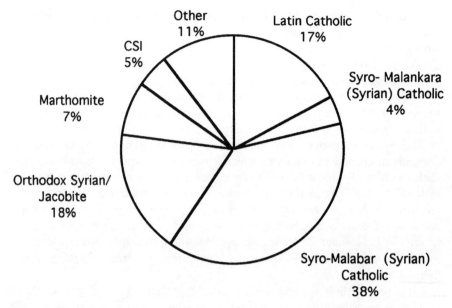

Figure 1. Distribution of denominations and rites among Kerala Christians. Statistics based on Bureau of Economics and Statistics, Government of Kerala (1969).

means of garnering political and economic support from the British through their missionary societies (see Figure 1).18

Because Keralite Protestants, like other Protestants worldwide, do not typically engage in saint devotion, this study focuses on the views and practices of Kerala's non-Protestant traditions—that is, Roman Catholic, Orthodox Syrian, and Jacobite. The Kottayam district where I carried out most of my research is primarily a Syrian Christian (and, more specifically, an Orthodox Syrian) stronghold, so Latin Catholic perceptions and devotional practices are not discussed as thoroughly as are Syrian Catholic, Orthodox, and Jacobite. Also included in the category "non-Protestant" are members of Hindu communities who, on the whole, are much more inclined than are Protestant Christians to take refuge in Christian saint traditions during times of duress or to celebrate the holy patrons of neighborhood churches during their annual festivals.

Sharing the Spotlight: St. George and Sr. Alphonsa

The following study of Kerala sainthood narrates tales of highly complex Christian diversity, of schisms within schisms; it also invokes an impressive array of heavenly figures. These include Keralite manifestations of some universally familiar saints such as Mary the mother of Jesus, St. Thomas the apostle, St. Sebastian, and St. Thérèse of Lisieux, as well as some less well-known native saints such as the Orthodox Syrian St. Gregorius and the Syrian Catholic Fr. Chavara. Two saints, however, play leading roles throughout this book, supported by other saints and Hindu deities who perform minor parts. They are Sr. Alphonsa of Bharananganam and St. George of seemingly everywhere, two saints who are dissimilar in almost every possible way and who deserve some introduction.

Sr. Alphonsa (1910–1946) was a Syrian Catholic Keralite nun from a Franciscan Clarist congregation who—although devotees regularly refer to her as "saint"—has yet to receive the official stamp of sainthood from the Vatican. In 1984 she was beatified and given the title "Blessed," just one rung below full canonization, and thus has moved relatively quickly through what is normally an agonizingly slow canonization process. Among the seven current Malayali candidates for sainthood, only Sr. Alphonsa and Fr. Chavara advanced to the position of "Blessed" in 1984. In late 1994, Bishop Thomas Kurialassery also joined the ranks of the "Blessed." The bishop's beatification did not capture the national attention that Alphonsa's and Chavara's had, however, as their ceremony a decade earlier was performed in Kerala by the pope himself. Sr. Alphonsa's claim to fame—beyond having inspired a papal visit to Kottayam—is her life of ascetic self-denial and suffering and, perhaps most importantly, her posthumous ability to bestow favors upon her devotees.

Hagiography depicts Kerala's St. George—in almost diametrical opposition to the rather passively construed Alphonsa—as a brave soldier who heroically saves a maiden and her village from the jaws (or deadly breath) of a fierce dragon. Commonly invoked by Keralites for protection against poisonous snakes (in menacing abundance in the tropics of India), the cult of St. George in southwest India appears to be nearly as old as Alphonsa's is young. Probably imported by Syrian merchants during the first few centuries of the common era, additional layers of St. George's cult were superimposed by the Portuguese during the sixteenth and seventeenth centuries and, again, with the arrival of the British. He was, and still is, the patron saint for both these western European nations.

In spite of the superficial differences between these two figures in terms of nationality and international scope, charism, gender, and cult history, each boasts a vast popular appeal largely unrivaled by other Kerala saints (see Figure 2). Among the group of seven Malayali Catholic saint candidates, Alphonsa's tomb shrine, with its constant stream of visiting pilgrims, is by far the busiest.[19] Compared to the many other "foreign" saint cults in Kerala, St. George's is remarkable in its universality; it is both undeniably popular and very diverse, attracting devotees from across a number of denominational and religious divides.[20] The dramatic differences between Sr. Alphonsa and St. George—in their lives as holy people and their relationships to Kerala's religious and cultural terrain—shape the following chapters.

The Foreign and the Foreigner: Juxtaposition and Misunderstanding

Given Christianity's firm standing upon south Indian soil, amid a predominantly Hindu culture, the following discussion of sainthood elicits comparisons of Hindu and Christian practices and beliefs. I also compare Kerala Christian saints and cultic practices with non-Indian—primarily European Catholic—saint traditions

Figure 2. As testimony to their popularity, Alphonsa and St. George are among the most visible of the Christian saints and Hindu deities whose names and images grace Kerala's buses, trucks, and autorickshaws.

in order to situate Kerala Christianity within a wider context and to help us to understand what might be uniquely Indian about Kerala Christian sainthood. At the same time, and perhaps more importantly, by exploring European cult practices and beliefs in the midst of a discussion about Keralite traditions, existing similarities between Christian and Hindu religious practices become all the more striking.

This kind of cross-cultural examination also allows for "critical questions from one society to another" to be brought into focus and addressed (Marcus and Fischer 1986: 117). As argued by Loring Danforth, such efforts should have the "jarring effect of making exotic worlds of cultural others appear more familiar, while simultaneously making the familiar world of the [ethnographer] more exotic. . . . It invites us in a provocative and occasionally unsettling way to subject ourselves

and our own discipline to the same critical gaze we so often cast only on others"
(1989: 8). For this reason, I have repeatedly chosen examples "closer to home"—
from European Catholic traditions—as a tool for contrasting Indian Christian
practices with those of non-Indian Christianity. Comparisons with other Asian
Christian traditions or those lived out in Latin America and the Caribbean would
not be as helpful in cutting across and therefore calling into question the deep-
seated biases implied by divisions such as East/West or third world/first world.[21]

The other non-Indian perceptions and practices infused into the following
discussion are my own. They represent, for the most part, personal responses to
Keralite opinion and practice while in the field. More often than not, the reactions
I relate represent types of ethnographic blunders: "mistakes" revealing misperceptions
about what is going on around me. Although I refer, at one point in the second
chapter, to the admission of a particular faux pas as one of my "true confessions,"
the reason for such disclosure extends beyond the implied contrition and desire for
absolution. The following chapters readily admit to these ethnographic
misunderstandings on the assumption that if the reader is, like me, a product of a
non-Indian or, simply, non-Kerala Christian culture, (s)he might have reacted in a
similar way, given the same series of events. My hope, therefore, is that the valuable
lessons I learned through making errors might be gleaned by reading about them.

An Inside Outsider: Methodology and Indian Christianity

Much of the data that have laid the foundation for this book emerge from an eleven-
month period—January through November, 1994—during which my husband, our
two sons, and I lived in Vadavathur, just outside the town of Kottayam, Kerala. Our
home was in a location central to the places I had chosen to carry out my research
and, by a stroke of luck, about a quarter mile down the road from a major Syrian
Catholic seminary (Syro-Malabar rite). Here, I was kindly allowed free access to the
library and found many opportunities to share ideas and opinions with several of the
professor-priests and seminarians who befriended us.

During the first part of our stay, I traveled regularly from our home to Alphonsa's
Bharananganam shrine (an hour-and-a-half windy bus ride into the foothills) to
speak with visiting pilgrims, local villager-devotees, and the Sisters in several of
the nearby Clarist convents. I was accompanied on these interviews, for the most
part, by Sr. Josephina, a retired Clarist nun in her middle sixties who, with seemingly
boundless energy and generosity, helped me in my efforts to learn shrine practice
and tradition and to approach visiting pilgrims for interviews.[22] She also did
everything she could to assist my understanding of Alphonsa the woman by
arranging interviews with dozens of people who knew her when she was alive.
During the latter half of my stay in Kerala, I occasionally conducted interviews by
myself or with the help of a lay woman assistant, to see whether Sr. Josephina's
presence was influencing participants' responses. Although her open and engaging
personality helped to make interviews, often with complete strangers, relatively
smooth and enjoyable, I wanted to know if people were perhaps giving me
information they felt would also please the Catholic nun standing by my side.

After trying a number of different interview strategies, I found that this was probably not the case.

Also during the latter half of our stay in Kerala, aside from occasional trips to Bharananganam, I concentrated on making visits to St. George shrines, most often at the Syro-Malabar Catholic church in Aruvithura near Bharananganam and the Orthodox Syrian church in Puthupally near Kottayam. During this period, I also made repeated visits to a number of churches and temples where a saint or god was rumored to have a special ecumenical relationship with the other tradition's neighboring god or saint.

In spite of my many trips to holy sites—to the geographical "sources" of my interests and topics of interview questions—I found that some of the best conversations about Kerala sainthood happened more spontaneously with strangers, traveling companions during long train or bus trips, or during lazy evening chats with neighbors and friends. Although devotees at churches and temples were almost without exception forthcoming and generous with their impressions and opinions, I was keenly aware of the fact that people visiting holy sites do not normally come prepared to be interviewed by a foreigner and her whirling tape recorder. The pilgrimage visit, often prompted by personal crisis or accumulated duress, is commonly not a social event at all; it is often carried out, particularly after one has arrived at the shrine, in relative isolation. Although large crowds may be present at a shrine, and devotees often arrive in pairs or even by noisy busloads, they usually come not to interact with others but to commune individually with the saint or deity, perform a vowed exchange, and then return home.[23]

Adding to the contrived and often awkward nature of many of my shrine encounters (mitigated greatly when accompanied by Sr. Josephina and her gentle magnetism), I was—unlike many "classical" anthropologists who build relationships and rapport within a particular community—an ethnographer-on-the-go. The fact that my work entailed spending time at nearly two dozen places of pilgrimage over the space of a year made an already uneasy endeavor all the more precarious. Furthermore, even at shrines where I eventually became a kind of "regular," the pilgrims were of course only sporadic visitors. As a result, I was nearly always and unavoidably a stranger to members of a perpetually migrating pilgrim population and, undoubtedly for many, a startling sight to chance upon.

Jill Dubisch, in her study of Tinos, a Greek pilgrimage shrine, writes about similar awkwardnesses with pilgrim interviewees and about her preference for collecting, when possible, information and opinions about shrine practice away from the shrine itself. She attributes her obstacles, in part, to the lack of established rapport between herself and pilgrims as well as to her own personality, which resists repeatedly striking up conversations with complete strangers.[24] Most frustrating, as Dubisch describes it, was her inability to coax anything but the most superficial responses from stranger-pilgrims:

> The major problem with my questions was that the pilgrims to whom I spoke did not necessarily "know" in the sense in which I wanted to know. "Why did you come here?" I would ask. "I have a vow" would be the reply. "Why is she on her knees?" I would ask the companion of a woman crawling up to the church. "She has a vow," the companion would say. Much of the time I would get no further than that and additional questions were met with a shrug. (1995: 104)

Aside from simply representing a different way of knowing among pilgrims (which Dubisch examines in convincing detail), these curt answers also seem to reflect a certain mistrust of outsiders. Dubisch identifies this skepticism as a part of a larger mistrust of an urban elite, triggered most recently by Greek journalists' recent interests in Tinos. Resenting patronizing outside perspectives that seem to suggest that they are "quaint" or "backward," and identifying Dubisch as part of the same class of elite, potential informants might understandably withhold information that could further incriminate them (1995: 104).

Although I was unmistakably an outsider at Kerala pilgrimage sites, and although repeated efforts to strike up conversations with strangers were sometimes awkward and wearing—perhaps for all concerned—Malayali pilgrims seemed rarely at a loss for words. Like Dubisch, I occasionally felt I was not getting what I considered to be "useful" information, but such instances seldom arose because of a lag in conversation. One reason for these differences in experience might be that the ideological gap between an educated urban elite and the minority who practice pilgrimage—seemingly significant in Greece—is not particularly relevant in Kerala. Though a small divide does exist, elite disdain for pilgrimage in Kerala seems nearly negligible, as is peer pressure among young people to abstain from such practices. Except among Protestant denominations (particularly Pentecostals), pilgrimage, like many other church or temple activities, is a generally accepted, routine part of religious expression.[25] Thus pilgrims' fears that I might portray them as quaint or backward seemed rarely to come into play during our interactions.

There were several occasions, however—not at the shrine, as it happens—when Keralite elites intimated their own concerns, however obliquely, that my work as an American ethnographer might add fodder to existing orientalist ideologies that aim to belittle or romanticize Indian society. This legitimate concern I did not and still do not take lightly. As a North American, I can never totally extricate myself from colonizing powers, and thus I have tried—both in the field and while writing—to be vigilant of tendencies intrinsic to my cultural heritage. Although I address the matter at different points throughout the book, I discuss it in greatest detail in the second chapter.[26] Here I come to the conclusion that the misunderstandings and mistakes of self-aware ethnographers, although problematic, are much less troublesome than what seems to be our other alternative: simply packing up and leaving the "field." The latter option may not only be impossible for many—as "home" and "field" are not necessarily clear-cut or separate—but for those for whom it would be possible, we run a greater risk of further perpetuating ignorance rather than curtailing it.[27]

Aside from conversations with people who voiced valid concerns about my status as a North American foreigner, I repeatedly found—again in contrast to Dubisch's experience—that my outsider status acted as a kind of welcome icebreaker. In places where tourists rarely tread, finding a foreigner in one's midst, one who can even converse (albeit imperfectly) in Malayalam, was often sufficient—I found to my relief—to start a conversation. Perhaps helping things along even further, particularly in Bharananganam, was the fact that I shared the same religious background as many of the people with whom I spoke. Feeling that this factor would somehow help to ease some people's reservations about talking to me, Sr. Josephina made a rather conspicuous effort, during a number of conversations with pilgrims and convent members, to contribute the fact that my background was Roman Catholic. She would often supplement this information by adding that, even though I was American, my grandparents were from Ireland, "perhaps the most Catholic of all European countries." The extent to which this information actually made people feel freer to speak with me about Alphonsa is, of course, uncertain. But if it helped to bridge a gap between myself and Sr. Josephina, it is possible that it had a similar effect on others, as well.

My choice to focus on religious practice and local tales rather than texts, making it necessary that I go to India and struggle with the various complications of the ethnographic process, has indeed something to do, I believe, with my religious background. Raised as I was with such traditions as lighting votive candles, giving up candy for Lent, walking through the stations of the cross, and reciting the rosary for deceased relatives, for me the meaning of religion has often weighed much more heavily upon practice than upon the written word. Because I am aligning myself with a discipline that has for so long associated religion with the literary and the literate, however, I feel the need to justify what seems to me a natural perspective.[28]

By discussing and theorizing such religious material as iconography, shrine and festival practice, oral mythology, and personal opinion, I aim, as Lawrence Sullivan puts it, to "give fair hearing and sight to the imaginal expressions that live well outside the singular expression of writing" (1990: 42). This approach is not meant to question the value of written religious texts for the study of religion; rather, it comes from a desire, as Sullivan views it, "to find or bring an end to an overly literary approach to the religious condition, because religious life has thrived without the written word" (58). Sullivan furthermore argues that it is precisely the field of religious studies that impels us to break with the "tyranny of text" embedded in Enlightenment cultural studies (45). He thus presents a number of studies that have recognized nontextual activities and phenomena (such as canoe making, shadows, sound, and weeping, to name a few) as a means by which certain cultures negotiate and understand the cosmos. Yet, among the litany of scholars whom he lists as successfully upholding the richness of this possibility, the reader finds, for the most part, anthropologists, folklorists, and ethnomusicologists. Although South Asianists within the field of history of religions currently show an increased interest in nontextual religious expressions, scholars who study nontextual or local manifestations of modern Catholicism and Eastern Orthodoxy are, by and large, anthropologists and folklorists.[29] It appears, therefore, that in spite of the wealth of evidence which supports the idea that religious imaginings can and should be accessed through nontextual articulations, some areas within the field of history of religions have been less than quick to take this up.[30]

The following study of primarily nontextual religious expressions gathered first-hand in the "field" thus gladly accepts Sullivan's proposition. Furthermore, in moving my emphasis from sacred text to lived practice I reap the benefits of a consequent shift in focus: away from the study of religion in relative isolation and toward one that must, particularly in the case of Kerala, take into account a complicated and richly pluralistic context. In any case, it is an approach to religion with which I feel very much "at home" in spite of its challenges and, hopefully, one that increasingly will find—especially in the study of modern Christianity—more of a home in the field of religious studies.

Chapter Road Map

The first chapter, "Me, St. George, and Other Foreigners," views sainthood as a means for forging and negotiating national identity among Kerala Christians. Keralite self-understandings, which form and are formed by this process, are often expressed more generally as part of an Indian "Easternness," in opposition to ideas of European or North American "Westernness."[31] I argue, however, that constructions of Kerala Christian identity, rather than representing a true polarization of East versus West, often rely upon an adoption and reinterpretation of non-Indian ideologies and traditions. It is through saint cults, among other things, that these superimpositions often find expression. By taking into account opinions and stories reflecting the "hybrid" traditions of St. George and Sr. Alphonsa, I offer two very different examples of how Keralites have reconfigured cultural and religious meanings in a way that reflects international identity, both in the past and today. It also becomes clear that in this process through which devotees borrow and renew foreign (colonial) systems, the relationship between colonizer and colonized is one of neither diametric opposition nor total domination/subordination. Through this creative process of reappropriation and hybridization, Keralite Christians have fashioned for themselves not only a certain distance from colonial and postcolonial powers but also some leverage in mitigating the foreigners' effect upon domestic culture.

Changing the register slightly from the first chapter's study of sainthood and the part it plays in carving national identities, the second chapter, "Siblings and Other Metaphors for Hindu-Christian Relations," explores the emblematic nature of sacred figures for local village communities. More specifically, it shows local saint traditions and other village-based expressions—both Christian and Hindu—as reflecting and sustaining intravillage communal relations within Kottayam district. Some of the most striking expressions of these relationships emerge through local stories and festival activities that assign the role of siblings—often ambivalently rivalrous yet interdependent—to village church saints and temple deities. I argue that family ties among sacred figures provide a fitting metaphor for Hindu-Christian communal relations in a context where the two communities have indeed shared the same roof—and with it, uncanny family resemblances—for nearly two thousand years.

Chapter 2 also explores perceptions of communal relations expressed by religious specialists and politicians, which project a very different set of circumstances. In contrast to local portrayals of sibling rivalry and reliance, these perspectives argue either for the obliteration of difference between Christianity and Hinduism or else for the irretrievable separateness of the two traditions. I argue that such portrayals, in opposition yet simultaneously static and unambiguous, effectively deny individuals and their communities their particular and complex histories. The often unanticipated and underestimated ability of local groups to challenge such totalizing representations is worthy of a closer look.

The third chapter, "Calamity Management and the Role of Sacred Ambivalence," explores relations between individual devotees and sacred figures, and highlights the notion of ambivalence once again, but from a very different angle. I focus on the cults of St. George and Sr. Alphonsa, and explore instances in which devotees view saintly action upon human soil as not entirely benevolent or even welcome. In contrast to most official hagiographical tales, which portray these saints—indeed all saints—as heavenly figures showering blessings from above, local accounts and practices often tell a very different story. Gaining access to saintly powers—not given unconditionally—through various types of material exchange, devotees potentially run the risk of receiving punishment as well as blessing. The abundance of similar portrayals of ambivalent sacred power in local European saint traditions and Hindu traditions, among others, suggests that such understandings of capricious sacred powers are not isolated. The chapter concludes by arguing for and providing some speculation about the resilience of these instances of materially accessible sacred ambivalence—a resilience that effectively ignores authoritatively prescribed disembodied and dichotomized powers of good or evil.

In the fourth chapter, entitled "The Life and Cult of Sr. Alphonsa: A Celebration of Complexity and Paradox," I discuss interreligious patterns for the construction of female sacrality, the wrestling of a particular woman with these preestablished categories, and the blossoming of a cult after her death. Whereas the first three chapters explore Kerala's saint cults as means for understanding the formation and expression of different kinds of identities and relationships, the final chapter talks more directly about an (almost) saint herself, revisiting themes and theories from earlier chapters in the process.

Exploration of some of the more well-known themes running through this Indian-Christian woman's hagiographical accounts provides a framework from which to compare once again Christian and Hindu perspectives—this time in regard to female asceticism. I argue, as I do in Chapter 2 (when comparing religious festival traditions cross-culturally and interreligiously) and in Chapter 3 (when comparing types of sacred ambivalence), that there is much in common between Christian and Hindu beliefs and practices. Some important differences between the two traditions emerge, as well, particularly when we consider the value each places upon female ascetic renunciation. Whereas Catholic Christianity commonly portrays the female renunciant—one who forswears material wealth as well as marriage and family—as the pinnacle of holiness for women, for some traditions within Hinduism, particularly Brahmanical Hinduism, this ascetic path is not encouraged for women.

This final chapter also makes use of theories of hybridity introduced in Chapter 1 to show that when a subordinate culture borrows from a dominant culture's traditions, a kind of hybridization emerges that sometimes helps to undercut the full force of domination. Here, I portray Alphonsa as following normative religious (that is, patriarchal) expectations for female behavior; by fulfilling them, she manages to transcend them, as well. Her suffering and complete self-effacement produce supernatural powers, along with the confidence to steer her relationships with God and male clergy, and though she is not free from the constraints of patriarchal orthodoxy, she is not completely bound by them, either.

By exploring the ways in which sainthood is composed, understood, and revered by nations, communities, and individuals, the scope of the following shifts from broad vistas to intimate encounters. These fluctuations in perspective produce a view which, during its more panoramic moments, allows for comparisons and connections between Kerala Christian and non-Christian (or non-Indian) traditions. During closer encounters, however, it focuses on the unique particularities of Kerala's saints and devotional practices.[32] As the title of the fourth chapter suggests, the following is indeed meant to be a celebration of the complexity and richness of the multifaceted phenomenon of sainthood, a medium through which an abundance of issues finds expression. As already mentioned, I understand my occupation as guide for this exploration of sainthood's many contours to include a further complication of issues through the occasional, self-conscious emergence of my own voice. I therefore aim to promote a certain mindfulness (for myself as well as for the reader) of the guide's responsibilities: setting the itinerary for travel destinations as well as providing the accompanying narrative. In so doing, I hope to bring attention to the ways in which the choices and perspectives inherent in these roles doubtlessly shape one's impressions of the saintly landscape.

And so we begin the first chapter with a trip—literally—through winding mountainous terrain in God's own country.

1

Me, St. George, and
Other Foreigners

Soon after I arrived in Kerala, during a period when I was making frequent visits to Alphonsa's shrine in Bharananganam, a few of the Clarist nuns decided that I should take a trip up into the nearby mountain range to meet a gentleman they thought would be of great help to me in my research.[1] I was told that Fr. Francis Acharya, an eighty-year-old Belgian priest, had spent most of his life and virtually all his career in Kerala as director of a Roman Catholic hermitage he founded in the 1950s.[2] Among other things, I learned how this hermitage, with its Catholic monks dressed as sannyasis, worked to integrate the spirituality of a Christian monastery with that of a Keralite ashram. Because my interests were very much like his, and because he was respected in Bharananganam as a wise and spiritually advanced man, I was enthusiastically urged to go, and I agreed.

The next day, Sr. Josephina, a newly retired nun who was my designated research collaborator, Sr. Anita, a younger nun who knew many of the monks personally, and I set off. From the bus stop opposite the Clarist convent we embarked on a journey along winding mountain roads high up into Kerala's tea country. After about two hours, the bus dropped us off at the edge of a dirt road where we hiked further into the mountains and eventually came to the beautifully maintained gardens of the monastery. Soon after we reached the main compound, we learned that Fr. Acharya was in his study but was hesitant to receive guests as his health, at the time, was poor. Not one to take "no" for an answer, Sr. Anita was eventually able to coax our way beyond the monks guarding his door and into his study, where the Belgian begrudgingly but politely received us. Hoping to ingratiate myself to him immediately, I quickly told him, by way of introduction, that my interests and his were actually quite similar. I had come to Kerala to learn more about the influences of Hinduism on Indian Christianity and, more particularly, on the cult of Alphonsa and other saints.

Rather than forging a comfortable alliance between us, however, my hasty introduction gave the Father an opportunity—also without skipping a beat—to wax eloquent on the atrocities of the "complete de-Indianization" of Christianity in Kerala, thanks to the Portuguese. He explained that, in many cases, the decimation wrought by these invaders was total: they purportedly burned to the ground ancient churches (which, unfortunately, were built from wood, like Hindu temples) and demolished religious paraphernalia such as vestments and other liturgical items. After sharply delivering this historical diatribe, the Father softened slightly by offering a parting challenge to my work on Alphonsa's cult: "I wish you lots of luck finding anything Indian about her devotion—it's been entirely Romanized." Not wanting to send me away empty handed, he allowed me, as an afterthought, to borrow an article written by a Brahman journalist about Alphonsa. The article argued that Alphonsa's family name hinted at an ancient Brahmanical heritage—which Fr. Acharya found surprising and interesting. Again, he voiced his disappointment that such allusions to Indianness are so often thoughtlessly swept aside by the authorities.

During our short meeting with Fr. Acharya and what sounded to me like an angry tirade against the destructive imperialist influences of the West upon Eastern Christianity, I stole glances at the two women who had accompanied me—nuns in Western habit—and nervously wondered what they were thinking. As soon as we were back out in the hallway, while I was scrambling to collect my thoughts, Sr. Josephina turned to me and announced in hushed tones, "he is a very holy man." Feeling embarrassed about what I felt to be insults to their Roman tradition implied by his words (juxtaposed with the contrast between his monastery full of ochre-robed men and these Clarist Sisters in their Roman habit), I responded that he seemed a bit bitter, didn't she think?[3] With a laugh and a shrug, she admitted I might have a point (see Figure 3).

Figure 3. A Malayali nun in Clarist habit, Sr. Alphonsa's statue, prominently displayed in front of St. Mary's Forane Church, Bharananganam, during her annual feast-day celebration.

This first chapter involves, in part, my rising to meet Fr. Acharya's challenge. I will leave until later a more detailed discussion of the ways Hindu culture has left, and continues to leave, an indelible mark on Kerala's Christian traditions. There is ample evidence to suggest that many of Alphonsa's cult practices and beliefs reflect a larger Hindu context. Presently my focus is to examine critically—with the help of Sr. Alphonsa, St. George, and others—the perception that Indian Christianity is or even could be "entirely Romanized" (or, more recently, Anglicized or Americanized) at either the popular or institutional levels.

I am suspicious of claims for the all-pervasiveness of foreign colonial domination over domestic traditions thanks, in part, to recent writings of postcolonial theorists. Their work has been sharply critical of an earlier brand of postcolonial theory, typified by Edward Said's *Orientalism* (1978), which largely overlooks the forces of anti-imperialist literature, resistance, and nationalist movements arising from colonized countries.[4] In keeping with this more recent theorizing, Said's *Culture and Imperialism* (1993) departs slightly but significantly from his earlier position. In this later work, Said draws our attention to the enduring presence of a tradition of writing—coming largely from the European and North American left—which is both anti-imperialist in acknowledging the atrocities colonizers inflict upon their subjects, and imperialist in not taking into account the ability of the colonized to critique and subvert colonial rule. Said believes resistance strategies staged by the colonized, wrongly ignored by these authors (a criticism rightly leveled at Said himself in his earlier writings), have something vital to say about native agency, which is capable of keeping total imperialist dominance at bay. Said argues that these widely held—and often well-meaning—beliefs that imperialism results in the absolute destruction of indigenous culture are founded on racist assumptions. Fueling these assumptions is the idea that "outlying regions of the world have no life, history, or culture to speak of, no independence or integrity worth representing without the West. And when there is something to be described it is . . . unutterably corrupt, degenerate, irredeemable" (1993: xix).

In the mountain monastery scene, both foreigners seem guilty of this mixed imperialist/anti-imperialist stance to which Said refers. During his tirade against total colonial imposition, the Belgian priest glosses over the possibility of Indian resilience and resistance against Portuguese traditions. As for myself, I took his argument seriously enough to feel apologetic toward my Indian friends. My apologetic mode was not so much for what had been done to them by foreign powers (this, I felt, we could all agree upon) but for what I felt to be the hurtful way the priest elaborated upon the pathetic state—the "de-Indianization"—of the tradition they hold so dear.

Sr. Josephina's shrug and laugh, acting at the time to ease my presumptuous embarrassment, can now be seen as a suitable response of detachment in the face of two foreigners' imperialist misunderstandings of her religious culture. These gestures of detached levity have therefore become for me a serious invitation to view Sr. Josephina's tradition as not merely a passive receptacle for foreign imposition, and thus the impossibility of its being "entirely de-Indianized."

I approach this matter in two segments, through a discussion of distinct but related sets of issues. Section 1 explores aspects of identity formation among Syrian

Christians, showing how it has been based, at times, upon popular constructions or stereotypes of a Western "other."[5] More specifically, the cult of Sr. Alphonsa—particularly as understood by members of the Syrian Catholic hierarchy—and the tradition of St. Thomas as founder of Christianity on the Malabar coast reveal a process of self-identification among Syrian Catholics that depends, in part, on a reversal of or differentiation from things "Western." The cults of Sr. Alphonsa and other Malayali saint-candidates furthermore reflect complications arising from keeping a certain distance from and opposition to the "West" by a community of people who identify themselves as Catholic Christian. In other words, although Kerala's Syrian Catholics repeatedly and proudly express stark distinctions between East (us) and West (them), they nonetheless often look westward for institutional guidance and approval, epitomized most strikingly by the Vatican canonization process.

Section 2 of this chapter recounts tales of Kerala's St. George cult from the perspective of its precolonial, colonial, and postcolonial history along the Malabar coast. Introduced by the Syrians, reintroduced by the Portuguese and the British, and presently up for debate in the Vatican, the St. George tradition in Kerala offers a multilayered view into the complex and often tangled dynamic between foreign authority and domestic culture.

1. Sr. Alphonsa: Indian/Roman Catholic Saint and Champion of Syrian Christian Self-Identification

Colonial Constructions and Indigenous Interpretations

That Kerala Christian identity formation relies to some degree on stereotypes of a Western "other" is a phenomenon by no means unique to Kerala. The idea that constructions of an "other" work to build and confirm self-perceptions has been discussed at length by postcolonial theorists, usually (until very recently) in reference to American or European identity, to the extent that it is based on narrow perceptions of non-European peoples and cultures. Based in part upon Derridean ideas of identity and difference, Edward Said's *Orientalism* insists that the formation of stereotypical caricatures of others, ultimately says more about the culture creating them than the culture being described (1978: 22).

It is apparent that these Kerala Christian fabrications of a Western "other" do not originate entirely in Kerala, however, but rather are a part of an East/West dichotomy invented by and inherited from colonial, primarily foreign, discourse. Keralite constructions of the West are, therefore, not merely a one-way reflection, as Said, in *Orientalism*, would have it. Instead, they bring back into focus aspects of European and American imperialist rhetoric, while at the same time they portray a specifically Kerala Christian view of their own culture. This domestic self-understanding is therefore the result not simply of borrowing European colonial constructions but rather of Keralite elaborations and reinterpretations of the same.

Said describes these colonial binary constructions in their "classical" manifestations—that is, from a European or American viewpoint—as being so lasting and consistent that they operate to form an elaborately self-contained network. This rigidly structured system works, in turn, to build a hegemonic discourse whose strength ultimately allows for "a Western style for dominating, restructuring and having authority over the Orient" (1978: 3). Aijaz Ahmad, writing from a Marxist perspective, finds fault with Said's logic, and insists that the history of Western domination has not been based on the particular strength of a written or spoken discourse but rather on "the power of colonial capitalism" (1992: 184). But these formulations are not mutually exclusive; the structures of colonial capitalism have undoubtedly contributed to the discourse to which Said refers, and vice versa—much like the relationship invariably found between power politics and religious rhetoric. In the case of Euro-American imperialist expansion, the two contribute to one another and cannot be separated. The point that needs to be made when thinking about Kerala Christian understandings of the West is that, no matter how consistent and powerful this discourse may appear to be, it lacks the kind of political, economic, and resulting rhetorical backing that comes from and contributes to a serious desire for domination over foreign cultures. There is much within the dynamics of Kerala Christian "othering" that appears familiar, but much that remains distinct.

The most familiar aspect of East/West distinctions as put forth by Malayali Christians is their content. Ronald Inden discusses in detail a number of Western constructions of India that position East and West as being divided between two essences (1990: 49–84; 1986: 404–36). Put simply, the East is understood in terms of its spirituality, philosophy, mythologies, and visual art forms, while the West is cast as its "opposite"—as rationalistic and technologically inclined. The positivist or empiricist view of India, as Inden describes it, argues for Western superiority based upon these essential differences between East and West. Romanticists, on the other hand, agree with the positivists and empiricists over both the fundamental split between East and West and the content of that split, yet give some value to what they consider "essentially" Indian. Whereas the empiricists and positivists view India's practices, spiritualities, and cosmologies as wasteful or deluded, romanticists—whom Inden identifies largely with scholars of art history and history of religions—find fascination in such things. Moreover, as Inden describes them, romanticists consider the division between East and West as "somehow embodying the antinomies of 'human nature,' the extremes to which men have gone" (1986: 433). He cites Joseph Campbell's *The Masks of God: Oriental Mythology* to bring home his point:

> Two completely opposed mythologies of the destiny and virtue of man, therefore, have come together in the modern world. And they are contributing in discord to whatever new society may be in the process of formation. For, of the tree that grows in the garden where God walks in the cool of the day, the wise men westward of Iran have partaken of the fruit of knowledge of good and evil, whereas those on the other side of that cultural divide, in India and the Far East, have relished only the fruit of eternal life. (1990: 80)[6]

To complicate matters slightly, Inden notes that some of the most important romanticist (orientalist) writers from 1875 through Independence were not

Americans or Europeans but rather prominent Indian nationalists, including Gandhi and Nehru (Inden 1986: 72). Inden's description of the orientalist discourse as a politically powerful Western construct is here only slightly complicated by the notion that it has, at times, changed hands over the East/West divide. Although this phenomenon, as Inden describes it, supports his argument for the all-pervasiveness of orientalist ideologies, he seems to fall somewhat short in his analysis. Because he does not call attention to the possibility that native use of orientalist ideas can represent something other than passive acceptance of a colonial mindset, Inden does not make room for the prospect that such borrowings require a certain conscious reinterpretation and disruption of the discourse itself. For example, in his article, "Orientalist Constructions of India," he suggests that the sheer forcefulness of colonial orientalism can be demonstrated by the fact that Indians themselves unwittingly live out the stereotype: "In many respects the intellectual activities of the Orientalist have even produced in India the very Orient which it constructed in its discourse. I doubt very much, for example, if Gandhi's concept of nonviolence would have played the central part it did in Indian nationalism had it not been singled out long ago as a defining trait of the Hindu character" (408). Obvious proof that the Indians in question, although possibly acting upon "imported" constructions, were not doing so in a passive manner lies in the unquestionably subversive goal of the nonviolent nationalist movement. This goal was to disentangle the subcontinent from exactly that power structure which "represented" them and thus held them bound. Although the new rhetoric echoes the old, the result differs considerably from a re-production in India of "the very Orient" created in the minds of the original, colonizing orientalists.

To complicate matters further, the means Gandhi used to carve out this "stereotypically Indian" movement were not always derived from Hindu texts or traditions but often from Christian ones. For instance, Gandhi's strategy for nonviolence was admittedly influenced by the Sermon on the Mount more than any other text (Nandy 1983: 51).[7] Gandhi and other Independence movement leaders also gained inspiration from writers such as Tolstoy, Thoreau, and John Ruskin when criticizing Western injustices (Bondurant 1958; Nandy 1983; 1987: 120–21). In reference to Gandhi's use of Christian rhetoric to support the cause of independence, Nandy argues that by appealing to the other, "softer," side of Christianity, he could criticize Western culture on its own terms, thus bringing "the battle to [Britain's] home ground" (1983: 100).[8]

Given this view of Gandhi's "typically Indian" movement—not only as a rejection of Western colonialism but also as a deliberate intercultural construction—we are forced to question on two related levels the potency, as proposed by Inden, of the orientalist discourse that is also described in Said's *Orientalism*. On one hand, the strength of this allegedly omnipresent discourse is highly suspect and, on the other, so is its ability to support tidy divisions between East and West. An acknowledgment of leaks in the system that allow for Indians to think beyond and manipulate an orientalist discourse—even, at times, turn it against itself—should not merely be a matter of exposing the weaknesses of a supposedly invincible structure. Rather, it should be viewed as a tribute to the complexity of cultures and their exchanges and, moreover, to the potency of human creativity.

(handwritten margin note: Gandhi– Sermon on the Mount)

Although Kerala Christian constructions of Europe and the United States indeed reflect, in content, an East/West dichotomy similar to the one Inden describes, the final interpretation given by Keralites differs conspicuously from that of Inden's orientalist positivists or romanticists. In the hands of Malayalis, this reverse orientalism helps them to argue for the supremacy of Indian—and, more particularly, south Indian Christian—culture over that of the West.[9] Kerala Christian inversions of imperialist constructions base themselves upon the "familiar" idea that Indian culture is fundamentally of a spiritual nature, whereas the "West" is preoccupied with modern technologies and comforts. The final assessment of this global arrangement, however, is that Western obsession with technology and material well-being ultimately leads many cultures—on the earth's "other" side—on a path to societal breakdown and spiritual bankruptcy.[10]

Western Excess and Alphonsa as Antidote

Because I undeniably look like a Westerner while in Kerala (Indian clothing seems to do little to bridge that divide), perceived differences between India—particularly, Kerala—and Europe or the United States surfaced regularly and spontaneously as a topic of conversation. Fortified by stereotypical portrayals of Western hedonism and moral decrepitude, particularly in the United States (largely fueled by American and Indian media), Malayalis often seemed to be under the impression that societal ills on my side of the globe had reached epic proportions.[11] People often offered comments about the spiritual and moral decay of the West—which was, after all, my home—in the form of pity or kind condolences. Implicit in this stereotyping and sympathy was the perception that Kerala is, thankfully, a radically different place, free from the same kinds of problems intrinsic to life Over There. Key to the idea that the Keralite lifestyle and value system was antithetical to the trappings of the hedonistic, morally corrupt West were oft-cited claims to an Indian life characterized by its simplicity. This identification with a simple (that is, non-materialistic, read non-Western) lifestyle implicitly and often explicitly set the stage for an understanding among Kerala Christians that their culture contained a level of commitment to spirituality lacking in Europe and North America.

Among priests and nuns in particular, praise of a simple lifestyle was sometimes extended to include a certain glorification of suffering, as well. Because the subject of suffering was so often a topic of conversation during my visits to Alphonsa's shrine, it began to hold a prominent place in my thoughts. One day during my morning walk to the bus stop, I was mulling over such things when I fell into stride with one of the professor-priests from the seminary located on the hillside above our house. This particular priest often tolerated me and my occasional theological musings, so I brought up what happened to be on my mind, telling him that I wanted to hear his perspective. Instead of addressing my concerns, as he had done on every occasion before and after this particular encounter, he simply waved his hand at me and laughed, "How do *you* expect to understand suffering? You are a Westerner!" After shaking his head for a moment he added, on a more serious note, "You Westerners try to build Utopia." Without waiting for me to respond, he then steered the conversation in an entirely different direction.

Through this skepticism about the benefits of worldly comforts and technology, as perceived in particular by clergy and nuns, Indian spirituality emerges not only as the opposite of but also as standing directly in opposition to the lure of (Western) materialism and its allied corrupting forces.[12] The attraction of this elusive but enticing Utopia to which my priest friend made reference is precisely what many members of religious hierarchies fear is threatening the fundamentally spiritual nature of their denominational communities. During conversations with priests and nuns about the decline in such things as religious vocations, devotion to saints, and church attendance among the youth, the reason almost always cited for this deterioration had to do with the bombardment of "Western" influences. These were often connected to the encroachment of Western technology or to undesirable messages delivered through the media, especially the American media.[13] Like British colonists before them, American society is often understood as imposing upon India a series of unwanted and unwelcome cultural values, against which many Keralites feel they have difficulty defending themselves. These enticements, moreover, can be construed as counteracting the spirituality that is, in many ways, the defining point of Kerala Christian culture.[14]

A tangible force that acts as a barrier between Kerala and the corrupting effects of material comforts and worldly values is, for some, symbolized in the life of suffering and self-denial exemplified by Sr. Alphonsa of Bharananganam. This view of Alphonsa, expressed to me in a number of conversations, particularly with Catholic nuns and clergymen, is commonly reflected in hagiographical and biographical accounts, as well. In her Master's thesis, Salomi P. L. writes that Alphonsa "reminds the materialistic world and inspires it to embrace suffering when it is not possible to avoid them [*sic*]" (1992: 82). She goes on to write that Alphonsa "understood the meaning and value of suffering. The modern man who seeks worldly pleasures and luxuries of life could not see anything special in Alphonsa's life of suffering" (89).

The fact that this kind of association is an enduring part of Alphonsa's charisma, not just a present-day trend, is reflected in Fr. T. N. Siquiera, S.J.'s 1948 introduction to the second edition of K. C. Chacko's *Sr. Alphonsa*. In this widely sold publication recounting the life of Sr. Alphonsa, Fr. Siquiera begins on a cautionary note.

> Surgery has become almost painless; diseases can be mostly prevented and if they do, could be easily and even pleasantly cured; electricity has neutralized the changes of weather and season; food and clothing and lodging have become as convenient and pleasant as they can be. And even in India, where our standard of living is still low, the upper and middle classes have made their lives much more comfortable than ever before. What, then, becomes of the law of suffering which is inexorable both in the natural and supernatural plane? (19)

Siquiera writes, furthermore, that suffering is a necessary part of life and the only way humanity can atone for its sins. The perfect harmony of God's world, which sinfulness throws out of balance, must be restored by suffering and pain. Fr. Siquiera goes on to equate material pleasures and comforts with sinfulness when he defines sin "as excess of enjoyment which is beyond what is allowed by nature or reason" (20). His call for the ascetic life as remedy for the material (that is, sinful) excesses of humanity is thus apparently all the more urgent in the increasingly comfortable world of the mid-twentieth century. The kind of lifestyle that is meant to return God's equilibrium to the troubled "pleasure-intoxicated" world is epitomized by the life of Sr. Alphonsa:

> After visiting the chapel where her body is buried and reading her Life by Mr. Chacko I have no doubt that God has sent this unknown, unimportant nun of a small convent in a small village of Travancore in this mid-twentieth century to teach us an important lesson. Just as Sister Thérèse of the Child Jesus was raised in France at a time when science and criticism were giving men a swelled head to teach them that unless they become as little children they cannot enter the kingdom of heaven, so, I think, Sister Alphonsa was meant by our good pedagogue, God, to teach us in this pleasure-intoxicated age that unless the grain of wheat fall to the ground and die, it cannot bear any fruit, that he that doth not carry his cross and follow Our crucified Master is not worthy of Him. (Siquiera 1948: 19)[15]

This description of Sr. Alphonsa alongside that of St. Thérèse of Lisieux as antidote to the values of the modern world is part of a series of similar comparisons in the Indian nun's hagiographical accounts. Noting the parallels between the two women's lives of simplicity, particularly in their acts of self-denial and penance, these comparisons show them as taking a similar road toward spiritual victory. In spite of these common hagiographical themes, the challenges to the lifestyles of St. Thérèse and Sr. Alphonsa are somewhat different. Whereas foreign technologies and comforts stand in contrast to Alphonsa's life of simplicity and suffering, St. Thérèse's adversary is domestic: nineteenth-century political and ideological challenges to the Catholic Church from within France itself. In both late nineteenth-century France and twentieth-century Kerala, however, these "enemy" forces, although historically distinct, represent a phenomenon generically understood as modernism.

Barbara Corrado Pope argues that the late nineteenth and early twentieth-century valorization of St. Thérèse and her lifestyle of suffering and self-denial was part of a larger trend beginning in mid-nineteenth-century France. This trend, which promoted a sentimentalized popular Catholic piety, functioned to combat undesirable forces of modernity. According to Pope, "The belief that innocence and suffering were the primary human virtues stood as a reproach to the secular world, which honored skepticism, materialism, rationalism and optimism" (1988: 55). Such ideas, however, have not always been so central to the Church's self-identification. This late nineteenth-century support of sentimental popular devotion was, in fact, a reversal of an earlier eighteenth-century campaign attempting to rid the Church of embarrassing devotions that "seemed to smack of superstition and emotionalism" (54). Pope argues that the fostering of these late nineteenth-century religious ideals was part of a larger social and political dynamic that emerged after the French Revolution. During this period, Church activities and teachings came under siege by republican and socialist politics resulting in a counter siege in which "a high evaluation of suffering, innocence, and faith became transmuted into either a political animosity toward those who doubted and mocked the church and its beliefs or a profound alienation from secular society" (55).

As implied by Pope, Thérèse Martin's meteoric posthumous rise to saintly prominence in the early 1900s indicates not only that her life resonated with the experiences of like-minded others but also that her cult devotion met a certain need at a particular time. As witnessed by the speedy production of Thérèse's canonization—on both official and local levels—it appears that the force of a particular group's ideology gained welcome strength and cohesion through identification with an iconic personality. This collective identification, which reflected a larger process of pitting one group against another (antirepublican Catholics against modern French society), is modeled by and also after the saint as, in her lifestyle, she emblematically stands in opposition to similar well-defined antagonistic forces.16

I argue that, given the centuries-old imperialist associations of things "Western" with the material, comfortable world and the adoption of these associations by Malayali Christians, Alphonsa as antidote to material excessiveness stands as antidote not only to the sinful secular world but also to the West itself. As with Thérèse of Lisieux, devotion to Alphonsa therefore helps to form and sustain a kind of corporate identity for those for whom she is emblematic. Devotees who understand Alphonsa's lifestyle as challenging sinful extravagance thus stand with her in opposition to the evils of the modern world and the foreign powers associated with them. The fact that Siqiera's introduction to Alphonsa's shrine pamphlet, so adamantly linking technology with sinfulness, was written roughly one year after the completion of India's Independence movement (with its corollary rhetoric of reverse orientalism) should not therefore come as a surprise. Furthermore, the fact that Alphonsa is an *Indian* candidate for sainthood—an unusual case, as there are no canonized Indian saints—fuels these East/West distinctions and their respective associations. Although the Belgian priest, Fr. Acharya, insisted that Alphonsa's cult has been "entirely Romanized," I counter that its challenge to the West through an emphasis upon a lifestyle of self-denial (not to mention her Indianness per se or many aspects of the devotional practice) can work toward forming a type of Indian identity. Such an identity is especially meaningful for many members of the Catholic hierarchy as well as laypersons for whom the encroachment of Westernism/modernism is threatening.17

Current concerns that Western forces threaten to weaken Kerala's spiritual (read also Indian) foundations are intensified and complicated, somewhat ironically, by the encroachment not only of secular modernism but also of Western religion—most visible today in the form of American-based Evangelical or Pentecostal groups. As viewed by many who stand outside these newly burgeoning religious traditions, lower economic classes of Hindus and Christians are especially enticed to join because of the promise of foreign material benefits.18 Citing the common claim that Indian converts are paid by American evangelists to proselytize other Indians, one Catholic man referred to them as "evangelists on commission." An Orthodox Syrian neighbor of ours explained that among the wealthier classes, Orthodox Syrians and Jacobites are particularly vulnerable to conversion. Catholics, on the other hand, seem able to provide an emotional outlet similar to that of the Pentecostal movement with their own Charismatic movement. As related by our neighbor, the notable aspects of the Syrian Christian tradition left behind after conversion are devotions to saints and death anniversary *śrāddham* feasts for ancestors (also practiced by Catholics but not necessarily challenged by the Charismatic movement).[19] The tragedy of their abandonment, he argued, is that these practices "are at the heart of the Orthodox and Jacobite traditions."[20]

Whether through secular or religious enticement, the perceived power of Western culture to lure members from their Syrian Christian affiliations, be they Jacobite, Orthodox Syrian, Syrian Catholic, or Mar Thomite, is seen as a problem not simply because it causes people to forsake important observances.[21] More troubling to many is that potential religious defection leads to disowning an ancient Keralite tradition, one that adherents understand as virtually indigenous or, at least, not forced upon them by outsiders. This claim to an indigenous Christian heritage often focuses on the belief that St. Thomas the apostle came to India after the death of Christ and converted a large number of Brahmans, who are ancestors of the bulk of today's Syrian Christians. The importance of this perception of a home-grown and ancient Kerala Christianity becomes clear in the frequently stated comments to the effect that Kerala was largely Christianized (and civilized through Hindu philosophical systems) "while much of Europe was still running around like barbarians." In essence, many a Kerala Christian's claim to dignity lies not only in a perceived spiritual ascendancy but also in a certain chronological supremacy over Western religious tradition. Keralites who join nonindigenous Christian traditions perhaps perceive themselves as maintaining a measure of spiritual and moral depth intrinsic to Kerala culture, but their conversion means they must let go of a unique and, for some, invaluable tie to an ancient history.[22]

Regarding the widely debated historical authenticity of St. Thomas's visit to Kerala, an Orthodox Syrian friend of mine explained that since the coming of the Europeans, efforts to debunk the validity of the ancient tradition abound. The intrusion of Western influence, this time in the form of scholarly cynicism, is thus seen once again to threaten Kerala Christianity, challenging an integral and formative aspect of its heritage. The specific target, in this case, is the foundational belief that their ancient tradition was not imposed by foreign colonizers but preached to them by one of the very apostles of Jesus himself.[23]

The West as Religious Authority and Kerala Catholic Ambivalence

Although some Kerala Christians believe "the West" and its influences to be meddlesome if not downright damaging to indigenous culture, a significant portion of them looks westward, on occasion, for religious guidance. This link with European powers is especially strong for Syrian Catholics, whose center of authority is Rome (as opposed to other Syrian Christian denominations).[24] Beyond the Roman theology and ecclesiology that are an undeniable authority for Kerala Catholics, other European Catholic customs and traditions work to inform and form the Church community, as well. For instance, judging from outward appearances (such as clerical vestments, religious habits, liturgical paraphernalia, and church architecture), Roman influences upon Syrian Catholicism often set it apart from its non-Catholic counterparts.[25] Occasionally, popular currents from Europe and North America (most recently, the Charismatic movement from the United States) become a significant part of Malayali Catholic practice, as well. But the most enduring and visible aspect of popular

Catholicism in Kerala was initially imported from Europe, although it is currently homegrown as well: devotion to saints.

I was well aware of the presence of foreign sainthood in Kerala, but it struck me with particular clarity one morning while attending a Syrian Catholic mass just outside Kottayam town. I was visiting this particular church for the first time, looking for a priest friend of mine whose home was on the nearby grounds. As described in that evening's journal entry, dated September 11, 1994,

> because this was a new parish for me, my foreign presence today seemed to draw more than the usual amount of whispers and stares. For some reason, I felt unusually uncomfortable with the attention I was drawing this morning, so I sat in the very back left-hand corner of the church wishing to myself that I could somehow appear less "obtrusive." I stared at the floor for a while running such things through my mind. When I looked up I was given kind of a start to see a row of European faces staring back down at me—pale-skinned saints' statues lining the walls. I know I've seen them all before (or something like them) in other churches, and in calmer moments felt that they looked out of place. But this morning, in this particular state of mind, they helped *me* to feel somehow less out of place (in a surreal kind of way).

It would not be difficult to argue that we European types—whether wooden or flesh— were indeed out of place that morning. But the saints are also arguably an intrinsic part of local Catholic tradition in Kerala, and herein seems to lie the source of some confusion or "ambivalence." As mentioned above, the history claimed by Kerala's St. Thomas Christians, along with their reinterpretations of orientalist distinctions, contribute to the positioning of their tradition as exemplar—both chronologically and spiritually—for European and American society. Devotion to European-looking saints might therefore be seen as challenging or even reversing ideas of Eastern spiritual superiority, as the ever-present "Western" cult of saints plays a major role in providing, to some extent, exemplary modes of human holiness for Kerala Christians, especially Catholics.[26]

An example of the ways in which light-skinned images offer a type of endorsement of a "Western" brand of holiness is the tentativeness with which Sr. Alphonsa's officially recognized cult began. It seems that, in spite of popularly held notions of Indian spiritual superiority over the "West," the very Indianness of Sr. Alphonsa initially acted as an obstacle to some people's ability to imagine her as a bona fide saint of the Church. Ironically, Alphonsa's Indianness was an obstruction not so much for the imaginings of the Roman authorities as for the Malayali nuns who lived with her, some of whom were otherwise convinced of her sanctity. During interviews with elderly nuns who knew Alphonsa when she was alive, there were several instances in which these women admitted to their initial disbelief that a non-European could ever become a saint. I heard this for the first time during a conversation in a Clarist convent with an eighty-three-year-old nun named Sister Marguerita as she described to me (and a few of her contemporaries listening intently around the table) the scene surrounding Alphonsa's death in July 1946: "There was great faith in her sanctity. People had gathered around her to touch some of their belongings to Alphonsa's body. I brought some of my own items with me and touched them to her. But did I consider her to be a saint? No, they were all European." This prompted the listening nuns to laugh, seemingly because of the anecdote's incongruence. By touching their belongings to her corpse, those crowded around the newly deceased Alphonsa expressed their Catholic faith in the power of holy relics—of the miraculous efficacy of materials that have come in physical contact with a saint's body. Whereas Sr. Marguerita's relic-making activities thus assume a conviction that Alphonsa was indeed a saint with saintly powers, the elderly nun ironically admits, on another level, to a certain disbelief.

Thomas Mootherdom, a Malayali priest and the second vice postulator in charge of Sr. Alphonsa's canonization, told me of an event that portrayed similar tensions in belief.27 While offering an account of his experiences with the canonization process, Fr. Mootherdom described a nine-year segment of time, beginning in 1953, in which officials took on the arduous task of compiling an assessment of Alphonsa's virtues. In the process of gathering information from people other than nuns (the priest felt the Vatican might perceive them as biased because of their special relationship with Alphonsa), these officials filed reports from 142 witnesses who gave testimony to the nature of Alphonsa's character. After completing interviews in Malayalam, the data was then laboriously translated into English; the finished product amounted to twelve volumes, a thousand pages each. In 1962, Bishop Sebastian Vayalil left for Rome with the twelve volumes only to learn that, as Fr. Mootherdom put it (throwing his hands up), "they had made a mistake—all these pages were not necessary." The bishop then retreated to Kerala, where he and his colleagues picked out what they felt to be the most relevant passages, shrinking the original twelve volumes into one volume of a thousand pages. Fr. Mootherdom and others attribute the eleven-thousand page "mistake" to the fact that Malayalis are new to the formalities of the canonization process and mistakes are inevitable, which is true. But to err on the side of such voluminous overproduction also suggests an overcompensation for the Indianness or, rather, the non-Europeanness of their potential saint, Sr. Alphonsa.

To offer another example of the mixed feelings many Keralites appear to have toward the "West" with its capacity to set the standard for—as well as pose a threat to—Kerala Christian spirituality, let us return to the omnipresent image of the European saint. Reminders that the vast majority of Catholic saint cults were originally European exports are everywhere in Kerala, particularly in Christian areas such as Kottayam. Whether in the form of statues in roadside shrines or churches, or paintings inside shops, homes, or buses, or images on the backs of trucks, the European-looking saint is an unavoidable part of everyday public life. Even the Holy Family (Mary, Joseph, and baby Jesus) normally appears quite Germanic, not at all what the Palestinian originals must have looked like. While I was discussing this issue over tea one afternoon with a young man who lived in the seminary near our house, he recalled seeing an Indian-looking Holy Family the previous December, printed on Christmas cards. These tastefully designed prints were on sale at the seminary, displayed alongside the more familiar fair-haired and blue-eyed Jesus, Mary, and Joseph. Apparently, the latter cards were nearly all snatched up, whereas the "Indian" selection barely sold.

The tastes of a good many seminarians and priests, reflected in their preferences, offer striking testimony not so much to the Europeanness of Kerala's canon of saints (this seems to be a given) but to an insistence upon the Europeanness of the saints' appearance. In spite of this, resident priests and seminarians associated with this particular institution are enthusiastically and vociferously devoted to the maintenance of their ancient St. Thomas (read non-European) tradition. Although they draw much from Rome in terms of theology and leadership, they clearly make it their business to uphold a firm connection with their Syro-Indian heritage when dealing with matters of theological nuance, liturgical symbol, and practice.[28] Efforts to sustain a connection with their ancient Christian tradition are so insistent that they occasionally create tension with the Vatican. In spite of this, the European-looking Holy Family is an image with which this group feels more comfortable—that is, it is somehow more Indian than the seemingly contrived Indian-looking Holy Family. Even among adherents of Eastern Christian denominations such as the Orthodox Syrians and Jacobites, Western European prints are generally more popular, although Eastern Orthodox iconography is sometimes used, as well.[29] It should not be surprising, therefore, that the northern European-looking Holy Family was produced by an Indian card company who understood the local market. The Indian cards, on the other hand, were designed by a European artist who had the misguided idea (audacity?) that one can simply switch one iconographic figure for another.

The Keralite cultural dynamics and foreign misunderstandings played out in this Christmas card affair in some ways parallel issues discussed earlier, in the juxtaposition of the Belgian priest with his ochre-robed monastics and the Malayali nuns in Western habit. The popularity of Northern European-looking saints and the failed attempt of a European artist to appeal to domestic tastes suggests, once again, that "Indianness" cannot be a simple, pure, or static construction. Efforts at fashioning pure strains of Indianness by foreigners in their (understandable and sometimes laudable) attempts to wipe away evidence of imperialist contact often miss the ways in which Indian identity itself has been and continues to be a complicated result of colonial/colonist exchange.[30]

Superficially European yet ultimately Indian, these saint figures express the potential ambiguity of colonial religious symbols and, to some extent, the inconsistency of Kerala Catholic perceptions of the West, that is, of their ambivalent stance toward its influences. Connecting these two somewhat separate issues is the question of the extent to which foreign structures are truly able to assert their influence upon Keralites, providing yet another layer of ambiguity or "ambivalence" to the dynamic. An example of this was neatly expressed for me during a conversation with a Syrian Catholic priest, Fr. Anthony. As we stood outside his parish church near Ernakulam, the young priest, dressed in the white cassock typical of Malayali clergy, passionately conveyed to me tales of the sixteenth-century Portuguese destruction of ancient Indian churches and liturgical items (although the portrait he drew was not quite as bleak as the one painted by the Belgian Fr. Acharya). Once finished with his point about Portuguese colonial cruelty, his narrative skipped ahead to the late twentieth century, extending the notion of foreign "invasion" to include current difficulties among today's youth due, once again, to "Western influences." The effects of these disturbing influences, according to the priest, emerged most problematically in a decline in young people's piety, reflected in a tendency to miss Mass on Sundays and holy days. The future of the youth and subsequently the Church were worrisome for Fr. Anthony but he said that, in spite of the general trend, he was optimistic. The past several years have shown a rebound in church attendance and religiosity among the youth, "thanks to the Charismatic movement"—an import from the United States.

The irony that different manifestations of the same "Western" force are simultaneously luring the youth from their churches and bringing them back was something neither of us appeared to grasp as we ended our conversation. Without reading too much into it, Fr. Anthony's statement seems to reflect both the ubiquitous presence of "Western influences" and his ambivalence toward them. It is important to add, however, that this impression of ever-present Euro-American influences may be misleading. The fact that this seemingly contradictory statement could be expressed so unflinchingly by the priest and pass completely unnoticed by me suggests that the "American" Charismatic movement has been assimilated and transformed by the Kerala Catholic community. Given the possibility for such a transformation, the extent to which the Charismatic movement represents an identifiably "Western" influence therefore becomes suspect. Along these lines, the extent to which Fr. Anthony and others like him are truly of two minds regarding the effects of Western influences is also questionable. What seems to the casual observer to be "native" uncertainty may in fact be something else.

What I am trying to describe here thus goes beyond a superficial ambivalence reflected in the priest's inconsistent opinion of things "Western" and points to an underlying inconsistency within the Kerala Charismatic movement itself. The term "ambivalence" more fully describes this latter phenomenon than does "ambiguity," because it points not only to the mixing of Indian and foreign properties but to a stance that is more expressly caught in tension. As suggested by Fr. Anthony's "contradictory" remarks, domestic adoption of this "Western" movement seems to have been so thorough as to enable it to be wielded by and on behalf of Malayali Christians as a means to combat what it used to be itself: "Western" influence. The fact that this foreign import has turned in on itself is what simultaneously gives it its ambivalence and prevents Fr. Anthony's statement from being contradictory.

In writing about the ambivalent authority of colonial phenomena—imports that become hybrids through native adoption and reconfiguration—postcolonial theorist Homi Bhabha describes such recontextualizations as forcing us to rethink traditional colonial categories of dominance/subordination: "It is this ambivalence that makes the boundaries of colonial 'positionality'—the division of self/other and the question of colonial power—the differentiation of the colonizer/colonized—different from both the Hegelian master/slave dialectic of the phenomenological projection of Otherness" (1985: 150).[31] As a tangible site from which boundaries are blurred and allegiances may be difficult to identify, the colonial hybrid representing a colonial "partial presence" furthermore "terrorizes authority with the ruse of recognition, its mimicry, its mockery" (157). As argued by Bhabha, colonial hybridity becomes disruptive to foreign authority because it does not play by the established "rules." As such, the hybrid represents the *problematic* of colonial representation and individuation that reverses the effects of the colonialist disavowal, so that other 'denied' knowledges enter upon the dominant discourse and estrange the basis of its authority—its rules of recognition" (156). Bhabha characterizes "colonialist disavowal" as something imperialists use in their attempts to mask differences between themselves and the native culture. These differences are denied in order that the necessary illusion of sameness be created in which "the 'part' (which must be the colonialist foreign body) must be representative of the 'whole' (the conquered country)" (153). This idea that the colonized are but inadequate copies of their colonizers produces, for the latter, the right of domination. Yet this construction of similarity is simultaneously (and ironically) built upon the "disavowed" idea of radical difference or opposition—basically, orientalist constructions of East versus West. The projection of total representation paving the way for total domination allows for an outsider's perception that a saint cult in Kerala can be "entirely Romanized" or, as Bhabha describes it, "the noisy command of colonialist authority or the silent repression of native traditions, rather than the actual effect of colonial power: the production of 'hybridization'" (154).

Examples of "problematic" (for the colonizer) hybridization include the originally foreign Charismatic movement used as a tool to combat unwanted outside influences, as well as local constructions of foreign-looking "Indian" saints, some of whom rally for domestic causes. (St. George's cult provides a particularly compelling case, as described below.) Although Bhabha's emphasis on the hybrid's ambiguity and ambivalence helps to make sense of complicated colonial exchanges and reflected power dynamics, it seems, from the context of Kerala Christian hybridity, the best view of ambivalence is often from the (disembodied) eyes of the hybrid itself. In other words, colonial hybridity, particularly when seen from the native's point of view, does not necessarily reflect ambivalence at all. For example, although the Charismatic movement itself may seem precariously juxtaposed between India and the United States, Fr. Anthony does not see it in this way. For him the movement is—particularly in its anti-Western stance—unambiguously Indian.

Indeed, there are ways outsiders can overestimate the hybrid's overall ambiguity and ambivalence and thus underestimate the tenacity and integrity of its domestic impulse. We have seen this in a European artist's attempt to provide an "indigenous" Holy Family for an Indian market and, in some ways, the replacement of European clerical garb with the ochre robes worn at the Belgian priest's monastery.[32] Indianizing the appearance of what began as a European-looking saint or cleric does not simply result in a domestication of what was originally a foreign—and perhaps even unwanted—import. Rather, it more likely will be an imposition of yet another unwanted (or, in the case of Christmas cards, unbought) "foreign" import. It is seen as a substitute for something that has undergone a centuries-long process of indigenization, a hybrid with which the majority of Malayali Christians presently identify. By extension, the domesticated "hybrid," in the minds of some, may cease to be a hybrid at all.

To flesh out Bhabha's theory that hybridization helps reintroduce differences that colonizers claim but "disavow," an example may be found in Kerala Christian self-identification achieved through borrowing (and manipulating) orientalist divisions between "East" and "West." The colonial construction of oppositions between India and Europe has been, over the years, unearthed by and for Keralites on a number of levels. On one level, the retrieval and reuse of East/West categories during the Independence movement has affected, to some degree, Indian self-perceptions throughout the subcontinent. Yet for Keralites who are, as a whole, well traveled and well educated, exposure to and reinterpretation of colonial literature and rhetoric that is not necessarily meant for the native appears to be more all-pervasive.[33] Added to this is Kerala Christianity's link with St. Thomas, giving further substance to reverse orientalist constructions—supportive of and supported by regional interpretations of history. The adoption of this foreign construction therefore gains considerable depth and potency in its domestic (that is, different) meaning, which argues for the superiority of Indian culture. The imported orientalist discourse, once foundational to colonial reasoning, thus plays a part in a conscious distancing of St. Thomas Christians from European and American culture and religious traditions and, with this, a certain conscious defiance against (post)colonial channels of power.

Although the historical distinctiveness of Kerala Christianity indeed provides a measure of autonomy from and recourse against the seemingly omnipresent influences of the "West," this does not, of course, tell the whole story. There remains, as we have seen, particularly among Roman Catholic nuns and clergy, a strongly felt "contradictory" need to maintain links with Europe in matters of institutional authority. Beyond Vatican texts and teachings, this foreign influence can also be found, for example, in the visual canon of European sainthood. Among the variety of ways Keralites incorporate and understand these foreign-looking saints, for some they retain visual cues to Vatican standards and thus wield a certain amount of foreign authority. This is particularly evident in the influence prevalent images and traditions of European sainthood apparently had upon Alphonsa's contemporaries. As we have seen, a number of people, although convinced of her sanctity, underestimated her potential for institutional greatness due to lurking suspicions that she was somehow too Indian to ever be a bona fide saint.

Nevertheless, beneath lingering doubts about Alphonsa's ability to meet Vatican expectations, people exercised subtle defiance against Rome as well, acting to diminish the force of its authority. The resulting dynamic enabled a sizable group of traditional women religious (and a number of priests) to view Alphonsa as sacred in her own right—articulated in their actions after her death—in spite of their belief that Rome would never canonize her.

2. St. George, the Indigenous Foreigner

A dragon slayer, depicted as a young soldier in a flowing red cape astride a white horse, St. George is a figure whose dramatic and abundant presence throughout Kottayam district makes him impossible to ignore. He is the most visible of Christian saint images, with lance thrust into the mouth of a fierce-looking dragon, painted conspicuously on the backs of trucks and industrial auto-rickshaws (see Figure 4). Statues of St. George are a common sight in roadside shrines, as are framed and garlanded images in shop fronts, bus fronts, and in houses. During his feast day, celebrated from late April through early May, people come in droves to the various centers of cult devotion to take part in elaborate festivities—complete with liturgical

Figure 4. St. George freshly painted on the back of a truck.

events, illustrious speakers, and ear-splitting fireworks.[34] Most Keralites agree that St. George is by far the most powerful or, at least, the most popular saint in their midst, with the occasional exception of Mary, the mother of Jesus. Furthermore, aside from Mary and St. Joseph, St. George is the only saint who could be considered a "universal" devotional figure among non-Protestant Christians in Kerala: Jacobites, Orthodox Syrians, and Catholics of both the Syrian and Latin rites, regardless of their doctrinal and political squabbles, all claim St. George as their own.[35] Devotion to St. George thus stands as one of the strongest and most enduring common denominators among the vast majority of Kerala Christians. In spite of this lofty position, which sets St. George apart from many of the other saints in Kerala, his appearance, when placed next to other Kerala saints, is quite unremarkable. His statue was no more startling than were his likewise pale companions on the church wall that day when they appeared to look down on me, a fellow "European."

Brought to India by a number of foreign powers, the Kerala cult of St. George—as with any other imported saint cult—should be examined not simply in terms of indigenous devotion but also in the context of how this devotion is shaped by and, more importantly, gives shape to what was at one stage the European colonizers' devotion. Upon his discovery that the healing figurines among the Cuna Indians were carved in the forms of European "types," Michael Taussig similarly confronts the limitations of ethnography solely confined to discussions of the "other": "For if I take the figurines seriously, it seems that I am honor-bound to respond to the mimicry of my-self in ways other than the defensive maneuver of the powerful by subjecting it to scrutiny as yet another primitive artifact, grist to the machinery of Euro-American anthropology. The very mimicry corrodes the alterity by which my science is nourished. For now I too am part of the object of study" (1993: 8). As in Taussig's study of the Cuna healing figures, to take seriously Kerala devotion to European-looking St. George means to look beyond Kerala and into issues of foreign contact/colonization. An examination of St. George's cult offers a ready site not only for reflection upon European power structures in Kerala but also for a view into their complexity. Brought by Syrian merchants, bolstered by Portuguese and British imperialists, and more recently called into question by the Vatican, devotion to St. George has left traces of culture and conflict from a vast area of the globe.

Nonetheless, the foreignness of Kerala's incarnation of the light-haired, fair-complexioned St. George is, in the final analysis, only skin deep. In spite of the saint's apparent mimicry of European countenance, fashion, and tradition, reflected in the initial defining and shaping of the cult by a steady stream of outsiders, St. George is not always what he first seems to be.[36] As framed by Keralite devotion—that is, by the domestic meaning brought to the saint's cult—he seems to have become, in essence, domesticated. By viewing St. George's cult from the perspective of the Malayalis who received him from abroad, recruited, and partially refashioned him, the practices of ideological differentiation and distancing, basic to the process of hybridization, are brought to the surface once again. Ultimately, this leads us again to wonder, from the standpoint of many Malayalis, if Kerala's St. George is really even a hybrid at all.

Because of Kerala's particularly strong allegiance to his cult and, as I will demonstrate, vice versa, St. George's soldiering has extended beyond the dragons of legend and repeatedly acted as a buffer against the very colonial powers— specifically, Portugal and Britain—who exported him. Somewhat similar to light-skinned Alphonsa pictured in her Roman habit, St. George is at times portrayed as a remedy or counterforce to encroaching "Western" powers, but from an earlier era. Here, again, it is through the manipulation of a dominant (that is, colonial) construct that an "ambivalent" and, from some perspectives, plainly antagonistic stance is made possible. Whereas Alphonsa acts as antidote to "the West" by representing Kerala Christian inversions of orientalist categories, St. George fends off colonial powers through a domestic reworking of the imported cult itself. The use and remaking of foreign structures to forge a certain distancing from the same is, in the case of traditions surrounding both St. Alphonsa and St. George, a matter of using to one's advantage "legitimate" channels of expression through which multivalent domestic meaning can emerge.

This process, in which groups make use of modes of expression legitimate in the eyes of a dominant (in these cases [post]colonial) culture, is similar to what James Scott describes as a "hidden transcript." Hidden transcripts, according to Scott, provide a means for marginalized communities to express themselves through such acceptable types of communication as rumors, gossip, folk tales, jokes, songs, rituals, codes, and euphemisms.[37] As such, these public, cryptically controversial, expressions often hide or make confusing local meanings within the context of the dominant culture. They lie somewhere between the openly "public transcript . . . which takes as its basis the flattering self-image of elites" and a private, contentious discourse which takes place completely "outside the intimidating gaze of power" (1990: 18). This third realm—that of the hidden transcript expressed publicly through validated channels—represents "a politics of disguise and anonymity that takes place in public view but is designed to have a double meaning or to shield the identity of the actors" (19). It is through a similar "doubleness" that St. George potentially emerges as a colonial hybrid and assumes a certain ambivalence toward or, at other times, a duplicitous reversal of his original, colonial manifestation.

In working out his theory of hidden transcripts, Scott assumes that the discourse of the oppressed is in opposition to and separate from that of the dominant order. He thus fails to highlight the extent to which the "double meaning" of a hidden transcript—through the expedient assimilation of colonial traditions by the colonized—could imply a doubleness or complicity in those who make use of it.[38] For example, on occasions when the domestic cult of St. George operates in an ambivalent way toward foreign powers, it is not always in the best interest of colonized communities—nor is it feasible—to be entirely separate from and opposed to colonial authority.[39] By adopting the religious symbols of their colonizers, I argue, Keralites negotiated necessary links with the Portuguese and the British yet, at the same time, set the stage for a less-than-ambivalent domestic stance.

Because both Scott's idea of hidden transcripts and Bhabha's notion of ambivalent hybridity help to rightly complicate understandings of power and resistance within a colonial context, I find them helpful in framing the following discussion of hybrid St. George. A significant difference between these two systems, for my purposes, is that whereas Scott argues for an emergence of intentional, albeit coded resistance, Bhabha's writings point to a more indirect and unintentional assertion of "difference." During instances when "hybrid" saint cults and other borrowings from colonial culture apparently help devotees assert resistance against colonial or postcolonial powers, Bhabha's ambivalent colonial hybridity seems less to the point than does Scott's hidden transcripts. However, during situations in which domestic appropriations of colonial structures express a level of expedient complicity with foreign powers, Bhabha's notion of colonial hybridity and his more subtle understanding of resistance help to further complicate the picture. Nonetheless, because I find it difficult to perceive power and resistance in immutable and monolithic terms, the usefulness of such theoretical frameworks will ultimately depend upon the given situation as well as the angle from which it is viewed. By connecting theoretical nuances to particular instances, perspectives, and places in history, I thus avoid planting myself in one camp or the other. Furthermore, as it is often undesirable if not impossible to identify for others their motivations and intentions, I regularly suggest possibilities but, in the end, leave such determining distinctions relatively unresolved.

Devotional and Narrative Background

Keralites usually mark the beginnings of St. George's cult on the Malabar coast with the arrival of Syrian merchant-immigrants during the first few centuries of the common era, long before the coming of the Portuguese and Roman Catholicism. Although there are no hard facts to support this position, many people back this argument by pointing out that the name "George" in Syrian, "Geevarghese," and its derivatives (Geevarughese, Varghese, Varkey) are commonly given to male members of Kerala's Syrian Christian communities. The name's popularity is such that many families belonging to the different Syrian denominations maintain a tradition in which one of their sons must be named Geevarghese or George. Another argument supporting the Syrian origins of St. George's cult in Kerala has to do with the fact that although the Portuguese brought a number of saint cults to Kerala, few were adopted by Syrian Christians, particularly not by those denominations unaffiliated with Roman Catholicism. It would therefore make little sense that the Portuguese initially introduced to Kerala this saint cult that later became so central to Syrian Christianity, particularly for members of the Jacobite and Orthodox traditions.

The earliest written legends about St. George, *The Acts of St. George*, are in Syriac and Greek, dated around the seventh century and later written in Latin, Armenian, Coptic, Ethiopic, and Turkish (Brooks 1895: 70). The earliest Syrian *Acts* portray St. George as a wealthy tribune to an evil Syrian king who threatens his Christian subjects with dire consequences if they do not sacrifice to the Roman gods. In spite of the king's threats, St. George claims his allegiance to Christ and consequently suffers a number of horrific tortures. In the meantime, George performs several miracles and survives his deadly torments in such a way that many convert to Christianity—most conspicuously, the king's wife, Alexandra. The story culminates with George's decapitation and consequent martyrdom for his Christian convictions.

Some accounts of St. George's life circulating in Kerala echo themes from the Syrian *Acts*, and relate the many tortures and eventual martyrdom of the saint at the hands of a pernicious king. A number of people aged fifty and older told me that when they were children, dramatic embellishments of St. George's tortures were especially popular. A frequently told tale was that of the martyr being sliced up into small pieces, fried, ground into a powder and thrown into the river seven times, only to have Christ himself retrieve and revive him each time.[40] More commonly today, however, stories that parallel the *Acts* are not part of local storytelling in Kerala but are almost exclusively found in official church biographies of the saint or in publications marking anniversary celebrations at St. George churches. These churches and their publications represent the spectrum of Kerala's non-Protestant Christian denominations.

The version of St. George's hagiography that Keralite devotees most commonly tell today deals primarily with the valiant defeat of a fierce dragon and rescue of a young princess. This story usually has little connection with the agonies of the *Acts* except for an occasional brief tag at the end of the story, in which St. George is martyred by a king who is angry that St. George's heroism spurred his subjects to join the Christian faith. In Europe, evidence of St. George's association with a dragon does not surface until the twelfth century, at which time it was widely disseminated by such popular writings as the *Golden Legend* by James Voragine (Butler 1985: 148; Hole 1965: 18). Because of their relatively late connection with the cult of St. George and with Kerala, the Portuguese may have imported this dragon-slaying aspect of the saint's character to Kerala or, if not, added flourishes to dragon-slaying motifs already introduced by the Syrians. In any case, Portuguese identification with St. George was undoubtedly strong by the time they arrived in Kerala in the fifteenth century as, by then, they had chosen him as their patron saint.

Based upon popular depictions not only in local stories but also in iconography, song, and ritual, St. George as dragon-slayer is central to Keralites' current understanding of the saint. As told to me one evening by two Syrian Catholic devotees, Ammini and her mother, Mariyamma, the saint's tale is altered little from its twelfth-century *Golden Legend* rendition. As we sat out on their porch during the late monsoon rains of August, watching the sun set and the puddles grow below us, the two women related the following, deferring one to the other as storyline details dimmed. Ammini's grandmother started off the narrative by quietly humming the tune of an old church song about the exploits of the dragon slayer.

> A snake was blocking the water hole where water was supposed to gush for the use of the people there. So the people used to prepare a grand lunch for the snake and wait for him. He would then move away from the place so that water could gush out. The people would then go to collect their water. Each lunch would include a human also. It was the turn of the princess one day, and she was standing there weeping.
>
> St. George happened to be passing by as he was going back to his homeland to meet his parents after his tedious work in the army. On his way, he saw the princess surrounded by a snake. He wanted to save the princess. He got down from his horse and went over to the snake and called out, "You Satan, come out from this place, it is I who am calling." But the snake hesitated. After some time, it went up to St. George to eat him. The snake tied its tail onto the legs of the horse on which St. George was sitting. But St. George took out his spear and pierced it into the snake's mouth. Then with his sword he cut it into pieces. Thus it was killed. The princess, relieved, dipped her hands in the blood of the snake and touched St. George's back in order to identify him, as there were a lot of people crowded there, and ran back to her house. Upon seeing her, the king was furious and he told her to go back to the snake or else the people would kill him. The princess narrated the whole story to him.
>
> With the help of bullock carts, the people lifted the dead snake away from the place. They all got enough water to drink and for their uses. The king was greatly pleased. He then proclaimed that he would give his daughter in marriage to that brave soldier. People rushed forward hearing the news, saying, "I am the person! I am the person!" but the princess said, "You are not the people, none of you is the one. I know the person." And from the group of people she identified St. George by the mark of blood on his coat and showed him to her father. St. George refused to marry her. He said, "I want everybody to be converted to Christianity; I don't want anything else." Everybody did as he wished.

Although the Syrians may possibly have beat out the Portuguese in bringing this legend of the pious and courageous George to Kerala, the latter are indisputably known for introducing saints' statues to the Malabar coast. Before the fifteenth-century arrival of the Portuguese, the Syrian Christians had no tradition of sacred statues, as they believed such replications of holy figures to be idolatrous.[41] The branch of Syrian Christians that became a part of the Roman Catholic tradition—via the Portuguese—was thus offered a new material dimension to its cult of saints and, as we will see below, fresh fodder for miracle stories.[42]

St. George as Portuguese Keralite

The Aruvithura St. George Syrian Catholic Church, one of two prominent pilgrimage sites honoring the saint in Kottayam district, was originally dedicated to Mary. According to a local novena pamphlet written by Joseph Pallickaparampil (1991), Portuguese influence brought about a sixteenth-century "renewal" of the church building and its liturgies as well as the conversion of its parishioners to Roman Catholicism. This transformation coincided with a rededication of the church to St. George, the patron saint of Portugal (see Figure 5). According to the pamphlet, this sixteenth-century rededication had much to do with a miraculous statue of the saint brought to the church by some outsiders two centuries earlier. To mark the occasion, parish officials moved St. George's statue to a position of prominence above the main altar when the church's physical reconstruction was complete.

In spite of the fact that Kerala's saint statues are commonly identified with Portuguese influence, people of the Aruvithura parish traditionally maintain that this particular statue of St. George was neither brought nor inspired by the Portuguese. Both lay people and clergy consider it to be of Syrian make, transported to Aruvithura in the (pre-Portuguese) fourteenth century from a distant parish that had earlier been destroyed (in some accounts by Muslim invaders). According to historian-priest Fr. Arayathinal, these parishioners carried with them to Aruvithura

> a statue of St. George, a veritable type of Oriental (Persian?) sculpture. Unlike the traditional likeness of the Saint as an armoured cavalier of 20 or 21, the statue represents a middle aged soldier, seated on a horse, thrusting his lance to the mouth of a dragon. The statue's lively appearance is an imposing feature. This very miraculous statue has been present here for the last six centuries without any change even of retouching by an artist. The present generation is proud of its possession and keeps it as an invaluable treasure. This antique statue dating back to the 13th century (or earlier) may certainly checkmate the contending historians who assert that there were no statues of saints in the Syrian churches of Malabar, prior to the coming of the Portuguese in the 15th century. . . . Ever since the advent of the statue, the people began to have unflinching faith in the saint and he has been particularly beneficial in bestowing favours on his clients. (1953: 13–14)

The idea that a group of fellow Syrian Christians rather than the Portuguese were responsible for bringing the miraculous St. George image to the church further underlines the statue's "Oriental" heritage—a point that is consistently central to

Figure 5. St. George Roman Catholic Church, Aruvithura.

contemporary explanations of the image.[43] Consequently, even though this community of Aruvithura Syrian Christians allied themselves with Rome via the Portuguese during the sixteenth century, parishioners have traditionally considered the efficacy of their church as a pilgrimage site to lie behind a conspicuously un-Portuguese power represented by their statue. An otherwise sure symbol of Portuguese tradition, this statue, which stands as an "exception to the rule," thus symbolizes a noncolonial indigenized power to which people have given their allegiance. It is true, at one level, that Portuguese influences effected a Romanization of the new church of Aruvithura both architecturally and liturgically. Nevertheless, the simultaneous rededication of the church to St. George resulted in the placement of a culturally hybridized saint (that is, the Portuguese patron in the form of what is believed to be a Syrian statue) at center stage above the main altar of this newly Romanized church. From a local perspective, the miraculous statue might thus have functioned as a type of "hidden transcript" in which the centrality and efficacy of an older indigenized tradition, embedded in the trappings of a more recently arrived foreign tradition, expresses anonymous domestic defiance against these new forces of power.

At the very least, the marking of Syrian St. George's territory upon a Portuguese establishment represents a more subtle kind of hybrid resistance in which a foreign-looking symbol challenges the dominant order simply because it assumes an alternative, indigenous interpretation. As Bhabha puts it, the site of hybridization is never neutral, although it is "not necessarily an oppositional act of political intention, nor is it the simple negation or exclusion of the 'content' of an other culture, as a difference once perceived" (Bhabha 1985: 153). Although it may be difficult to impose Scott's category of the hidden transcript and its implied intentional resistance to sixteenth-century Aruvithura St. George devotion (as we know it), Bhabha's subtle description of distancing might be too muted. Although events in Aruvithura may indeed reflect perceived differences and ambivalences rather than intentional (and perhaps impossible) opposition to Portuguese power, we cannot discount their potential for providing a diagnosis of underlying—and undocumented—antagonisms and resistances, as well.

St. George the British Keralite

The arrival of the British two centuries after the Portuguese was preceded by Dutch colonizers whose brief presence on the Malabar coast appears to have been—in terms of contributing to Kerala's pantheon of saints—rather uneventful. Anglican Britain was also not much concerned with the tradition of sainthood by the eighteenth century, except to denounce it—with one exception.

Traces of St. George's cult had been in evidence since the seventh to eighth centuries in England, but his later promotion to national patron had to do with legends related by British crusaders upon their return from Middle Eastern conquests. Especially famous are tales of the saint's miraculous assistance in the First Crusade during the 1098 battle of Antioch—sacred aid that led to the eventual defeat of the Saracens. In spite of the Reformation, devotion to St. George retained its popularity in England through the beginning of the eighteenth century. At this time, the British initiated "virulent attacks against the cult of saints," and devotion consequently declined (Gerould 1916: 332). In spite of these attacks, public vestiges of English allegiance to St. George remained during the era of British colonial presence in Kerala, making a decided impression upon Malayali Christians. Citing his status as England's patron saint during colonial times along with the flying of St. George's flag by the British military, Keralites today commonly associate St. George with Britain.[44]

Regarding relations between Britain and Kerala Christians, J. W. Gladstone (1984) maintains that British missionary groups during the nineteenth and twentieth centuries specifically targeted for conversion the Syrian Christian community in Kerala. As a result of this vigorous campaign, Bayly describes the Malabar coast as being, at the time, "the most active missionary field in India" (1989: 285). Missionary activity in this context was not necessarily evangelical but was avowedly carried out in order to secure British control by means of support from "a respectable body of Christians" (Gladstone 1984: 63).[45] The more religiously based (and therefore more overtly pronounced) goal was to restore among non-Catholic Syrian Christians "the pure principles of faith and practice which prevailed before the arrival of the Portuguese" (63). The aim of what British missionaries termed its "mission of rescue" was to cleanse the Syrians of the "heathenish practices" and "popish superstitions" they believed Malayali Christians had acquired only since the sixteenth century. The British missionaries, in their post-Reformation fervor, found saint devotion to be particularly despicable (Bayly 1989: 294).

In spite of these prevailing tensions, non-Catholic Syrian communities occasionally turned to Anglican British missionaries for the purpose of garnering a favorable political position. An Orthodox Syrian friend of mine described this phenomenon as a response to the Jacobite Church's frustration over the growing political clout and position of those who had aligned themselves with the Vatican. Because so many churches originally of the ancient Syrian rite had now joined Roman Catholicism (and consequently experienced economic and political advantage), some people feared that the Jacobite tradition might disappear completely. Ironically, Jacobite clergy and parishioners often felt that the only hope for their denomination's survival was through the political and economic leverage made possible through alliances with the British. As described by my friend, if Jacobite members promised leaders of the English Church Missionary Society (C.M.S.) that they would convert their churches to C.M.S., they would receive whatever economic aid they needed for "keeping these churches away from the Catholics." Quite often, however, a community would secure its monetary and political benefits from the British and then not keep its promise to convert to C.M.S.[46]

According to its locally told history, the building and dedication of the St. George Orthodox Syrian Church of Puthupally (one of the most prominent St. George pilgrimage sites in Kottayam district, rivaled only by the St. George Catholic Church in Aruvithura) reflect a similar kind of ambivalence toward the British presence in Kerala (see Figure 6). The parish church built before the present one was also non-Catholic Syrian (Jacobite at the time),[47] dedicated to St. Behanan and constructed in 1640, preceded by yet another, dedicated to Mary. St. Behanan's Church, located a short distance from the present building, is said to have had a number of C.M.S. converts among its parishioners. One wealthy convert named Mathu wanted to convert the entire church—building and all—to C.M.S. Before he could carry out this highly controversial plan, however, St. Behanan's parishioners chose to demolish their church. This demolition was ostensibly the result of an oracle's proclamation from the nearby Kālī temple, announcing that the church bell was disturbing and angering the goddess.[48] Erected in its place was the St. George Church in what is today called Puthupally (literally, "new church" in Malayalam). In contrast with the earlier trends set by some of St. Behanan's parishioners, the new church was built and maintained under the auspices of the Syrian tradition, not the British. When I asked parishioners about the impetus behind the church's concurrent rededication to St. George, people most commonly answered that it was due to British influence. In fact, many parishioners consider colonial Britain (rather than

Figure 6. St. George Orthodox Syrian Church, Puthupally.

Syria or Portugal) to be one of the driving forces behind the popularity of contemporary St. George devotion.

Given this perspective, the demolition of St. Behanan's church in lieu of its transformation into an Anglican parish emerges as a possible defiance against the encroachment of British traditions (with some help from the local goddess). The adoption of the so-called "British" St. George as the patron of the new non-Anglican church, however, represents a curious mix of allegiance with and disdain for the colonial endeavor. Because of the multivalence of nineteenth-century devotion to St. George, the conceivable strategies that lie behind the dedication of the Puthupally church to this saint are (and probably were) varied. The decision to make St. George the patron saint of this consciously un-Anglican Syrian church could have helped Keralites to reclaim and reestablish this cult tradition as their own—for the martyr to whom the old Syrian songbooks pay tribute (versus the British or Portuguese St. George). However, given the need for the Orthodox Church to compete in stature with the surrounding Romanized churches, another rationale also seems plausible. The dedication of the Puthupally Syrian church to a "British" St. George may also have acted as a means for harnessing a foreign colonial power without being entirely subject to it.

Along these conjectural lines, Susan Bayly, in her wide-ranging historical discussion of religion in south India, maintains that "For all [royal] subjects and worshippers, royal power and the forces of the supernatural formed part of the same continuum of accessible but awesome power and energy" (1989: 453). This assertion supports her argument that colonizers have used techniques of "conspicuous piety" in the form of shrines, pilgrimage sites, and other "repositories of sacred power and landscape" in order to increase their domain (453). Citing a number of examples in which foreign powers, notably the Portuguese, have used these methods for their imperial expansion, Bayly is clear that south Indians were not passive recipients of colonial domination. Rather, she describes cult traditions as eventually being reinterpreted or indigenized once in the hands of local devotees.

The circumstances surrounding the founding of Puthupally's cult of St. George, however, begs an extension of Bayly's argument. Although his cult probably provided a sacred conduit for mundane power structures, similar to the examples Bayly provides, its establishment in Puthupally does not appear to have been the result of colonial "technique" later indigenized. Instead, the saint appears to have been domestically designated as patron for the Puthupally parish. As such, he probably acted as a tool for, or at least was complicit in, an ambivalent resistance to the colonial powers who also claimed him. "Framed" in such a way, the hybrid St. George of Puthupally appears more like a traitor or spy (depending upon your perspective) than an imposed model of holiness parishioners later refashioned.

Scars from the Vatican: St. George in Question

The foreign authority presently making its mark on Keralite devotion to St. George—and vice versa—is the Vatican and its (highly selective) contemporary concern with empiricism and historicity. As a result of the Bollandist's investigation of Catholic sainthood in the 1960s, Rome has called into question the actual historicity of the dragon-slayer's life, along with a number of other saints' lives. Subsequently, St. George has undergone a demotion in status from a full-fledged canonized saint to a holy person of lesser rank, or "Servant of God"—two rungs down on the Vatican ladder to canonization.[49] As a result, the official calendar of saints no longer includes his feast day, and any new Catholic devotion, including the building of new churches in St. George's honor, has been prohibited. An Orthodox Syrian friend of mine, although not typically concerned with Vatican proclamations, described the period when St. George's "demotion" was made known to Keralites as a "painful time" that affected Keralite non-Protestant Christians regardless of their denomination.

There are some Malayalis (mostly Catholics), however, who seem to be somewhat sympathetic to the recent Vatican stance toward St. George, as witnessed by a tendency to downplay their association with his cult. I found myself in conversations with both Latin and Syrian Catholics, mainly priests, who—although admitting to the popularity of his devotion—tried to distance themselves and their traditions from the saint. This was done, in some instances, by ascribing his popularity to the other branch of Catholicism. One Latin Catholic priest stationed in Kollam dismissed my questions about the saint with a wave of his hand, saying, "St. George is a part of the Syrian tradition." By this, he seemed to imply that his parishioners had very little to do with St. George—which I later discovered was not at all the case. A Syrian Catholic priest in Kottayam town, when asked about St. George, admitted that devotion to the saint was very strong among all non-Protestant Christians in Kerala. Nonetheless, he believed that the tradition was brought by the Portuguese and was therefore even stronger among the Latin Catholics than the Syrians. Upon second thought, the priest noted that the popularity of Syrian names for George might be an indication of the cult's Middle Eastern origin but, nonetheless, devotion within the Latin community, he insisted, was stronger. Judging from many other conversations with Syrian Christians, Catholics and non-Catholics, as well as from the abundant presence of St. George churches and iconography in the predominantly Syrian Christian district of Kottayam, it seems safe to say that the Syrian Christian devotion to St. George is just as strong if not stronger than that of the Latin Catholics. Perhaps this priest would have reconsidered his position about St. George's popularity (as he had about the origin of the cult) if he had given the matter more thought. The point to be made here, however, is that hasty disclaimers by Catholic clergy about their congregations' association with St. George express the fact that the Vatican has, on some level, made its mark on Keralite devotion. Papal questioning of the saint's historicity has resulted in certain misgivings and embarrassment about the perseverance of his cult.

In some cases, I found that surface skepticism about St. George gave way to a more fundamental devotional alliance with the saint. Such was the case with a middle-aged Syrian Catholic man, Mr. Joseph, who spoke with me at his home in Bharananganam, not far from Alphonsa's shrine. I was led there by Sr. Josephina to meet Mr. Joseph and his ailing mother, as their family had a particularly strong devotion to Sr. Alphonsa. After speaking in lengthy detail about their family's indebtedness to this local saint, our conversation turned to sainthood in general. When I asked Mr. Joseph about his relationship to St. George, his response came back to me very quickly, "Oh, St. George! He's been cast off by the pope. He's now only recognized by the Orthodox Syrians and the Jacobites." Not able to hold my tongue, I responded that it seemed to me that St. George was still quite popular among many Catholics. After brief deliberation, Mr. Joseph admitted that perhaps elderly Catholics continued to keep their devotion to St. George. This time I kept my thoughts to myself, and Mr. Joseph also sat in silence for a few moments before blurting out that even he prayed to St. George: "OK, I guess I still pray to him." To explain what he seemed to think was an inconsistency, he continued, "The pope may try to cast out a saint, but he or she may still remain in our hearts nonetheless."

Among the well-educated younger generation in Kerala, forces less well defined than the Vatican—amorphously associated with modern or "Western" influences—sometimes evoke embarrassment about or call into question, often superficially, the cult of St. George and other saints.[50] Jacob, a well-educated neighbor of ours in his early twenties from a devout Orthodox Syrian family (thus not directly affected by Vatican decrees) regularly spoke of his skepticism, somewhat typical of his age group and education level, about saint devotion. During a discussion about religion in Kerala that he, my husband, and I were having one evening at our home, Jacob described his opinion about the cult of St. George—that it was particularly ridden with superstition—and, ultimately, his disdain for it. Because Keralites traditionally associate St. George with protection against poisonous snakes, Jacob's train of thought led our conversation to an incident in which he was asked by some elderly neighbors to kill a great hooded viper near the couple's house. While Jacob animatedly described to us his face-to-face encounter with the frighteningly large hooded creature, my husband interjected, wondering if thoughts of St. George crossed his mind at the time. Jacob chuckled to himself for a moment then announced, "Oh yes, they did! I said in a loud voice, 'St. George, save me!' and then came down with the instrument and killed the snake."

In spite of the number of Keralites who presently disown St. George's cult, either completely or superficially, this is by no means the only response to current institutional and societal forces. During conversations with young and old alike, people most commonly expressed a hearty defense of the dragon-slayer and his cult. As a means of describing Kerala's overall support of the saint, a Syrian Orthodox English professor in his forties, Abraham John, claimed that the recent Vatican decree demoting St. George "was rejected in Kerala like nowhere else on earth." This rejection, in its various forms, is maintained today by a wide spectrum of people—by clergy members as well as the laity and by people in the upper as well as lower classes.

In his recent (1993) edition of St. George's hagiography, an Orthodox priest, Fr. Perumal Joseph, expresses current stepped-up desires to defend the efficacies of the saint against foreign decrees and forces of rationalism.[51] Here, the priest offers a few words on behalf of St. George apparently not necessary in an earlier version of the hagiography.

> There have been divergent versions which have appeared about the holy martyr George in books subsequently written [after his 1973 edition]. Rationalists contend that many stories relating to him were but fables. In the light of rationalists and atheists maintaining the same view about even the miracles wrought by Christ the Savior of the World in his earthly sojourn, one need not attach much importance to the rationalist contention about St. George. No matter whoever may try to disregard or reject St. George on the basis of needing sufficient historical documents, this saint will continue to remain enthroned in the hearts of the devotees. . . . The unprecedented crowds of devotees that are drawn to these churches on the feast day of the saint are almost inexplicably large. Such astounding crowds of the devotees are sufficiently eloquent witness to the blessings received through the saint's intercession. (n.p.)

Arguments in support of devotion to St. George espoused by Catholic and non-Catholic clergy as well as educated Christians are at times less concerned with the saint's miraculous powers than with his cult's long-standing Kerala tradition. A number of people with whom I spoke felt St. George devotion to be a venerable institution in Kerala, something undesirable if not impossible to erase. Many Christians consider him an "old friend" whose name their father, grandfather, or they themselves share. To turn on St. George would therefore be akin to denouncing a family member.

Reading from meticulously written notes prepared for our meeting, Abraham John (the Orthodox Syrian English professor mentioned above) argued that St. George's appeal has to do with his indigenous and, therefore, accessible nature. Professor John reasoned, for instance, that St. George attained saintliness through his work as a brave soldier and thus could easily be understood within the Hindu framework of karma yoga. Because doing his job well was the path St. George took toward saintliness—rather than the usual asceticism or "purity," as the professor put it—the dragon-slayer was not a typical Christian holy figure. Because St. George did not live a life of extreme austerity or abstinence, Professor John reasoned that most of his devotees could understand and perhaps even realistically emulate him. Another way in which the professor understood St. George to be at home within his Hindu surroundings was that his powers, similar to those of some of the more ferocious deities in the Hindu pantheon, dramatically wreak havoc with the powers of evil (symbolized by the dragon/snake). He noted that this physical forcefulness made St. George, again, an unusual saint among other Christian saints, but that it made him all the more appealing. This capacity for ferocity, according to the professor, meant that the highly capable St. George could be called upon as "a friend in need. . . . When we are in need of help, sometimes force is what we are hoping for, not just love."

Although an appreciation for St. George's character or for his association with Hindu patterns of holiness are not uncommon among Keralites, the impulse that most tenaciously drives his cult's vast popularity is a faith in and reliance upon the great strength of his powers. A male board member at the St. George Catholic Church in Aruvithura laughed during our conversation about the saint's Vatican demotion, saying, "The people sided with the saint, not the pope." Overhearing our conversation from a few feet away, a nun added to it by stating that St. George is, for his Keralite devotees, "their own." Elaborating upon her interjection, she insisted, "The people's negative reaction to the decree was based upon their own personal experience of his miraculous power. Such things the pope can never understand."

St. George the Keralite

It is not merely the efficacy but the particular nature of St. George's powers that enlivens Keralites' dogged claim that the saint is "their own." Christian devotees (and many Hindus) rely on this dragon-slaying saint more than any other to provide protection from a particularly Keralite threat: poisonous snakes.[52] Snakes are a daily hazard for Keralites and, according to Kumaran Vaidyar, an Ayurvedic snakebite doctor practicing in northern Kerala, the incidence of snakebite is currently on the rise. He surmises that this probably has to do with the relatively recent arrival of electricity and urbanization. As a result, "People keep wandering around long after dusk and keep getting bitten all the time." Doctors in an Ayurvedic snakebite clinic outside Kottayam town see the same trend in central Kerala (see Figure 7). During our discussion about the connection between the looming threat of poisonous snakes and the strength of St. George devotion, an Orthodox Syrian bishop illustrated for me the extent to which snakes pose a daily hazard for Keralites. He recalled an occasion about a year earlier when the seminary hired some "professional snake catchers" to come to their grounds (approximately four acres) and round up the stray snakes. In a single day, they managed to catch eighty-three.

Contributing to his role as a balm for indigenous concerns, the local imagining of St. George, in spite of his iconographically depicted Europeanness, is often not of a foreign figure at all. He is an indigenous saint caught up in domestic affairs. When we were talking once about St. George's popularity in Kerala, Meena, our cook, explained to me that "Christians came to be in Kerala only after the arrival of St. Thomas. In the days of St. George, people were not worshiping the real

Figure 7. Display of local vermin at the entrance of Ayurvedic snakebite hospital near Kottayam.

God, but kings and idols. After this incident [when the princess was saved by the snake], everyone turned to God. There is a saying that the snake incident happened in Kerala, so people in Kerala worship St. George more than outsiders."[53]

The popular understanding of St. George as a holy figure indigenous to Kerala is further validated by tales of sibling relations to other saints and Hindu deities, discussed at length in the following chapter. For instance, as long as locals can remember, Hindus and Christians have associated St. George of Puthupally and the nearby Hindu goddess Bhadrakālī as brother and sister. One of the ways devotees elaborate upon this sibling connection is through the idea that St. George's church bells sweetly awaken Bhadrakālī each morning. (This is the same goddess for whom St. Behanan's bells were earlier so annoying.) Furthermore, additional domestication of St. George's cult throughout Kerala occurs many times over through the investment of his power in a variety of miraculous images such as the statue in the Aruvithura church. Devotees do not invoke his powers as remote heavenly abstractions but as earthly forces located just a short pilgrimage away.

The rededication of the newly renovated/rebuilt Aruvithura and Puthupally churches to St. George seems to signify, from the evidence left to us, a certain ambivalence toward the colonial powers of their day. It appears, however, that current local devotion to St. George, concerning itself with homespun issues (which probably has always, to some degree, been true of local St. George devotion), is seemingly impervious to—or uninterested in—foreign authorities and their decrees. The recent relocation of Aruvithura's miraculous statue from its sixteenth-century place of prominence over to a side altar, although done to appease Vatican authorities who wish to deemphasize devotion to the saint, appears to have had little effect on devotees. In spite of this logistical adjustment, in other words, the miraculous efficacy of the statue is no less revered (see Figure 8). The vast majority of the many pilgrims (currently increasing in numbers, according to parish estimates) who come to the Aruvithura Church to pray and light candles crowd before St. George's side altar, often leaving the main church building virtually empty.[54] Arriving on the Malabar coast in the company of three different waves of foreigners and claimed by many Keralites as their own, the cult of St. George does not appear to be so easily swept aside by yet another wave of foreign influence.

This chapter began as a response to the Belgian priest's challenge that Alphonsa's—and, by implication, *any* saint's—cult in Kerala has been "entirely Romanized." I have demonstrated, instead, that a complete "Romanization" (or colonization) of domestic traditions is unlikely, as foreign impositions so often become hybridized through indigenous interpretations. Yet this chapter also leads us to consider the extent to which colonial imports can, in the eyes of many Kerala Christians, cease to be hybrids in spite of outward appearances. Whether we are speaking of the recently introduced Charismatic movement, Christmas cards decorated with European-looking Holy Families, or (shrugging) nuns in Western habits, claims that such phenomena are indisputably less "Indian" than other, perhaps less complicated, Keralite traditions are problematic. Such assertions are troublesome, as they tend to be founded upon nostalgic and impossible assumptions that cultures stem from original, pure states rather than being a product of continual exchange and change. As for (the still Euro-looking) contemporary St. George, the fact that many Keralite Christians continue to keep the faith through popular disjunction with and widespread inattention to foreign edict represents a striking response, on a local level, to Fr. Acharya's concerns about the debilitating contamination—that is, "Romanization"—of Kerala Christianity.

To understand the dogged nature of St. George's popularity in contemporary Kerala as a deliberate defiance against the statutes of Rome would be, I think, an oversimplification. Rather, as the Sister said, it probably has more to do with the fact that such proclamations do not resonate with people's experiences of the saint and his powers. As can also be seen in the establishment of the "Portuguese" Aruvithura and "British" Puthupally cults, Kerala devotees and Vatican officials are not referring to quite the same "St. George."

Figure 8. Vendor with religious trinkets at St. George Aruvithura festival. The forward-facing St. George image displayed below the picture of Jesus is a replica of the church's miraculous statue. The image below that, depicting St. George from the side, is the more typically seen iconography.

In spite of arguments that Kerala Christian "hybrid" traditions reflect processes of distancing from and/or defiance against foreign authorities—depending on one's perspective—it bears remembering that today's Malayali Christians do not commonly conceive of themselves as any less Christian than their European and American counterparts. If anything, Keralites' perceived moral superiority (validated by such things as reverse orientalism and Sr. Alphonsa's impending canonization) and chronological superiority (Christianized "while much of Europe was still running around like barbarians") help distinguish themselves as better—if not more—Christian than their counterparts in the "West."[55] Furthermore, Syrian Christians, who trace their heritage to the peaceful conversion of Brahmans by the apostle Thomas, typically understand themselves as being just as Indian as any Hindu. The international negotiations and antagonisms reflected in the many-layered antics of Kerala's St. George cult over the centuries express the fact that these Indian Christians have, in their own way, held their ground against the same colonial and postcolonial "others" as have their Hindu neighbors. It is thus important to emphasize that being simultaneously Indian and Christian is not, from the standpoint of most of today's Kerala Christians—and in spite of undeniable complexities and implicit tensions—a watered-down state of being or a contradiction in terms.

2

Siblings and Other Metaphors for Christian-Hindu Relations

In keeping with the idea that Kerala's present-day cult of St. George represents, ultimately, an indigenous tradition, best understood within the context of life on the Malabar coast, this chapter shifts our focus from international power relations to interreligious dynamics within the village community. I relate contemporary local traditions such as church saint and temple deity stories, tales of church origins, and shared Hindu-Christian religious practices as a means to contrast the complexity of communal relationships voiced locally with more simplified prescriptions advanced, for the most part, by clergy and ritual specialists.

Section 1 relates village tales of sibling ties between temple deities and church saints as a basis for exploring perceptions of communal relations between the sacred figures' constituent communities. In the second section, I discuss clerical attitudes and official religious rhetoric that challenge local village notions of Hindu-Christian relations reflected in stories, interreligious tales, and rituals. The third section returns to local sacred sibling stories, but from the perspective of their performance to an ethnographer and her tape recorder.

1. Siblings and Neighbors: Models for the Divine and Human

A short while after my return to the United States from Kerala, I had the chance to view the internationally acclaimed Anand Patwardhan film, *Father, Son and Holy War*, which—among other things—portrays north Indian communal violence at its worst. A scene that made a particularly strong impression on me was that of a Kṛṣṇa procession during a temple festival in Ahmadabad. Here, the camera takes the viewer to a portion of the procession route where it passes through a Muslim neighborhood. As they make their way through the narrow streets, male Hindu devotees of Kṛṣṇa walk alongside an elaborate float and shout devotional words to their god along with what appear to be taunts directed at the surrounding Muslim neighborhood. While the narrator tells us that this portion of the annual festival is frequently a site of violence each year, angered Muslim onlookers throw rocks at the vociferous Kṛṣṇa devotees and the armed police, who later claim that they "have no other choice," fire bullets into the increasingly unruly neighborhood crowd.[1]

Such an image demonstrates how public occasions can provide powerful forums not only for celebrating devotees' ties with a sacred figure but also for acting out underlying interreligious community relations. What follows, however, will not be a narration of the well-publicized communal conflicts that continue to erupt throughout India. Rather I offer examples of relative communal harmony, performed regularly during Kerala's local saint and deity festivals, which are virtually ignored by much of national and international media and big-time filmmakers.[2] This ready association of India with communal conflict—both within Indian politics and internationally—is a separate matter of concern, taken up in section 2 of this chapter.

Christian Saint and Hindu Deity: Forging Communal Identities

The following invokes the category of siblings—traditionally used by Kerala's Christian and Hindu devotees to depict relations between church saints and temple deities—as a means to describe, metaphorically, interreligious communal relations. In doing so, I assume a certain connection between patron saints or deities and their constituent human community of devotees. We have already seen how religious figures such as Thérèse of Lisieux, Sr. Alphonsa, and St. George potentially reflect and forge national identities; here we find that saints and deities of particular churches and temples help to express local identities of (or within) village communities. According to William Christian, the formation of identity through ties between communities and their sacred figures is most strikingly pronounced at the local level. About contemporary Spain, he notes that "Certain shrines seemed to correspond fairly well with certain levels of identity, indeed, they seemed to be utilized as symbols for that identity. This was especially true, of course, for shrines organized to that end—some of the national shrines, the shrine that was shaped to fit the new provincial identity; a couple of shrines that had come to stand for vales; and above all the shrines that stood for villages" (1972: 99). Timothy Mitchell likewise states that "Ethnologists and theologians alike agree that the cult of patron saints has been the most potent and decisive vehicle of local identity in Spain" (1988: 36).[3]

In south India, ethnographers similarly describe local Hindu communities as garnering identity through their ties with a village deity. In the case of the goddess Māriyamman, Brenda Beck (1971) notes the intrinsic connection between a community and the deity as mirroring the perception that the village and its inhabitants are the very body of the goddess herself. When the goddess becomes sick or angry, the community simultaneously experiences some sort of adversity—or vice versa. Richard Brubaker argues that village festivals performed in answer to a particular crisis provide an occasion when this dynamic is played out most strikingly: "In some places it is imperative that every inhabitant remain within the village for the duration of the festival [generally seven days in length] and/or that all outsiders be excluded. . . . Thus it is on these occasions of crisis and ritual response . . . that both the villagers' dependence on their goddess and their own corporate interdependence are most dramatically expressed" (1979: 130–31).

Christian festival activities that honor local saints likewise express intimate connections between heavenly patrons and their communities. In her study of Portuguese saint festivals, Caroline Bretell maintains that these celebrations "serve to define and reinforce community identity" (1990: 59). She notes that for village emigrants, festivals provide an occasion when they can return home and reassert their ties with a local patron and his or her constituent community: "They time their summer vacation in conjunction with its celebration. The saint, in short, is a symbolic representation of their identity" (63).4 In a setting similar to the one Brubaker describes, William Christian notes that Spanish religious officials and group expectations strictly enforce participation in saints' festival processions as well as the correct observance of special vowed days honoring particular village saints. Furthermore, an imposition of fines and public humiliation often fall upon those guilty of noncompliance. Citing a rather extreme example, Christian describes a sixteenth-century Spanish town in which membership to the brotherhood of St. Benedict was required (originally vowed in the fifteenth century) or else individuals would "lose their rights as village members" (1981: 58–59).

As in the north Indian procession portrayed above, communal identification with a European patron saint—heightened during festival celebrations—sets the stage for the devout to act out intercommunal conflicts, as well.5 Mitchell asserts that, given the strong bonds between a community and its saint, it is a "small wonder, then, that a patronal festival can include real skirmishes between locals and outsiders as an unprogrammed side-effect of the festivities" (1988: 36). William Christian likewise notes that regional shrines that attract more than one village are often the site of altercations that erupt "around boundary disputes, stray animals and common lands." In an attempt to avoid these kinds of flare-ups, festival organizers often arrange for different villages' processions to take place on separate days (1981: 118).6

Communal Discord and Harmony in Kerala

In contrast to the climate of interreligious cooperation that typically prevails in Kerala today, Susan Bayly (1989) describes a nineteenth-century breakdown in relations between Syrian Christians and Hindus that she credits to British missionary-colonizers. In short, Bayly argues that this collapse in communal relations was due to English misunderstandings of shared customs traditionally carried out by members of the two traditions. She refers to the British misinterpretation of the practice in which village church and temple members provided funding and materials for the celebration of each others' religious festivals and/or for the building of sacred structures. Although this ecumenical patronage apparently played a part in establishing Hindu and Christian rank in society and reflected a healthy affirmation of the communities' allegiances to one another, the British interpreted it as outright extortion—solely on the part of the Hindu community. Identifying with and wishing to "protect" the Christian traditions from such inappropriate activities, Bayly describes colonial authorities as harshly punishing the Hindus for their deviant behavior. The restrictions and penalties imposed upon the Hindu community—and the "aid" offered the Christians—set into motion a series of events that reflected seriously disrupted relations between the two religious groups (1989: 281–89).

During the late nineteenth and early twentieth centuries, animosity between Hindus and Christians reached its height, seen most visibly during festivals honoring patron saints or deities. According to Bayly, underlying tensions erupted most commonly over the logistics of festival processions and the performance of religious music outside rival temples and churches (313).[7] During the early twentieth century, a Syrian Christian man describes annual festival processions as providing opportunities for Hindu and Syrian participants to march past one another's shrines "howling, screaming and crying out obscene words" (294). One of the worst clashes occurred in 1891, when the Malabar Pūram festival and Easter fell on the same day, and fierce rioting broke out throughout the region. According to Bayly, where once these occasions were opportunities for "the sharing of rites and regalia . . . they now provided a focus for the expression of exclusive communal identities" (313).

Today, although Kerala's church and temple festivals continue to express distinct communal identities, they are most commonly identities not entirely antagonistic toward or even disconnected from communal "others." In any case, contemporary religious festivals almost always reflect, to some degree, relationships radically changed from the days of direct British influence. Most fundamentally, contemporary Christian and Hindu festivals are not "exclusive" events: representatives from both traditions will probably be present at the celebrations. In stark contrast to Bayly's description of communal mayhem unleashed at the Pūram festival one hundred years ago are the traditions currently in vogue at Kerala's famous Pūram festival in Thrissur.[8] For instance, prominent members of society, including a fair share of Christians and Muslims as well as Hindus, perform the prestigious task of offering (that is, feeding) the temple elephants white-stemmed buds from the coconut tree.[9] This tradition is ceremoniously carried out in front of vast crowds of onlookers as the animals, decked out in festival finery, make their way from one end of the procession route to the other. Not only is this kind of interreligious festival participation a sign of communal interdependence common throughout Kerala society today, it is also a sign that imposed colonial structures, such as resentments once generated by British misinterpretations, are often more superficial and precarious than they appear.[10]

Sacred Siblings and Their Festivals

Sibling ties between Kerala's village church saints and temple deities, metaphoric portraits of interreligious cooperation and interdependence, also find public expression during festival activities and events. The festival tradition of rooster sacrifice at St. George's Church in Puthupally provides a basis for one such example. In this village, where locals commonly associate the church saint and the goddess Kālī from a nearby temple as brother and sister, some devotees describe the sacrificial offering as being performed on behalf of sister Kālī, who has a particular thirst for blood. She leaves the meat portion of the sacrifice, in turn, for her brother, St. George.[11] Proof of this sibling cooperation is the claim by witnesses that no blood is spilled during or after the sacrifice. In Manarkad, locals' stories relate similar reciprocation between the village temple goddess, Kaṇṇaki, and her sister, Mary, patron saint of the church up the road. Although fowl sacrifice seems to have died out during the last three decades at the Manarkad church, elderly villagers remember a time when it was an integral part of the church festival event. Similar to the offering St. George shares with Kālī, Mary honored her sister Kaṇṇaki's request that the blood be fed to her bloodthirsty bodyguards. In turn, these *bhūtagaṇangaḷ* saved the leftover meat for Mary.

A more commonly and tangibly recognized sign of sacred sibling ties during festivals takes place during processions honoring the saint or deity. Manarkad's Mary and Kaṇṇaki processions are one pair of examples, among many, that conspicuously contrast with the well-publicized animosity and danger at festival processions elsewhere in India. During Kaṇṇaki's December festival, as she ventures out into the village on an elephant accompanied by her oracle (*veḷiccappāṭa*) and a ceremonial band, people along the way, regardless of their religious beliefs, pay their respects to the goddess by giving her offerings. Likewise, when Mary's September procession (*raza*) winds its way through the Manarkad streets with music and fanfare, those whose homes line the route, whether Hindu or Christian, decorate their entrances as a form of greeting. This is most commonly done with displays artistically set on small tables of tender coconut buds and a lighted traditional oil lamp (*nilaviḷakkà*) or candle, and occasionally an icon or picture of Mary.

A particularly memorable sign of the Manarkad *devī's* ecumenism occurred about forty years ago during her April Pattāmudayam festival. During this celebration, people traditionally dress up as the bird Garuḍa and perform a dance standing on a chariot pulled by a special rope called a *cāṭu*. If all goes according to plan, devotees crowd around the chariot and, grabbing hold of the *cāṭu*, pull the chariot in procession from the main gate to the temple. Yet on this particular occasion, according to an elderly member of the Hindu community, "the chariot bearing the eleven dancers refused to budge from the main gate. Even an elephant was put to task but to no avail. Then the oracle-priest (*veḷiccappāṭa*) for the *devī* went into a trance. Through the *veḷiccappāṭa*, the *devī* asked for her Perumphayathu family, which is Christian. The members of the family were brought on the scene and when they joined in to pull the *cāṭu*, it moved. Since then, at every Pattāmudayam festival, a member of this family must touch the *cāṭu* before [the procession] starts."

When I talked to a senior member of the Perumphayathu family he said that although it was once specified that a certain family member touch the *cāṭu*, it is now acceptable for any Christian to touch it before the chariot can move. In any case, this gentleman did not seem to feel this was a particularly urgent matter. He remarked offhandedly, "every Christian in this area will take part in the festival of the temple. Even the Christians will take part in the *kumpodam* [an event where people pierce their cheeks and chant and jump as a vow and as entertainment for others]." As community members consider it a blessing to take part in pulling the chariot, he reasoned that there would invariably be Christians among the many who are struggling to and occasionally successful in touching the *cāṭu*.[12]

Another instance of Hindu-Christian interdependence during festival time, involving members of the Piravam Śiva temple and those of the nearby Jacobite

Church of the Three Magi, commemorates friendship ties (an alternative to sibling ties) between the deity and the three "saints." According to local tradition, Śiva and the three kings became close comrades during their long and arduous journey to a common destination.[13] As they neared Piravam, the four reached the impressive Meenachil River and, distraught at the prospect of getting across it, stopped dead in their tracks. To their great relief, a Nair gentleman named Chalassery Panikkar came to their rescue with his boat and kindly ferried them across.[14] Once these four "men" arrived in Piravam, devotees recognized that they were not mere mortals and installed them in their places of worship. Because the resulting establishments and divine/saintly presences could not have been possible without the generosity (and good timing) of boatman Chalassery Panikkar, the Piravam community has commemorated his good deed ever since. Even today, his descendants receive gifts from both Hindu and Christian institutions during festival occasions and, before the Magi festival procession can begin, a Panikkar family member must light the church's *nilaviḷakkā* oil lamp.

Sacred Spats and Sibling Rivalries

In spite of innumerable examples of interreligious cooperation portrayed through public festival practices and lore, sacred sibling (and traveling companion) anecdotes can also reflect a more balanced view of such alliances—that is, of their potential indelicacies. In Manarkad, in addition to the tales of harmony cited above, stories also circulate about the petty side of the sisters' relationship. One such account, related by an elderly Hindu gentleman, explains that the large crack in St. Mary's church bell is due to the fact that its tolling was so annoying to Kaṇṇaki in her neighboring temple that she angrily damaged it. In retaliation, Mary produced a crack in the rare right-spiraled conch that temple officials blow during her Hindu sister's *pūjā*.

According to local tradition in Piravam, the four traveling companions, once settled into their respective places of worship/devotion, display mischievous tendencies and fiery tempers that make for a less than idyllic relationship. In a type of "neighborly quarrel" similar to that of the sacred sisters, retaliatory antics once again result in damage—this time, permanent bodily injury. As told to me by a Syrian Catholic middle-aged gentleman employed as a driver,

> On certain days, flowers typically used by Hindus [*tuḷasi* and *cetti*] were found in the church. This was considered to be an insult to the kings. In retaliation, the Magi threw frankincense into the Hindu temple. One day, the Magi found that oil offerings for the church [to light the lamps] were missing, so they kept watch at night to see who was stealing it. During their vigil they found out that Śiva was the culprit. The kings became angry and hit Śiva with their scepter. Thus one arm was severed and the other was broken in two.

Portraying more explicitly a fit of jealous rivalry between Christian and Hindu figures is the tale of St. Sebastian and his sister from the local temple in Thodapuzha. This story was narrated by a Syrian Catholic man, our Kottayam neighbor's brother, over a sumptuous midday meal of water buffalo and assorted curries prepared by his wife.

During the annual St. Sebastian festival, there is a procession from the chapel to the church in which the statue of St. Sebastian is a key figure. It is said that the statue of St. Sebastian refused to move forward one year. The statue itself was supposed to have perspired with the effort. Suddenly, people in the procession heard a big sound. It seemed that invisible obstacles were thus removed and the procession was made clear and moved on. People who were in the temple at this time rushed to the spot of the procession and explained that the loud noise was the *devi* being thrown into the pool. The story is that the *devi*, as the sister of St. Sebastian, wanted him to be with her and not go to church. There was thus a tussle that St. Sebastian won by pushing her into the pool.

A Puthupally story about Kālī and St. George likewise reflects competition between siblings, not only through the community's interpretation of experienced events but also through the actions devotees chose to take based upon their understanding of sacred sibling dynamics. As proposed by the storyteller, an Orthodox Syrian middle-aged gentleman, this community's course of action, which took place during a smallpox epidemic, reflects the Hindu belief that when one god becomes angry and therefore destructive, another is sent in to prevail over the catastrophe and to set things right. As a former resident of Puthupally, he related the following as part of his childhood memories.

> As it was believed that the smallpox was brought on by Kālī's anger, the members of the community, both Hindu and Christian, decided that they should appeal to St. George for their release from the disease. They conducted a procession, complete with drumming, music, and prayers to which they marched all along the village roads. That night, when the people were all in bed it is said that the sound of horse hooves could be heard. The next morning, the disease had vanished. Word of this incident became well known by people all around, and so worship of St. George grew beyond the Orthodox Christian community, especially among Hindus.

Sacred Harmony and Communal Accord

As intimated by these last few stories, the well-being of the community itself— whether having to do with its members' physical health or ability to perform rituals—may rely significantly upon a happy balance between sacred siblings. Local stories do not simply portray saints and deities as tending exclusively to their respective religious communities, but often connect the keeping of peace between the sibling duo with the well-being of all concerned, Christians and Hindus alike. Sibling tales that illustrate the benefit of the larger community as reliant upon harmonious saint-deity ties thus emphasize not only the common interests of both human communities but a certain interdependence between the sacred and earthly realms, as well. A Syrian Catholic man in his fifties provided an example of this multifaceted dynamic through his tale of Manarkad Mary and Kaṇṇaki. Once again, the two are engaged in a sisterly spat.

> These two females are generally on good terms. One day, however, when there was a procession for one of the figures, the two did not look at each other. One of them, I think it was the *devi*, became offended because she was not acknowledged by the other. Following this, there was an epidemic of chicken pox. An oracle-priest

(*veḷiccappāṭā*) cast his shells and found out the reason, which was that the *devī* was offended by the other. Because the people were affected by the quarrel, the two sisters needed to come to a reconciliation and thus today they are friends again.

A similar situation, this time taking place in Bharananganam, again illustrates how human catastrophe can result from broken exchanges between sacred companions (these two, like the Magi and Śiva, are traveling buddies, not brothers). As told to me by Bino, a Hindu man in his twenties, however, the troubled relations between Bharananganam's Kṛṣṇa and St. Sebastian had less to do with the celestial whims of the saint or deity than with a faulty human agenda. According to local tradition, the bond between these two sacred figures was forged during their lengthy travels by boat along the Meenachil River, which eventually brought them to their respective places of honor. After simultaneously installing the two of them in a temple and church close to one another, devotees have, ever since, ritually remembered this common installation and friendship during their annual festivals—with the fateful exception of one year. This was described by Bino at a seaside Kerala resort where he worked as a lifeguard (far from his home in Bharananganam).

> The annual feast of the temple and the main feast of the church occur on the same day in January—I forget the date. Many traditions are followed during these festivities. That day a *muttukuṭam* [specially decorated temple umbrella used by both churches and temples] is given to the temple from the church and a *nilaviḷakkā* [Indian oil lamp traditionally used in temples but also in churches] is given to the church from the temple. During the processions this *muttukuṭam* is held in front of the main deity and the *nilaviḷakkā* is carried before the statue of St. Sebastian.
>
> Some twenty-five years back, a group of nuns and priests petitioned to the bishop to give permission to stop this exchange. That year the church procession was held without the *nilaviḷakkā* from the temple. The adverse effects due to this started from the very beginning. The statue of St. Sebastian became unusually heavy and it was difficult to lift, even with the help of many people. When the procession reached the northern turn, a private bus lost control and ran into the crowd, killing ten to fourteen people and injuring many. Ever since, even now, the *nilaviḷakkā* is held before the statue of St. Sebastian during processions.

Another story that relates human negligence, this time seemingly invoking the spite of the deity rather than the saint, takes place outside Ernakulam. This anecdote of catastrophe was related to me by a young Syrian Catholic priest, Fr. Anthony. Unlike the previous story (and perhaps not coincidentally), Fr. Anthony's tells of the short-sightedness of Hindu extremists rather than the closed-minded "mistakes" of Catholic nuns and clergy. Moreover, in this case the resulting "punishment" affected only the erring party's community, not both. Involving yet another manifestation of St. Sebastian, this tale reflects Kannur's traditional linking of the saint and his Latin Catholic community with the goddess Kālī and her temple devotees.

As described by the priest, a Kannur tradition carried out during St. Sebastian's festival procession has been, as long as anyone can remember, to open the main temple doors so that the goddess can greet her brother as he passes her turf. Four to five years ago, local members of the R.S.S., a "fundamentalist" Hindu political party, decided that this local tradition of Hindu-Christian familial relations had gone on long enough. As a tangible symbol of their position, they convinced the temple officials to keep Kālī's doors closed during St. Sebastian's annual jaunt. Following that year's procession, a number of misfortunes occurred in the Hindu community. As a result, members reasoned—with the support of the *pūjāri* at the temple—that the goddess was angry for being kept from her annual viewing of her brother and was therefore seeking revenge by causing trouble. Convinced that interreligious exchange between sacred figures was more to their benefit than exclusivity, the temple resumed its yearly practice of opening its doors to the passing Christians and their saint.

These stories of short-sighted human omission and divine punishment—of reparation and apparent forgiveness—emphasize mutual reliance among sacred figures and between the sacred and earthly realms, as well. Although the tale of Mary and Kaṇṇaki demonstrates that the well-being of humanity depends upon sacred civility, the latter two stories show how saints and deities themselves rely upon communal cooperation in order that their own material needs be met. As I argue in the next chapter, tangible, physical interdependence between sacred figures and their human devotees is central to local religious practice, expressed most vividly through vowed exchanges by members (that is, saints and deities as well as earthly beings) of both traditions.

Tamil Family Ties within the Hindu Tradition

In their separate studies of Madurai temple poetry and tradition, William Harman and Dennis Hudson describe sibling relations between two of the Madurai region's major temple gods, Viṣṇu (known locally as Aḷagar) and Śiva (known locally as Sundareśvara). They find, furthermore, that these Tamil sibling ties reflect lived interactions between their constituent communities. By creating family connections between deities, the communities forge, as Hudson puts it, "an alliance characteristic of South Indian thought today" (1996: 17–18). Harman describes the sacred kinship metaphor as providing a social basis from which humans work out their interactions: "They define those on whom we can depend, from whom we can expect helpful or indifferent behaviors; they provide us with norms for interpersonal relations" (1989: 146–47).

The story as related by Trivikrama's eighth-century Tamil temple poetry depicts the goddess Pārvatī (known locally as Mīnākṣī) as the sister of Viṣṇu (Aḷagar)—the same relationship described in the Sanskrit *Bhāgavata Purāṇa*. The Tamil account further entrenches sacred family connections by marrying Mīnākṣī to Sundareśvara, making the two male deities brothers-in-law. The Madurai legend as locally told elaborates upon this temple tradition by adding a familiar twist to the tenor of the male deities' sibling tie—one which, unlike that of the temple poetry, rests on an unresolved if not discordant note. In this oral rendition, Sundareśvara notifies his future brother-in-law of a wedding date, prompting the latter to make a rather lengthy journey to the celebration, wedding gift in hand. After traveling twelve miles, Aḷagar arrives at the outskirts of the village where the wedding is to take place only to discover that Sundareśvara had mistakenly given him the wrong date. Consequently he misses his sister's wedding. In anger, Aḷagar refuses to cross over the river bordering Sundareśvara and Mīnākṣī's village. He passes on his present to a messenger rather than deliver it to the couple himself. After several days, the slighted Aḷagar trudges back home to his temple.

As Harman and Hudson describe it, Madurai inhabitants tell this story of divine siblings as a backdrop or means for bringing together two separate temple festivals occurring in the area. Taking place during the full moon of the month of Citrā, the festivals of the Mīnākṣī-Sundareśvara and Aḷagar temples coincide every year. The first temple festival annually reenacts Mīnākṣī and Sundareśvara's wedding, while the latter plays out a journey taken by Aḷagar as a means for offering *darśan* to his devotees. Possible impetus for the combining of the two festivals and for the origins of this local story—posited by Hudson and later elaborated upon by Harman—is the personal and political agenda of Tirumalai Nāyakkar, a seventeenth-century ruler of Madurai. The two authors agree that this Vaiṣṇava ruler would probably have benefited from strengthening the popularity of the Aḷagar (Vaiṣṇava) temple in a region historically known to be a Śaiva stronghold. An effective means for doing so would be to bond as brothers-in-law the Śaiva and Vaiṣṇava deities. Such bonds seemed to have assuaged the often troublesome communal ties between Śaiva and Vaiṣṇava factions, forging for Tirumalai Nāyakkar the political allegiance necessary to help him reestablish the Pāṇḍya kingdom recently broken from the Vijayanagara empire (Hudson, 1977: 111–13; 1982: 137–39; Harman 1989: 80–83).

Aside from the fact that this Tamil example of divine sibling relations offers an interesting parallel to dynamics between sacred siblings and their communities in Kerala, the overtly political dimensions of the Tamil story are worth exploring. Of particular note are the discrepancies between majority understandings of sacred sibling relations and the more formalized or official conceptions: local portrayals of the divine brothers-in-law are fraught with tensions and ambivalences, whereas official channels construct the family relationship with much less ambiguity, if any at all.

On one hand, let us accept for the moment Hudson's and Harman's elaborately and convincingly argued case that the seventeenth-century Vaiṣṇava ruler composed or at least promoted the currently popular brother-in-law tradition. Although it was undoubtedly expedient for Tirumalai Nāyakkar to create (or perhaps to promote a preexisting) ritual and narrative means for bridging the gap between the Vaiṣṇava and Śaiva communities, it does not make sense that a politically motivated rendition of the story would have included an insulted Aḷagar who stops short at the river's edge only to return home, slighted and angry. Hudson indeed describes the tension in the local myth as accurately portraying ancient rivalries between lower-caste devotees of Aḷagar and members of the Brahman-led Mīnākṣī-Sundareśvara temple (1982: 139; 1977: 110). Yet it seems questionable that symbolic representations of these tensions would have willingly been promoted by a ruler whose interest is communal cohesion. If Tirumalai Nāyakkar was interested in furthering Madurai's local brother-in-law tradition, which is likely, he would undoubtedly have reconstructed—or at least embellished—the story line to make it less contentious. Nevertheless, although the story lacks a happy ending, the ongoing local tradition connecting the two temple festivals indicates a perseverance of sectarian cohesion that reflects, in Hudson's words, "the ideal and hope of unity while recognizing at the same time its flawed nature" (1977: 117).[15]

In contrast with the agenda of cohesion probably held by the seventeenth-century ruler, the contemporary "official" stance is that the two Madurai festivals are in no way associated. Temple officials apparently understand the Mīnākṣī-Sundareśvara festival as simply celebrating a wedding, while the other temple festival commemorates Aḷagar's journey—neither of which has anything to do with the other. The only recognized connection between the two is the fact that they fall during the same approximate time period. The two temples and their respective communities are therefore currently related only through popular tradition rather than official precept. Nevertheless, it seems that the tradition of brothers-in-law and their precarious alliance ultimately wins out over official perceptions as, according to Hudson, the public gives it much more importance than the separate stories assigned to the two temples (1982: 135).

By speculating upon and drawing attention to the differences between popularized and official discourses, both past and present, I am suggesting that the nonofficial Tamil tradition assumes a certain life of its own. The dynamics of sacred siblings (in-law) portrayed by local traditions seem to be reinforced by the fact that they accurately convey tensions and ambivalences intrinsic to communal (as well as familial) relations. In light of the previous chapter's discussion of colonial hybridization, it should not be surprising that the village tradition's resilient life of its own maintains elements of dominant ideologies—that is, Tirumalai Nāyakkar's agenda is still carried out, as are the officially recognized separate religious festivals. Yet, at the same time, local traditions insistently reinterpret and reshape official ideologies and prescriptions.[16] I argue that nonofficial traditions of ambivalence and hybridity often enjoy an enduring quality because they reflect important political realities not in accord with (contrived) discourses promoted at times through official channels.

2. Beyond Siblings: Portrayals of Exclusivity, Unanimity, and Ambiguity

The discrepancy between majority perceptions of ambivalent relations and the more rigid constructions often promoted by religious and political officials may also be seen in Kerala. The latter perspective can be explored, using saints and saint mediums as the basis for most examples, first in the Kerala Hindu and Christian public prescriptions for religious exclusivism and, second, in arguments for the negation of religious difference. Although these two viewpoints represent opposing ideologies, they share a similar tendency to simplify and rigidify religious identities and delineations.

Prescriptions for Religious Exclusivity

The experiences of a young Hindu woman, Renuka, who acts as a medium for Sr. Alphonsa provide an interesting forum from which to view promotions for religious exclusivism. Renuka's prophetic abilities—which she understands as being transmitted by the deceased nun-saint—began at a young age, after she experienced a miraculous cure attributed to Alphonsa's healing powers. Renuka's fame is such that large numbers of clients—Hindus, Christians and Muslims alike—regularly make visits to her house for consultation.

Renuka, a petite, attractive young woman, was seventeen years old in 1994 when I visited her with two of my friends. She lived at her parents' home, located on a busy road outside the town of Thrissur. With poise and confidence Renuka explained her special relationship to Alphonsa by tracing her early history and miraculous transformation. She told us that, as a young child, she was able neither to walk nor talk. After years of extensive treatment the doctors finally gave up on a medical cure and told her parents that they must simply go home and pray. Before they left the hospital, the superintendent of the institution, a nun, presented Renuka's family with a picture of Alphonsa, and directed them to frame and keep it in her room. Renuka describes the sequence of events that followed.

> When we brought the picture home, the people here told us that she's just an ordinary nun and not a god to be prayed to. The people who said this were Christians, so my parents thought that if a Christian says this, then it must be true. My parents didn't tear up the picture, however. They just thought that there was no harm in praying, so let's pray to her. We took the photo to our *pūjā* room and lighted a candle before the photo which was fixed on the wall of the *pūjā* room.
>
> On July 28, the death anniversary of Sr. Alphonsa, I was able to talk. I called out, "Amma!" [Mother] but everybody thought that it was my younger brother who called out. My brother was sleeping with my mother in the hall, but I was sleeping in the room nearby with my sister. After calling "Amma!" several times, I walked up to her and called "Amma!" again. My mother turned around and saw me near her bed, like a normal child. My mother asked me how I got there. I said that I had the help of the *ammumma* [grandmother]. Hindus have a belief that dead people can visit their loved ones. My mother immediately asked me, "How was she dressed?" I said that she was dressed in a long white cloth and that she wore a black cloth on her head. I was speaking so well. I continued that she [Alphonsa] told me, "Come near me and I will give you a rose." My mother showed me St. Alphonsa's picture and asked me if I saw this person and I said, "Yes.". . . After that incident, I was transformed into a normal child.

People began making trips to see and get advice from Renuka in 1983, shortly after her cure, when she was six years old. Her first experience of prophecy, as Renuka explains it, involved the saving of her father's life. One morning, as he was setting out to catch the bus for work, she implored him to stay home for fear of his life. After a short while, she changed her mind and told him that he could go. Her family later learned that the bus her father normally took was in a serious accident, killing many of the passengers. When people asked Renuka how she knew there would be an accident, she reportedly replied, "It was the same mother who was in the picture."

The steady flow to Renuka's house of clients from a variety of religious backgrounds is testimony to the fact that many people have little difficulty with the idea that a Christian "saint" is making use of a Hindu woman as a conduit for her communication. As stated by Renuka, "Alphonsa cannot be in the world now, but through children like me, she can proclaim the presence of God." There are others, however, who are troubled by this ecumenical combination. For instance, Hindu sannyasis occasionally come to Renuka's home and try to convince her that she should not, as a Hindu, pray to Christian saints. More commonly, however, she receives visits from local nuns and priests who insist that she must convert to Christianity. On her periodic sojourns to Bharananganam, some of the Sisters at Alphonsa's convent also try to convince Renuka to convert to Christianity and, furthermore, to become a nun like Sr. Alphonsa.[17] Although she has no intention of doing so, Renuka did not consider such propositions insulting but, rather, an affirmation of her life and relationship with Alphonsa.

Renuka also recalled some of the more drastic measures meant to put her in her place, performed by members of the Catholic hierarchy—which she related with a mixed sense of amusement and annoyance. She described one such occasion, which occurred soon after her childhood cure, involving a skeptical and meddlesome local priest.

> Every day my mother keeps a flower on the place where Alphonsa was found.[18] One day, I told my mother that I too would like to keep a flower. Then two flowers were kept in that place. The next day, we saw that the one kept by me remained fresh while the other dried up. We went and informed some of the Sisters in the nearby convent. One of the priests from there came to our house. He was a bit suspicious. Without anyone noticing, he took one petal from the same flower and sneaked it to the back of the picture. Then he went away. On the next day, when he returned, he saw that the petal dried up but the flower remained fresh.

Another example of the more invasive tactics meant to set Renuka and her family straight was related by Renuka's mother. As she described it, some nuns from a nearby convent insisted that if their family did not convert to Christianity they would be cursed. As might be expected, the elder woman panicked and seriously considered conversion. Responding to her mother's fears, Renuka prayed to Sr. Alphonsa and was told by the saintly nun that there was no reason to convert to Christianity and, furthermore, that they should pray that the sins of these presumptuous people be forgiven.

Back in Bharananganam, I reported to Sr. Josephina that I had made a trip to Thrissur to visit Renuka. She said that she knew about the young woman but added that the Church did not officially endorse her as a medium. Authorities are apparently uncertain as to whether Renuka's messages are truly transmitted from Sr. Alphonsa or from some other source not necessarily holy. As Sr. Josephina reasoned, "It's hard to know who is genuine and who is mentally unstable." But, always ready to keep an open mind, she did not want to rule out the possibility that the Hindu woman was communicating with Sr. Alphonsa in spite of ecclesial suspicions. Citing examples such as Joan of Arc and Galileo, Sr. Josephina spoke of individuals who have presented great threats to the institution but later were accepted or even, in the case of Joan of Arc, canonized. In any case, Renuka seemed to her to be "a sweet, pious girl, no doubt." Reflecting for a moment on the often-cited slogan for religious unity in Kerala, "God is One," Sr. Josephina summed up her ambivalent stance on the matter: "I know that God is One, I'm just not sure if He's at the temple or not."

Prescriptions for Unity and the Negation of Religious Boundaries

The desire for religious unity, typified by the statement, "God is One," represents an alternative—and in some ways, opposing—perspective to that of religious exclusivism. In spite of their conflicting ideologies, these two approaches are similar in their aim to portray or promote an unambivalent and fixed relationship between Christians and Hindus in Kerala, in contrast to the complexity offered through such traditions as sacred sibling stories.

The ideology of religious unity underlying the popular Indian saying, "God is One," is one that Keralite members of Christian traditions seem to hold more tentatively than do members of Hindu traditions. The phrase, "one caste, one religion, one God for man" is the most often quoted of the many aphorisms coined by Sri Narayana Guru, a highly influential Keralite sannyasi and vocal philosopher-humanist of the late nineteenth and early twentieth centuries.[19] In Kerala, contemporary devotees of Sri Narayana Guru—those who maintain and visit his shrines scattered throughout the state—are largely members of the Hindu Izhava caste. Yet his teachings enjoy a much wider audience not only within the Hindu community but throughout Kerala's Christian and Islamic communities, as well. It is in his honor that during a variety of Hindu festivals, a Sarva Mata Sammēlanam is held in which speakers from a variety of religious backgrounds come to give lectures on the topic of virtuous living. As insisted by Sri Narayana Guru, it is not religious adherence that determines the sanctity of an individual but rather his or her upright character.

In spite of the occasional ecumenical forum that supports the unity of all peoples and religions, this position—in its most extreme form, arguing for a complete negation of religious boundaries—is held most commonly by Hindu ritual specialists and priests (*pūjāris*) rather than by lay people. A Hindu astrologer in Kollam, to whom a number of Christians and Muslims regularly come for consultation, is among those for whom religious distinction seems to be arbitrary. Well versed in the Christian pantheon of saints and their attributes, this astrologer told me that he recommends devotion to saints for his Christian clients—"but only," he added, "because this is their faith. I ask them what their faith is and then proceed." In spite of the religious distinctions he draws for his clients, he does not see any difference between the Christian saints and Hindu gods—all are equally efficacious. After reflecting upon this ecumenical pantheon of equals, the astrologer flatly stated, "I don't see any divisions between religions, all are one."

Although many lay Hindus, and some Christians, likewise dispose of religious boundaries for their own purposes, their comments to this effect are conveyed more often with a degree of reservation. Many may regard religious distinctions as arbitrary in theory, but they admit to the ways they are, in practice, very real. In Renuka's family *pūjā* room, for example, her mother foregrounds images of Hindu deities with the traditional Hindu oil lamp. Conspicuously set before Alphonsa's picture is a candle, which is customarily associated with Christian devotion.[20] She does this in spite of the understanding this family shares (as does Alphonsa through her messages to Renuka) that "God is One."

During a conversation with a young *pūjāri* and a layman friend of his in his sixties outside the Manarkad *devī* temple, I learned that the connection Hindu devotees made between Mary and Kaṇṇaki often had to do with the sacred females' shared Brahmanical family background. Although the *pūjāri* left the story at that (implying that the sisters are "one" in terms not only of a common religion but a common caste and family, as well) his friend offered an addendum to the story. He underscored the fact that in spite of the sisters' unity, the separate religious traditions practiced by their devotees are a lived reality.

> *Pūjāri:* It's a belief [that Mary and Kaṇṇaki are sisters] that is quite accepted tradition-ally by the local people. There were two *illangal* [Brahman family homes] called Ochi-mattathy Cherumutta *illangal*—they're cousins, both with the same names. They were sons of two sisters. These families worshiped these sisters and it was understood that one of them was the St. Mary of the Manarkad Church and the other family wor-shiped the deity of the temple.
>
> Friend: Both families actually worshiped a single power but later it was separated into Hindu and Christian. At first, these families knew that both powers were one, but when people began to be connected to Christianity, there came a great rift between the two sisters—the great rift of religion. As time passed, because of their religion, they were looked upon as two although they were actually one.

A middle-aged Hindu man who owns a photo processing shop in Ettumanur just south of Kottayam likewise expressed the "unfortunate" reality of separate religious traditions in spite of his belief in an underlying unity. On the topic of Hindu/Christian sacred sibling stories, Mr. Nair proposed that religious officials fabricated them so that they could convince the deluded public of the correct belief that religions are, in fact, united and not separate: "All of us are interrelated. We have some relation or other to speak of. These stories have been created because people in the old days were mostly false-believing and so they had to have some sort of silly stories to help them believe that all the gods are one and to make religious harmony."

Although I found Hindus in Kerala to be more accepting of arguments for religious unity, a Christian priest was the first to bring such a position to my attention. During my first visit to the inside of an Orthodox Syrian church, I was fortunate to be accompanied by Fr. Varghese, who graciously agreed to lead me on an extended tour. As we were finishing our rounds, I asked him a few questions about his tradition. Because I had recently arrived in Kerala, I was curious about how local Hinduism influenced his tradition, but was unsure as to whether or not this kind of question would be an affront to a Christian priest. After I made several feeble attempts at tangentially approaching the subject, Fr. Varghese finally understood the gist of my questions and announced with great pride, "I am a Hindu!" After a moment of confusion about who he actually was and in what religious building we really were, I was able to compose myself and continue our discussion. Fr. Varghese explained that the prevailing culture for everyone residing in India, regardless of their religion, is the same. "We are all Hindus in India," he said. While he prays to a Christian god and someone else may follow a Hindu or Muslim god, all are performing rites and practicing rituals that are essentially Hindu. This kind of thinking, argued Fr. Varghese, may be unpopular among most Christians as well as among Hindu extremists, but it is absolutely necessary for the future harmony of the country—"we must all think of ourselves as one if our nation is going to survive."[21]

After this initial exchange with Fr. Varghese, during the rest of my stay in Kerala I tried out his philosophy on a number of other Keralites. I found that Hindus from a variety of religious and political persuasions were largely supportive of the priest's words. Christians, on the other hand, were not as eager to adopt his position. The exceptions to this, and there were a few, were limited primarily to priests and mainly during conversations tending toward the abstract or philosophical.

Interreligious "Sibling" Resemblances

Regardless of whether or not Christians consciously adopt Fr. Varghese's idea that they are, in fact, "Hindus," there is no doubt that many Christian practices in Kerala, fully approved by their respective denominations, are derived from the prevailing cultural context. The assimilation of a surrounding culture within which a religious tradition has flourished and developed over many centuries should not be surprising, nor is it by any means unique to Kerala. Although customs and rites shared by Malayali Hindus and Christians show many external similarities, however, divergent interpretations of these practices—particularly on the official level—help to lend distinctiveness to the various communities. Somewhat like the colonial hybridization discussed in the first chapter, Christian traditions as practiced in Kerala often balance themselves between an appearance of assimilation with and an asserted identity decidedly separate from the culturally dominant, in this case Hindu, traditions. Rather than expressing concern over the encroachment of foreign "modernity," ecclesial leaders in this context seem forever to be debating the extent to which Christian practices have become too domesticated—that is, too Hindu.[22] Such debates reflect from yet another angle the tensions intrinsic to Kerala Christianity's complex hybridity.

Among the resemblances between Kerala's Christian and Hindu communities, most familiar to the public (because they are the most visible) are church and temple festival processions and their trappings. The procession as a main festival event is not, as we have seen, an exclusively Indian phenomenon; many Christians outside India typically honor saints in a similar manner. Nevertheless, some of the compulsory procession details in Kerala Christian festivals reflect influences that are decidedly south Indian. For example, during Hindu and Christian processions, traditional south Indian royal paraphernalia add flourish and pomp to the event and to the statue or icon of the honored holy figure—always garlanded with flowers as it brings up the rear. Placed on the elephant carrying the Hindu deity or waved near the relic or statue of the saint during processions are *ālavaṭṭaṅgaḷ* (made from peacock feathers) and *veṇcāmaraṅgaḷ* (made from deer tail hair), fanlike objects associated with Hindu royalty. Commonly festooning the festival grounds and often carried by participants in church and temple processions are *muttukuṭaṅgaḷ*, large brightly colored umbrellas, also a south Indian symbol of royalty or privilege (see Figure 9).[23] At the head of most festival processions, whether Christian or Hindu, is *ceṇḍamēḷam*, intricate and explosive drum music traditionally played by members of the Hindu Marar caste who are, by heritage, temple musicians (see Figure 10). According to a Syrian Catholic priest, no festival procession is complete without this uniquely Keralite drumming leading the way.

Figure 9. Schoolboys with *muttukuṭam* umbrellas moments before Alphonsa's evening festival procession from St. Mary's Church to the Clarist Convent chapel, Bharananganam.

Other south Indian Hindu traditions often integral to Kerala Christianity include a number of rituals marking significant life events. These rituals include a milk-boiling ceremony (*pāl kāccá*) that takes place during the blessing of a newly built house (see Figure 11), the groom's tying of a golden leaf-shaped piece of jewelry (*tāli*) around the bride's neck during the wedding ceremony, and the yearly celebration of a *śrāddham* (or *cattam*) feast commemorating a relative's death. Such ritual events, among others, are not only acceptable in the eyes of most Syrian Catholic, Jacobite, and Orthodox church leaders, including some Protestants, they are often an expected part of Christian life in Kerala.[24] But although Christians perform these rites in a way similar to Hindus, subtle differences in ritual detail or theological nuance often emerge, working, for some, to keep a certain distance from the tradition of the domestic "other." An example of a nuanced difference between Christian and Hindu common practices is that of the wedding *tāli*. Although the tradition of tying a *tāli* around the bride's neck during a wedding ceremony may have similar significance for Hindus and Christians, the design of the *tāli* itself expresses a difference. It can be embellished in a number of ways, depending on the taste and economic status of the owners, but the Christian *tāli*, because it is decorated with a cross, is conspicuously unlike the Hindu one.[25]

In spite of the fact that many Christian denominations officially encourage the presence and further adoption of Indian religious culture into Christian practice—deemed positively as "inculturation" by the Vatican—there are some "Hindu-looking" practices performed by many Christians of which clergy do not always approve. But although they are Hindu in appearance, it is not necessarily true that

Figure 10. Fulfilling a vow, a St. George devotee circumambulates the Aruvithura church with a festival umbrella (*muttukuṭam*), stopping to talk with a lone *ceṇḍamēḷam* drummer. In the background, people line up to receive *kaḷunnà*, small arrows carried as a vow to St. Sebastian.

official Christian disapproval renders them non-Christian. For example, it appears likely that the Middle Eastern and European Christian traditions, when they arrived in Kerala, brought with them the same practices that have currently fallen into disfavor. Two such controversial practices are menstruation restrictions and astrology.[26]

Although the fact that a menstruating Hindu woman will rarely enter a temple during her period is well known in India, I was not aware of this practice among Christian women until Meena, our cook, and I were discussing our plans for going to St. Mary's festival in nearby Manarkad.[27] Meena told me that she and her family looked forward to attending this festival each year. They were planning to go several

Figure 11. Orthodox Syrian priests light incense and *nilaviḷakkả* oil lamps before beginning a house blessing, milk boiling (*pāl kāccả*) ceremony.

times during the eight-day period, especially to see the procession and the *naṭa turakkūka*—a twenty-four hour unveiling of Mary's picture and spiritual high point of the festival (see Figure 12). A few days before the festival was to start, however, Meena, who had earlier been so enthusiastic, commented that she was not sure whether she would be going. She explained that she was expecting her period and was not certain when it would arrive. If it happened soon she could go; if not she would have to stay home during part of the festival while the rest of her family went without her.

As I had never heard the nuns or pilgrims in Bharananganam speak of such things—and because I had spent so much time there I assumed that it would have come up in conversation somehow—I asked Meena to explain this to me. This restriction, as she described it, only applied to certain churches, namely, St.

Figure 12. Miraculous painting of Mary and Jesus during its 24-hour festival exposition (*naṭa tuṟakkūka*), St. Mary Jacobite Church, Manarkad.

Sebastian's in Ettumanur, St. George's in Puthupally, Infant Jesus' in Cherpunkal, and St. Mary's in Manarkad. These four churches are by far the most popular pilgrimage spots in the immediate area, are imbued with particularly impressive powers, and thus require certain restrictions not necessarily applicable to other, less powerful, churches. I later learned from Meena that she regularly attends mass in her nearby (less powerful) church during her period but refrains from receiving communion. I asked her if, in either case, her priest asks that women keep their distance when they are having their periods. A wry smile spread across her face at this suggestion, after which she became very adamant, "No! This is just something that we all know about and do. The priest has nothing to do with it."

Because it appeared to me—judging from Meena's response and from the general silence on the matter—that menstruation restrictions are discouraged by the Catholic hierarchy, I broached the subject with some of the Sisters in Bharananganam during my next visit. Sr. Rita, a younger Sister in her early forties, told me that she had never heard of such a thing and that this woman (Meena) must not really be Christian.[28] After I convinced her that she was indeed, and a Catholic at that, Sr. Rita looked disappointed, "What happens to our bodies is good and natural; there's no need for this." Instead of expressing shock, Sr. Josephina, on the other hand, said that she was well aware of the practice. Women often come to Alphonsa's museum and shrine and ask permission for entrance during their periods, and of course she tells them that there is no need to stay away. Sr. Josephina explained that the belief that women were polluting during menstruation was actually a part of the Hindu tradition and not really Christian, although some women practice it. She suggested that perhaps Meena spent a lot of time with Hindus and was thus influenced. When I next saw Meena I told her what I had learned—that the nuns went to communion during their periods. Seemingly aware of this, she flatly answered, "Yes, I know they do" and, with a shrug, left it at that. Her casual acceptance of this fact suggests to me that nuns are, for Meena, women of a different category. The rules that apply to them do not necessarily apply to the lay woman.

After my initial discussions with Meena and the Sisters at Bharananganam about menstrual taboos, I learned of their practice among women of other denominations, as well. Because they are not officially mandated by any Christian denomination, practitioners appear to observe these restrictions in a variety of ways and to different degrees. An Anglican neighbor of ours whose daughter receives communion during her period does not do so herself because she feels that during this time of the month she is not "mentally prepared." An Orthodox Syrian friend said that his wife will not enter a church during her period but will attend a major festival as long as she stays outside the church building. He felt that this is common practice among Orthodox Syrian and Jacobite women, in spite of the fact that their bishops commonly discourage such behavior. These officials assert that menstruation is a natural part of God's plan and is therefore not polluting. Defending the practice against such accusations, my friend presented the (rather collapsible) argument that menstruating women did not refrain from receiving sacraments or attending religious events due to "superstitious fear" of pollution, but rather out of respect for the liturgy and for the rest of the congregation.

Astrological predictions—which Christians commonly observe in spite of a lack of official sanction—are again an involvement that varies among denominational communities as well as among individuals within the same denomination. Although Catholicism strictly discourages visits to astrologers, Orthodox Syrians and Jacobites are vaguer in their disapproval. Until the beginning of this century it was common, in fact, for Syrian Christian clergy to perform astrological consultations for their parishioners (Bayly 1989: 267). Protestant church members, although not as likely to "sneak off and consult an astrologer," as put by Sr. Josephina, still often pay attention to *muhūrttam*, an Indian system for marking auspicious and inauspicious time periods during each day, as do other Christians. An Orthodox friend told me, with a chuckle, about his Protestant uncle who ridicules all such "superstition." He nonetheless "makes excuses, and says things like 'just wait, someone else is still coming'" in order to delay an event such as a house blessing. In doing so, he surreptitiously orchestrates (as my friend sees it) important rituals so that they fall within auspicious time periods.

In addition to the sway Hindu culture holds over Kerala Christianity, influences of secular India also contribute to the shaping of Christian practice. A clear example of this is the effect that India's policy on population control has had on an otherwise very conservative Catholic contingent, theoretically opposed to artificial forms of birth control.[29] An ex-Catholic priest, when I asked him about these practices so freely and frequently mentioned to me by Catholic women from all social and economic levels, told me a "joke" he had heard as a seminarian. Years ago, during a visit he paid to an elderly priest who was pastor of the Three Magi Catholic Church just west of Kottayam, the two of them found themselves discussing the pope's stance on family planning. The elderly priest commented that throughout his entire parish, he only knew of four members who did not practice birth control. When my friend asked who these "loyal people" might be, the pastor replied with a big laugh, "the Three Magi and myself." The elder priest concluded his witticism on a more serious note: "Why should the people listen to the pope on issues such as birth control?"

A recent statement regarding Indian influences upon Kerala Christianity was published by the 1994 Vatican Sacred Congregation for the Oriental Churches. Here, the Vatican Congregation identifies a "crisis of identity" for Kerala Christians of all denominations. The author describes this situation as emerging from the fact that "Kerala's Christians are neither Hindu nor are they Christian in the 'traditional' European sense" (1994: 75). The solution proposed by the Congregation is not what might be expected—the retrieval of a more European-looking Christianity. On the contrary, the report bemoans the presence of a "'westernization' of a colonial type, of a type which is estranging and unjustified and which is visible in innumerable elements that make up or color the life of certain Christian milieu (particularly among the clergy and the more 'evolved classes')" (75).

This concern expressed by the Vatican seems to be in sympathy with recent efforts of some members of the Indian clergy—with the approval of Rome—to undo the centuries of "Western" influences imposed upon St. Thomas Christians, beginning with the Portuguese. To support these efforts, the Congregation proposes first, that all Syrian Catholic seminarians learn Syriac to better understand their religious roots, and second, that the Catholic Church work toward a fuller integration within Indian culture. This latter proposition includes the suggestion that Christians take on "a serious study and understanding of Hinduism," as it is a "fundamental component of this culture" (76). What exactly is done with the study and understanding of Hinduism is, however, of crucial interest to the Congregation. The writers of the report caution their readers to

> bear always in mind that there are inseparable and radical differences between the ethicaoreligious [sic] perspective of Hinduism—of any Hinduism—and that of Christianity. It does nobody any good—and is contrary to the truth—to pass under silence or pretend to ignore such differences, cutting out for oneself a Hinduism according to one's wishes, made out to suit Christianity, or accumulating false "parallels" which cannot convince anyone and which manifest only superficiality and cultural "approximation" thereby being unjust to Hinduism no less than to Christianity itself and laying oneself open, not unfoundedly, to the accusation or the suspicion on the part of sensitive Hindus of "spiritual imperialism" and of insincere maneuvers. (76)

These concerns expressed by the Congregation appear to be part of a reaction—as might be expected—to recent efforts made by Indian clergy-liturgists to incorporate a number of Hindu motifs and symbols into the Catholic mass. The excerpts of the report quoted here are an epilogue to a lengthy and detailed critique of what the Congregation considers to be unacceptable liturgical hybridization. Although it appears that the Vatican Congregation is aware—and perhaps even repentant—of Catholicism's history of colonial imposition upon domestic culture, there seems to be a limit as to how far these current efforts toward inculturation can comfortably go. Although the local Christian practices described in this chapter reflect a certain degree of hybridization, with and without church approval, the formal liturgy itself appears to represent one of the more impregnable bastions of Hindu-Christian separation within the Kerala Catholic tradition. The tension between those members of the Catholic hierarchy who eagerly push for liturgical reform and those who struggle to maintain what they believe is essentially Christian—a tension out of which this Vatican report emerges—marks a polarization of official desires somewhat similar to that which this chapter repeatedly describes.[30]

Constructions of Communalism: Familiar Dichotomies

For yet another example of rigidly perceived and conceived interreligious relations, let us return to events such as the Indian festival upheaval depicted at the beginning of this chapter. Gyanendra Pandey (1990) argues that the use of the term "communalism" in reference to violent and irrational relations between Indian religious groups is largely a construct of British colonizers, but he also notes that this term and its associated meaning was later put into use by Indian nationalists, as well. Although the two groups had opposite agendas, the perspectives put forward by both tend to reflect, once again, the kinds of totalizing prescriptions described throughout this chapter.

In Pandey's discussion of communalism as a British construction, he notes that interreligious communal tensions naturally arose out of local issues that stemmed from such mundane matters as land disputes—practicalities foreign colonists tended to overlook. Because of their tendency to overdetermine an "all-India" Muslim or Hindu community, British administrators often reduced complex communal tensions to disputes about religion (1990: 16).[31] Beginning in the nineteenth century, the term "communalism" was often used to describe violent flare-ups between Muslim and Hindu groups, associating them with the perceived religious fanaticism and irrationality of the masses. British officials considered this divisive impulse to be an intrinsic part of the Indian race's primitive culture; it was the opposite of colonialism's natural tendency toward cohesiveness and a counterforce to the rationality this cohesiveness required (10).

According to Pandey, India's nationalist movement ironically assimilated into its own rhetoric a notion of communalism similar to that conceived by British colonizers. Although not identical to British constructions of communalism, nationalist understandings likewise linked the phenomenon of local religious antagonisms with primitive and irrational impulses—aberrant behavior that blocked the way for a successful nationalist movement (247). The colonialist belief that Indian culture is essentially divided and divisive was countered by nationalist rhetoric arguing, in many cases, for Indian culture's true spirit of oneness. As described by Pandey, this perceived Indian destiny of unity became configured by nationalists as its "Essence, an already existing Oneness, seeking to realize its eternal mission" (151). It is this essential unity, and the secularism and rationalism that it presupposes, which nationalists perceived communalism as consistently thwarting.

By juxtaposing these two different portrayals of communalism, Pandey makes the case that nationalist portrayals not only of the nature of communalism but of nationalism itself acted to perpetuate colonial notions of an eternal and fixed Indian culture. He goes on to argue that the making of what has been construed as irrational "communal" impulses by the colonial powers, and no less by nationalists, ultimately robs individuals and groups of their histories and of their ability to act within those histories (21). Pandey, along with a number of other postcolonial scholars, thus makes an appeal for the dismantling of perceived dyads such as nationalism/communalism or secularism/communalism, and ultimately challenges the "imperialism" and the "givenness" of these kinds of categories (22).

The notion that Indian culture is essentially united or split—as promoted by nationalists and imperialists, respectively—echoes this chapter's portrayal of rigid prescriptions put forth by religious and political officials in Kerala and Tamil Nadu. Furthermore, the argument that Hindus and Christians are either irrevocably at odds or else united as "one" provokes reservations similar to the ones Pandey expresses. The idea that Hindus and Christians are capable of having traditionwide relations that are either entirely cohesive or separate implies a monolithic "Christianity" or "Hinduism" and conveniently ignores potential regional, economic, or historical differences and/or commonalties. Furthermore, the construction of a static relationship between entire traditions, whether forever at odds or essentially united, eliminates the possibility that different groups—or individuals, for that matter—have histories of their own. Evidence that myriad histories and perspectives exist within the boundaries of a religious tradition repeatedly emerges in Kottayam district through the fact that tensions in that area are far more likely to erupt over interdenominational than interreligious squabbles.[32]

Ultimately, by eradicating complex histories and the varieties of possible denouements, people and their communities are denied a political stance grounded in everyday life as well as a role in molding these lives. Although the notion that "God is One" is a noble one, often argued in the interest of interfaith peace and harmony, its potential shortcoming is in the blurring of distinctions vital to individual and/or communal identities. And, as local sibling stories demonstrate, differences in identity, although potentially problematic, do not necessarily lead to catastrophe.

Beyond Sibling Tales: Christian-Hindu Reliance and Rivalry Revisited

Removed from the rigidifying tendencies of nationalist policy, colonialist perception, or the honing of "ethicaoreligious" discrepancies (as coined by the Vatican), a number of local traditions, which include interreligious village rites as well as local tales of church origins, are worth exploring. Similar to sibling tales, these traditions reflect concerns that seem to be more comfortable with the ambiguities of life in Kerala's religiously plural context.

For example, interreligious purification rites, described to me by people from different parts of Kerala, provide concrete instances of the interconnected but separate nature of many Christian and Hindu communities. In a number of Hindu temples throughout the state, for instance, oil used for ritual purposes must be made pure by the touch of a Christian. Although it is less common, some churches require a Brahman from within the village community to touch the church oil before it can be used for their lamps. Describing a similar observance, an elderly man seated in the shade outside the Śiva temple in Ettumanur told me that "in the old days" a new temple needed the touch of a Christian and a new church the touch of a Hindu in order that they be purified for future worship. These locally designated rituals acknowledge both religious distinctiveness and the groups' interdependence within the village context.

Stories that recount the construction of churches also tend to highlight the realities of separate but related communities—for better and for worse. The Puthupally St. George church building, for instance, boasts truly ecumenical origins and continues this tradition of interreligious cooperation into the present day. During the church's construction, different members of the community, both Hindu and Christian, offered their professional skills. Today they continue to exert their "right" to provide these services for the upkeep of the building in order that the saint continue to bestow blessings and favors in return. From a crowded and clattering tea stall next to the church, an eighty-two-year-old Orthodox Syrian gentleman enthusiastically told me about the different Hindu castes who came and continue to come to the aid of their Christian neighbors and their saint.

> From the very ancient days of the construction of the church up to the present, different castes had their own separate claims, including carpenters even up to the Brahmans. Digging the grave is done by the Ullatans. The flag mast is prepared by the carpenters and they have their own separate rights. They bring offerings like a chair or wooden pieces to the church and for this they are given favors. Panams are the tailors—they make and repair the silken umbrellas. They also claim and are given certain rights. Another group will bring a mat. Upon this mat is placed the *appam* [rice cake] for the [festival] feast. Ironsmiths come and also claim certain rights—the service I do not know. All these different castes of people cooperate for the building and maintenance of the church. As for the sacrificing of the roosters, Ullatans cut down trees in the forest so they were in charge of cutting the roosters' necks with their instruments. The *pūjāri* is the officiating person of the temple—he comes to cleanse the oil for the oil lamp.

A good many church origin stories I have heard and read describe a wealthy Hindu king or prominent Hindu family who offers a piece of land to the Christians so they can build their church.[33] The tale behind the original St. Mary's Church in Bharananganam describes the local ruler or *kartha* as not only encouraging the Christian community to construct their building in the vicinity but helping them to settle a heated dispute about its future location. This widely circulated story, told to me by church officials as well as by locals, recounts an argument between eleventh-century Christians living on either side of the river Meenachil. Each group, understandably, wanted the church to be built on its side of the river. Unable to settle the matter themselves, they approached the local *kartha*, who devised a plan agreed upon by both parties. An elephant was to be led to the middle of the river where a rock, tied to a rope, was to be hung from its trunk. It was then allowed to wander freely. People would watch to see where the elephant happened to drop the rock, and there the church would be built (see Figure 13). As described by the story, the elephant eventually let go of the stone on property owned by the Mekkakat Nair family and, at the insistence of the *kartha*, this land was gifted to the Christians. Ever since then, this Hindu Nair family is given two silver *cakram* coins for every wedding performed at the church. The gift is collected once a year by a representative of the family, who offers fifty-one *neyappam* rice cakes and fifty-one plantains in exchange for the silver.[34]

A college professor and lifetime resident of Bharananganam—uncle and brother to two of the Clarist Sisters—expanded on this church origin story for me with the following more localized and, appropriately, less idyllic version.

> The priest who built the church, Fr. Vallianthadan, made the first structure out of bamboo and palm leaves. This he did and promptly said mass in it. The same day in the evening, some Brahmans came and threw the church in the river. This was a Brahman center and these people—particularly the twenty-two families who had a superiority complex—resented the church being there. After this happened, the Father was understandably distraught. While he was brooding silently in his home, a Nair woman came to pay him a visit. She found him silent and sullen and, not getting an

Figure 13. Monument to local ruler's famous decision-making elephant with rock, St. Mary's Forane Church, Bharananganam.

answer from him, she went to his mother to find out what the matter was. The mother told her the story and the woman was outraged. This *ceṟiyamma* [a term often used to refer to a Nair woman] thus gave a plot of land to the church.[35] While the church was being built, she carried a sword to protect the Father and the church. Now, every year, the church Fathers give money to this same family as a thank-you for their ancestor's bravery and support.

A local story about the Manarkad church's origins likewise centers on a theme of community discord, and includes, once again, a Nair rescue. An elderly Jacobite gentleman told me this tale from his home near the Manarkad temple as part of his answer to my questions about the connection between Mary and Kaṇṇaki.

> There were only a few Christian families in this area at that time [before the church was built]. They did not have a church of their own here, so if they had to conduct a funeral or wedding, they had to go all the way to far-off places. They started fasting for a church in the area. When the people were fasting, they got a vision of a cow and a calf standing in a certain location, and from this vision they were asked to build the church in that place. They began to build the church but as soon as the building was up, the Hindus came and destroyed it. They destroyed it because it was standing on their property. A particular family had a tradition of going through this place with a lighted lamp before a wedding. Because they did not want to disrupt their traditions they began to cause trouble for the Christians.
>
> The oracle of the temple was Elumpilakkattu Narayanan, who was a Nair living in that area. The Christians went to him and bribed him, and thus won him over to their side. The owner of the temple was Tekkumkattu Tamburan [the king]. When the king came on one of his usual visits to the temple, the oracle took his sword and began to scold him, "You have kept closed my place there in the west, you must light a lamp there for me!" This place was the area which the Christians chose for their church. Thus the king came to understand that the *devī* was willing to give a place for the construction of the church. The right of the Christians was established in this way.

The theme of Brahman bullies and Nair rescues relates, on the one hand, a kind of Christian ambivalence toward the larger Hindu community, but it more specifically marks the reality—from the point of view of local experience—that Hinduism is not a monolithic tradition, nor is its relationship to Christianity. While members of one segment of the Hindu community may try to keep Christians from their worship, members of another offer land or risk life and reputation to preserve it. It is likely that the casting of Nairs as the (sometimes dubious) hero(in)es of these stories is not a coincidence. Historically, Nairs and Syrian Christians both belonged to a warrior "caste." Skilled in the martial arts, these two groups often shared their training and fought together in battle. Due to these commonalities in the workplace, Bayly has argued that before the British era, the two communities probably held comparable high-caste standing in Kerala society. They therefore appear to have followed similar customs and observed similar ritual restrictions, perhaps even intermarrying during the fifteenth and sixteenth centuries (1984; 1989: 249, 294). Although this ancient relationship is rarely referred to in regular conversation—Syrian Christians speak with much greater frequency of a Brahman heritage—amiable ties between Christians and Hindu Nairs are remembered through the telling of these local stories.[36]

The Discourse of Ambivalence versus the Rhetoric of Power

Whether portraying the Christian and Hindu communities as separate yet interdependent or as alternately rivalrous and reliant upon one another, these stories of community relations, like the sacred sibling tales, reflect a perspective that resists simplification. Bakhtin speaks of a similar kind of honesty expressed through popular festival images, and constrasts these expressions with the contrived perspectives of "officialdom." According to Bakhtin, official perspectives often portray eternal and unchanging truths, while popular culture "makes a mockery of such arrogant claims" (1968: 212). Nonofficial expressions, often known for their blurring of officially designated categories such as good and evil or sacred and profane, thus become "a powerful means for grasping reality; they serve as a basis for an authentic and deep realism" (211).

The realism and honesty of Kerala's local sacred sibling stories, interreligious rites, and tales of church origins lie in their ability to portray aptly the tensions and relational ambiguities that are an unavoidable part of their pluralistic context. Rather than promoting "eternal truths" couched in representations of static absolutes, stories of church origins and sacred siblings clearly reflect the complicated and multivalent state of affairs evoked by daily life. From a Marxist perspective, Fredric Jameson (1981) also argues that narrative, regardless of what may seem to be private—or poetically abstract, as in the case of sacred sibling stories—is inextricably connected to political realities. To believe otherwise

> becomes something worse than an error: namely a symptom and a reinforcement of the reification and privatization of contemporary life. Such distinction reconfirms that structural, experiential and existential gap between the public and private, between social and psychological, or the political and the poetic, between history or society and the "individual" which—the tendential law of social life under capitalism—maims our existence as individual subjects and paralyzes our thinking about time and change just as surely as it alienates us from our speech itself. (1981: 20)

Jameson's argument describes the significance of narrative in a way that clearly differs from my understanding of Kerala's local stories and rites. He does not view political reality and narrative as having parallel meanings, but rather sees stories as "more specifically symbolic resolutions of real social and political contradictions" (80). Furthermore, Jameson argues that conventional sociology of literature and culture, which "feels that its work is done when it shows how a given artifact 'reflects' its social background, is utterly unacceptable" (81). He considers the interpretation of narrative as "dreamed resolution to a lived contradiction" to be "particularly appropriate for folk genres—thus reaffirming their marginalized status. Affirming without seeing the narrative for its subversive strategies is useless, however" (86).

Although I do not find it difficult to argue that, in many cases, Jameson's formula for folk genres holds true, the "subversive" element of Kerala's local stories appears to be precisely the reverse of what Jameson describes. These "folk" tales do not represent a dreamed resolution of a lived political contradiction but, rather, the honest complication of officialdom's tendency toward abstract, one-dimensional resolutions.

Among the examples that contradict Jameson's formula are Madurai's local sacred sibling narratives—particularly when compared with the Tamil ruler's hypothesized desire for a communally united front or temple officials' denial of ritual connection between the two temple communities. These latter two positions represent officialdoms' dreamed resolutions to perceived political problems, whereas the popularized expression reflects more honestly the complicated relations between neighboring communities. In this case, the local community's tradition stands as a mouthpiece for societal "contradictions" or ambivalences rather than for their resolution. Likewise, Pandey's description of colonialist and nationalist fabrications of an essential Indian "character" provides further examples of dreamed resolutions meant to advance fraught political agendas. As mentioned above, the notion that Indian culture is—or should be—by nature either divided or united serves to mask the variety of histories lived out by individuals and their immediate communities. In contrast to Jameson's thinking, official rhetoric that promotes dreamed resolutions or desired truth works against community narratives and symbolic acts that argue—and in some ways subversively—for ambiguity.[37]

The reasons why the examples of nonofficial expressions narrated here do not support Jameson's theories call for some speculation. As I see it, Jameson's formula does not fit these data because, in these cases, economic deprivation or exploitation are not necessarily at the root of societal tensions or contradictions, as Jameson would have it. As these local narratives and rites indicate, nondominant groups—although they are commonly victim to material deprivation and exploitation—can and do produce symbolic expressions reflecting realities at a remove from these kinds of problems.

Nonetheless, Jameson's formula can be helpful in that dreamed resolutions can be a diagnostic device for perceived societal tensions and contradictions that, furthermore, often have to do with issues of economics and power. What I am arguing, therefore, is that the dreamed resolutions put out by "officialdom" in the form of rigid and totalizing prescriptions suggest, on this nonlocal level, felt tensions between religious communities or nations. Suggested by these narratives—often in the form of religious or political rhetoric—are relationships perceived as troubled or troubling by those who produce them. Regarding Hindu-Christian relations, therefore, the issue of contradiction or "fight," in the examples I have given, is not on the local level—judging from local narratives' ease with hybridity and ambivalence—but rather on the ecclesial or official level. The official need to proclaim or prescribe dreamed resolutions—that different traditions or cultures are either united or irreparably splintered—points to certain kinds of tensions not necessarily felt by the local community. This relative immunity from particular tensions—a privileged position in many ways—is something to which I will return shortly.

Local Disdain for Sibling Stories and the Negotiation of Identity

Given my position as foreign ethnographer, poised with tape recorder before the storyteller, an additional layer of politics (and thus complexity) emerges through the performance of locally based tales, especially those about sacred siblings. To address this level of expression, I take on the uncomfortable task of scrutinizing not only my status as outsider in this ethnographic setting but also an imbalance of power that is often a part of such endeavors. By taking a look at sibling stories from this performative and, more overtly, political perspective, I am given another angle from which to explore the tensions underlying "dreamed" resolutions and totalizing discourses.

The Performative Layer: "Of Course These Stories Are Not True . . . "

In his study of oral traditions, Richard Bauman argues that the performative aspect of oral narrative offers a crucial opportunity for interpretation and thus cannot be ignored. As he puts it, a story's performance "provides an especially rich focus for the relationship between oral literature and social life because part of the special nature of narrative is to be doubly anchored in human events" (1986: 2). Similarly, Bakhtin writes that in our daily interpretation of meaning "we do not separate discourse from the personality speaking it" (1981: 341). Moreover, "the entire speaking situation is very important: who is present during it, with what expression of mimicry is uttered, with what intonation? . . . In this personalized representation lies in the double-voiced and even double-languaged representation of another's words" (341).

The performance of sacred sibling tales, graciously carried out for me by many a storyteller in a variety of situations, provides an additional layer of meaning not only politically fraught but also surprisingly consistent. The message, in many variations, that was repeatedly embedded in a prologue to the actual telling of sacred sibling stories diminished or belittled their worth. Such sentiments are typified by statements such as, "Of course you know that no one actually believes these stories." On a number of occasions, a potential storyteller would, in fact, seem very uninterested in telling the "silly" stories that "only my grandmother knows," until my pestering finally made her or him give in.

The meanings behind this performative prologue are no doubt varied. One significant implication, however, was fairly well spelled out to me by Dr. John, an English professor at a Kottayam college. This gentleman was a tremendous help to me in my research on popular devotion, but when it came to the telling of sacred sibling stories he consistently tried to cast them aside as silly or as irrelevant to my interests. Finally, in a supreme effort to accommodate my wishes, he agreed to relate some sibling anecdotes he had heard as a child living in Puthupally, but nonetheless added the reservation, "I just don't want you to get the wrong idea." When I asked him what he meant by this, he told me another kind of story, which he had read the previous year in the newspaper. His tale involved another young woman from New York who happens to be a Christian missionary. She, like me, comes to visit Kerala, but only for a short while. Upon returning to New York she reports to her church authorities that the poor people of Kerala are indeed backward and in need of domestication. To back up her claims, she describes, among other things, traditional Malayali eating habits, in which people sit on the floor and scoop up their food with their bare hands, using banana leaves as plates. Through vivid descriptions such as these, she convinces her church leaders in New York that these "primitives" are indeed needy of direction and assistance, and thus she is given the necessary funding to return. Aghast at the story, I assured Dr. Joseph that I was appalled by this woman's audacity and, furthermore, by her complete misreading of cultural differences. He then kindly proceeded with the "silly" sibling stories I had requested.

Although I was able to convince Dr. Joseph that I was not one of those imperialistically ignorant foreigners who are written up in the newspaper, I was left with a sense of unease. Had the divide between us that he perceived really been lifted through my assurances and, moreover, was I entirely unlike that irrefutably demeaning woman from New York who knew what was "best" for Keralites?

In Jean Langford's study of Ayurvedic medicine in north India, she lays bare a similar ethnographic conundrum. For instance, one Ayurvedic physician whom she interviewed changed the course of their conversation by commenting that one of his "worries" about her research was what he believed to be her "fascination" with Ayurveda. Langford guesses that, beyond her interest in Ayurveda, this doctor sensed fascinations "perhaps with India more generally. He is reluctant to say more for fear of being misunderstood" (1995: 359). Langford describes this reticence as stemming from a perceived ideological rift between herself and many of the Ayurvedic doctors whom she interviewed, and identifies this rift with the investment the physicians commonly have in an imperially introduced distinction between a "Western" scientific approach to medicine and Ayurveda. As supporters of the latter system, many Indian physicians have struggled for decades for the recognition of Ayurveda as a science in its own right.[38] As evidenced by many of Langford's conversations with these doctors, they were also, in their different ways, somewhat engaged in this struggle. Because she was aware of this dynamic, Langford attempted to frame her questions in a way she felt was sympathetic to the Indians' point of view. No matter how hard she tried to build a sense of solidarity, however, interviewees appeared to view her, as she puts it, "as the spokesperson for an opposing epistemology in all our conversations" (342).

A similarly felt divide between myself and potential storytellers is, I believe, brought into focus through Keralites' spoken disdain for sibling tales. Concerns about the stories' lack of literal truth—which no doubt contribute to their current decline—are probably magnified by my presence in the audience. In spite of my efforts to reassure potential storytellers of my appreciation for their local sibling stories, I seemed to be, nonetheless, representative of a larger, less accepting "audience" made up of a long history of colonial and postcolonial forces and expectations. I suspect that in some significant ways I represented a perceived "Western" or "modern" agenda that values rationalism and positivism and that the storytellers understood as having little time for poetic or mythic discourse.[39]

As it turns out, I repeatedly reacted to such disdain by leaping to the defense of poetic narrative traditions, arguing that they were worthwhile reflections of Kerala's uniquely peaceful pluralism. This defense was in part, as I begrudgingly recognized at the time, typical of postmodern scholarly efforts to dismantle and devalue the same rigid "literal truth" with which I was unwittingly associated. Through Keralite insistence on empiricism and my counterinsistence to the contrary, we seemed to be turning (or twisting) some of the ideological tables of the colonial project.

Langford describes a similar twisting of colonial ideologies during interviews with a self-professedly "modern" Ayurvedic doctor. "Frequently our conversations together devolve into arguments in which I am embarrassed to find myself trying to argue Ayurveda as a type of ethnomedicine. Dr. Karnik seems to delight in dismissing each

example of Ayurvedic essence that I try to offer. Paradoxically, despite his allegiance
to medical modernism, he undermines my anthropological modernism. He will not
let me claim Ayurveda as a healing balm for modernity's excesses" (1995: 347–48).

Privilege and the Appreciation of Sacred Sibling Stories

It is important to know that not everyone put me in the awkward position of trying
to defend local narrative traditions. An exception to this norm that caught me off
guard surfaced during an interview granted to me by an elderly Orthodox Syrian
bishop, Dr. Paulos Mar Gregorios.[40] A highly esteemed gentleman not only throughout Kerala but internationally as well, Dr. Paulos served as secretary general for the
World Council of Churches. As a result of his many travels, he and I found we had
common friends and acquaintances at the Graduate Theological Union in Berkeley,
where I received my Master's degree. Before my interview with him in his spacious
office at the Orthodox Syrian Seminary just outside Kottayam town, I had jotted
down a number of issues I wanted him to address regarding local devotion and Kerala
Christian history. Because I approached almost everyone with questions about sacred
sibling relationships, I planned to ask the bishop for stories as well, but decided to
keep the subject at the bottom of my list. I did not want to lose credibility as a
"serious" scholar in the eyes of a man who was of such stature, at least at the start of
our conversation.

To my great surprise, however, early in our discussion of Keralite devotion to St.
George, the bishop enthusiastically volunteered an anecdote about his home village
of Karinyachira, where parishioners of his church consider the patron, St. George, to
be the brother of Viṣṇu from the nearby temple. The bishop fondly reminisced that
when he was a little boy, the participants of both the temple and church processions
would halt and respectfully bow before the other "brother's" place of worship before
continuing on. Upon hearing this unsolicited account, I animatedly told the bishop
of my interest in Kerala's sibling traditions and of my appreciation for the ways they
express a communal harmony for which Malayalis are so proud. The bishop responded
that he too enjoyed these stories, and was glad that I was finding time to listen to
them now, before they die out. Surprised that the bishop seemed to share my unbridled
enthusiasm, I recounted for him some of the many conversations I had with people
who felt sibling tales were "silly" or simply not worth telling. At this, the bishop
became very serious. He slowly shook his head and said, "the rationalist training that
people have been getting these days has made them incapable of appreciating the
finer things in life."

As I understand it, Dr. Paulos' unapologetic appreciation for sacred sibling stories
suggests that his position suspended him from the need to make clear to me his
allegiance to literal truth. His cosmopolitan background allowed him in some ways
to be "at home" in European and North American culture as well as in Kerala, and
thus helped to dissolve some of the traditionally construed oppositions between East
and West. Furthermore, because he had held a position of authority within an
organization that included European and American participants, I would guess that
the radical imbalance of global political power felt by most other Keralites was, on a
personal level, further relieved. The prevailing tensions between domestic traditions

and "modern" expectations—the latter identified as banal rationalism by Mar Gregorios—felt by the average well-educated Keralite seemed to be quelled by the truly privileged perspective of the bishop. He was able, in turn, to be appreciative if not romantic about sacred sibling stories as a part of his own heritage and offer them to me without reservation.

Totalizing Discourses and the Problem of Identity

A comparison of the bishop's appreciation for sacred sibling stories with the more commonly expressed concern for their literal accuracy is suggestive of the contrast between local village traditions, which are more likely to portray groups as ambiguously rivalrous yet reliant, on the one hand, and the need for officialdom to create static categories and distinctions, on the other. The creation of hierarchical distinctions such as rationalism/tradition or modernity/tradition by local storytellers, Ayurvedic physicians, and ethnographers (although here the hierarchy is often reversed) once again suggests a troubled relationship between members of a group and their perceived "others." Although many of the examples of rigidly constructed religious delineations (such as Hindu-Christian and Vaiṣṇava-Śaiva) express concerns that are largely intranational, the distinctions that contrast modernity and rationality with indigenous tradition reflect troubled relations of an international (colonial and postcolonial) scope. These latter examples could also include the perceived "essence" of India demonstrated by the reverse orientalism of some Kerala Christian nuns and clergy. The associated rigid "dreamed" distinctions of East/West, tradition/modernity, spirituality/technology appear to represent reverberations of uneasy past as well as current international relations.[41] In the exceptional case of Mar Gregorios, his long-term position of international authority and privilege seems to contribute to a stance in which dichotomies such as "modern" versus "traditional" are not consistently prioritized or necessarily held in tension.

As Edward Said's *Orientalism* describes it, the creation of absolute distinctions between opposite entities is a byproduct of troubled identity negotiations. More specifically, the creation of oppositions between East and West has been a part of a process of Euro-American identity formation as against an East understood as the Other. As Said puts it, "European culture gained in strength and identity setting itself off against the Orient as a surrogate or underground self" (1978: 3). In *Culture and Imperialism* (1993), Said includes colonized groups' promotion of nationalism through separatism and nativism as likewise being "guilty" of dreaming up rigid oppositions between cultures for the sake of their own identity. The examples of static distinctions offered by this chapter may stretch Said's notion of binary opposition and, moreover, include instances in which distance or distinction between self and other is collapsed completely. Nonetheless, I posit that a similar issue—identity formation—is at stake in different groups' tendencies to dream up such fixed conceptions. I argue that the dreamed resolutions this chapter describes, acting either to exaggerate or banish differences between communities, have largely come about in answer to trouble or stress which, more specifically, may indicate an uneasy sense of identity. It is significant that the Vatican Congregation, in its discussion of the problem of both colonial and Hindu influences on Kerala Christianity, uses precisely the phrase "crisis of identity" to name what it feels lies at the root of today's often polarized clerical disputes. Likewise, the reverse orientalist formula, rarely referred to by lay and less-educated Malayalis, seemed to be taken for granted among many clergy and nuns for whom the pull of international authority affects the way they think about themselves.

Kerala's village-based traditions, such as sibling stories, interreligious rites, or church origin tales, show that totalizing prescriptions are not the only way for groups to understand identity and otherness, as we have seen. Local means for articulating such matters, emerging from these shared Christian and Hindu traditions, are neither reductive nor do they serve to set up exclusive oppositions. Ultimately, these self-reflective expressions seem to be a sign of "privilege"—somewhat like Mar Gregorios's—that convey, in other words, that the troubled need to assert a static categories of self and other is conspicuously absent.

Said's more recent work chastises imperialist and nationalist groups alike for "insisting upon the radical purity or priority of one's own voice," as such insistence so often leads to "the awful din of unending strife, and a bloody political mess" (1993: xxi). The consequences of most of the rigid perspectives given above, however, are certainly less dramatic. Furthermore, the less "organized" examples (such as disillusioned storytellers and modern Ayurvedic physicians) do not necessarily reflect an established political stance or even the primacy of one's own voice over an "other's." They simply represent a certain contending with and contesting of categories imposed by colonial structures. I therefore look upon these expressions as reflecting types of identity management not so much to be critiqued as to serve as valuable indicators of existing tensions.

I remain wary of the outcome of such polarized distinctions, however, even when they fall short of becoming a "bloody political mess." Such constructions ultimately act to obscure how cultures are indeed complicated mixes of overlapping traditions, thus, as posited by Said, they cause us to miss sight of "the diversity and complexity of experience that works beneath [such] totalizing discourses" (1993: xxiv).[42]

Complicity and Guilt: True Confessions of an Ethnographer

To conclude this chapter, I venture to discuss further the part I have played in this problematic. If I can claim that Keralite storytellers who defend the status of literal truth and clergy and nuns who subvert colonial categories are "guilty" of promoting static distinctions between modernity and tradition, my preference for "tradition" over the colonial legacy of empiricism and positivism is no less rigid and "guilty." Like Langford, who begrudgingly admits that what she had hoped for in Ayurveda was a "healing balm for modernism's excesses," my dogged appreciation for mythic tradition appears to support the kind of thinking that pits East against West, tradition against modernity, as well.

My response to such imperfect ethnography might be to quit the enterprise entirely or to make unconvincing claims that I have sworn off this kind of colonial baggage, promising never to let it happen again. Considering the impossibility of these options, however—the illusion that one can study only what is purely "familiar" or that one can claim an immunity from colonial biases—I posit that there remains an important place for ethnography and its inevitable flaws.

To add my voice to the cacophony of ethnographers who argue for the validity of their enterprise, let me first review a critique of one of the scholarly options to the study of colonial or postcolonial cultures. This approach—referred to by Sara Suleri as an "alterist reading" of cultural colonial studies—denies the plausibility of study-ing the "other" because foreign cultures are essentially unknowable and, certainly, unrepresentable. Although this perspective avoids the trap of reproducing the same colonial categories to which many European and American ethnographers and his-torians have fallen prey, Suleri agues that it recreates its own, equally problematic, distinctions. She views the alterist reading, which begins "as a critical and theoreti-cal revision of a Eurocentric or Orientalist study of the literatures of colonialism" (1990: 12), to be misguided in its claim for an irretrievable core of difference or "otherness" between colonizer and colonized. Suleri writes, "The very insistence on the centrality of difference as an unreadable entity can serve to obfuscate and indeed to sensationalize that which still remains to be read" (11). She goes on to argue that alterist readings which pose the "other" as unknowable represent a "postmodernist substitute for the very Orientalism that they seek to dismantle" (13) as well as "a repetitive monumentalization of the academy's continuing fear of its own ignorance" (12).

Although the reemergence of colonialist distinctions as seen in the writings of ethnographers may look somewhat different from the polarizations Suleri accuses alterist readers of promoting, there appears to be common ground between us. As I have argued up to this point, the creation of rigid boundaries between self and other commonly arise from a perceived troubled or troubling relationship stemming from and in turn affecting a process of identity negotiation. By the same token, both the alterist silence about colonial culture and ethnography's potential imperfections seem to be a consequence and reflection of an ongoing identity negotiation and counternegotiation between the "culture" of the scholar and that which she or he is "studying."[43]

Beyond the idea that our scholarly creation of static categories points to troubled postcolonial relations and self perceptions, something more specific can be said about the role scholars play in this dynamic. As a means for describing what this is, I return to Suleri's analysis. The relationship between colonized and colonizer identified by Suleri—in contrast to what an alterist view would have us believe—is one of intimacy based on complicity and guilt. This allows us to understand the dynamic between members of the two cultures as one that fails to "cohere around the master-myth that proclaims static lines of demarcation between imperial power and disempowered culture, between colonizer and colonized" (1990: 3). Euro-American scholars still contend with the reverberations of guilt that are the product of this "intimacy" of the colonial—and, as I see it, ethnographic—encounter.[44] Langford's and my ideological somersaults as well as the scholarly "generosity" of alterist readings—both attempting to erase the impact of colonial impositions—come, I believe, as a result of this guilt currently at work. An ironic byproduct of our tangled stance and the defensive position of our informants is the unwitting complicity of *all* concerned in the perpetuation of colonial categories.

Rather than resigning myself to the impossibility of an unsullied understanding of the "other" and thus promoting scholarly silence—and therefore ignorance—I suggest that the imperfect exchanges basic to ethnographic settings are helpful precisely when acknowledged for their imperfections.[45] By calling attention to the redundancy of the term "imperfect ethnography" I admit to the fact that the intimate exchange between ethnographer and informant will necessarily echo the troubled intimacies of colonialism. To claim an ability to somehow transcend such contamination is to deny these intimacies and mistakenly assume the possibility of a "correct" stance, disentangled from such troubles. As Suleri suggests, it is by paying attention to complicity and guilt and the resultant ambiguities of such intimacies that we can disorient our rigid understandings of self and other. These are the kinds of expressions—as valuable alternatives to wooden, preestablished categories—deserving of our careful attention. Without scrutinizing the intimacies and disorienting ambivalences of the ethnographic exchange, its inherent "imperfections" can act instead to reinforce rather than disrupt these all-too-familiar distinctions.

I began this chapter by recounting the escapades of sacred siblings, and noted that the embedded themes of rivalry and reliance challenge the static prescriptions of religious and political officialdom. I end by discussing possibilities for a similar ideological stance which, in effect, question the rigid polarization of East/West, colonized/colonizer, and tradition/modernity. Yet such possibilities find unfortunate distinction in the fact that they are just that: "dreamed resolutions" not yet actualized. Although I have argued that local sibling stories and their portrayal of communal intimacies and resultant hybridities reflect, on a certain level, a climate of relatively untroubled privilege, a similarly "privileged" exchange of postcolonial ethnographic intimacies remains to be seen.[46] Indeed, the fact that these kinds of ideological shifts need recommendation, as posited by Kamala Visweswaran, "mark(s) decolonization as an active ongoing process—incomplete and certainly not one to be memorialized as a past historical moment" (1994: 113).

3

Calamity Management and the
Role of Sacred Ambivalence

As we try to understand the nature of local saint-devotee relationships, if we view the saint as one who eases or manages calamity in the lives of the devotees, the theme of ambivalence surfaces once again. And if we look at the larger contexts of Christian and Hindu modes of calamity management, we can see, from another angle, what these local practices have—and do not have—in common. By juxtaposing local Hindu traditions with those of both Indian and European Christianity, I challenge the conventional belief that Hindu elements have necessarily seeped into many Kerala Christian saint cult practices, rendering the latter radically different from non-Indian Christianity.

A main theme running throughout this chapter's multivoiced conversation is the way in which institutional Christianity conspicuously promotes a sure victory of good over evil as well as the privileging of the spiritual over the material realm. When viewing saints in their cross-cultural capacity as calamity managers, on the other hand, such institutional preferences fade into the background. In such instances, dualistically oriented prescriptions are eclipsed by or replaced with a stance more comfortable with notions of materially accessible sacred powers. Furthermore such powers, as portrayed locally, are more often ambivalent than they are benign. As such, rigid distinctions between good and evil, spirituality and materiality, become less recognizable and perhaps even arbitrary and—in some respects—so do some of the perceived differences between Hindu and Christian traditions themselves.

To begin, Alphonsa's cult provides an example of how a saint can be cast as either heroine or healer: two roles, often assigned to the same figure, that presume radically different relations between devotee and saint. These disparate functions, in turn, help to distinguish between sainthood as part of authoritative institutional prescription and as part of local expression and practice.

Cross-Cultural Collision

As I began to make plans for my year's fieldwork in Kerala, much of my research, theorizing, and grant proposal writing had to do with the cult of Sr. Alphonsa of Bharananganam. According to my well-laid plans, I intended to hear devotees' stories about this holy figure, legends that had flowered along with her devotional tradition and that (as I led myself to believe) would be as varied as the tellers of the stories themselves: people from every walk of life, economic stratum, religion, political persuasion, and so on. Bolstered by these high hopes, I arrived at Alphonsa's village shrine and introduced and explained myself to the Clarist Sisters of Bharananganam. The nuns, who had been forewarned about me, seemed very happy to know more about my interest in "their" saint, but also rather puzzled at my particular agenda. Responding most directly and diplomatically to my grand ideas, sixty-five-year-old Sr. Josephina, my future research collaborator, said, "This sounds very interesting. But I think you will find that nine out of ten people who come here are seeking favors from Alphonsa and relief from their troubles." Wondering why Sr. Josephina felt that the motives of devotees would hinder their ability to tell stories, I proceeded as planned.

After two weeks of interviewing nearly a hundred pilgrims—who indeed did come from all walks of life, and so on—I learned that people were in fact visiting Alphonsa's shrine to ask or give thanks for favors, which was not surprising. But I also learned that my agenda was not entirely applicable. People were very generous about offering stories in great detail to me and Sr. Josephina about this (almost) saint, but they related events that occurred *after* her death: miracles that confirmed her legendary posthumous efficacy. Although these stories fascinated me, my dogged determination to learn about pilgrims' portrayals of Alphonsa herself through tales and anecdotes from her life was repeatedly met with an abrupt decline in storytelling momentum. Most people were resigned to the fact that they really knew very little of her life aside from sketchy ideas of a few seemingly crucial details. Many suggested that I talk to the nuns or relatives who actually knew her. Those who had read the church-sponsored shrine pamphlet would recite some of the better-remembered points that they felt to be of greatest importance.[1]

In spite of this dearth of detail, an overriding theme in Alphonsa's life clearly emerged from the pilgrims' accounts, consistently described to us in a variety of ways: she had led an agonizing life. Whether due to mistreatment from family members or the nuns in her convent, or through mental or, most commonly, physical anguish, Alphonsa—as universally understood by her devotees—was a woman who lived a life marked by excruciating pain. The composite depiction of Sr. Alphonsa, repeatedly illustrated regardless of the pilgrim's background, was of a nun who had been beaten down by life and who, after her death, became a healer of legendary proportions.

As time wore on, it became clear to me that I was not going to get to "know" Alphonsa and her various devotional communities through songs sung or tales told about her life. I thus turned my attention to the notion of a powerful, suffering Alphonsa whose posthumous story was primarily one of deals struck between herself and her devotees—of human vows promised and saintly miracles fulfilled.

Although I am intellectually aware of Christianity's glorification of suffering and of the connection between asceticism and merit and/or powerfulness, I was, as I have said, diagnosed by the seminary priest as being too "Western" to fully understand such things. Perhaps there is a grain of truth to this. I am from a post-Vatican II generation within a North American culture that understands saints, for the most part, as providing models for human behavior rather than as intercessors to solve problems.[2] Furthermore, the saints who enjoy the most visibility in the Catholicism that is familiar to me are not known for their asceticism but, rather, are made appealing through their heroism—if not through their actions, at least through their faith. My "Protestantized" North American Catholicism thus created a rift between my personal understanding of sainthood and the rather "classical" Keralite attraction to this saint whose identity is so tightly connected to suffering. Further widening this rift was the fact that pilgrims repeatedly described to me the ways they sought and found refuge in Alphonsa as sufferer—as a means to *end* suffering.

Suffering's Emulation and Eradication: Institutional and Local Perspectives

Within the Kerala Catholic community, there are members who consider this emphasis upon Alphonsa's role as antidote to suffering not so much a "confusion" as a perspective slightly off track. Official hagiographical accounts and some members of the hierarchy commonly see Alphonsa's suffering as central to her role rather than as antidote to material comfort and excess. The resulting portrayal of Alphonsa as a model of asceticism for her devotees to follow, promoted by this sector of Catholicism, thus gives a very different meaning to suffering. The local interpretation and apparent reversal of institutional prescription views Sr. Alphonsa, on the other hand, not only as a means for ending bodily suffering but also for winning "material" favors such as employment, house ownership, or contracting a marriage alliance.[3]

Although local and institutionally authoritative perceptions of a suffering Sr. Alphonsa are no doubt different, they are not, upon closer inspection, diametrically opposed. Devotees who hope to win favors from Alphonsa, whether for healing or for a job, often perform a vow in the form of an ascetic act—through begging, fasting, or other physically and psychologically demanding acts. Many devotees thus view suffering and self-denial as a necessary means to a desired, materially "positive" end. Moreover, people who understand Alphonsa as a model of asceticism to follow—an understanding expressed mainly through institutional channels— also recognize her powers to bestow healing and material abundance, available to those who ask for her intercession. After all, miracles of healing play a vital role in her recognition by the Vatican and for her "promotions" toward full-fledged, canonized sainthood.

The difference between these two Alphonsas—the champion world-renunciate to be emulated and the one who provides release from deprivation—reflects, for the most part, a conflict in expectation between a religion's (often but not always clerical and/or elite) minority and the overwhelming majority of its adherents. Such differences in perception and the ways they take shape within particular traditions (commonly labeled orthodox/popular religion in Christianity and great/little traditions in

Hinduism) are a topic of academic concern and controversy among scholars not only of Christianity but of Hinduism, as well.[4] Although the following does not intend to solve any controversies, it attempts to clarify—and problematize—these distinctions for the purposes of this chapter.

When discussing the religious inclinations and practices of the majority, I avoid the term "popular," and refer instead to such practices as "local" (or sometimes "regional"). I do this, in part, because the term "popular" so often conjures up pejorative (however romanticized) images of uneducated and primitive "folk" contrasted with the elite, civilized sectors of society. In fact, no such tidiness exists. Rather, there seems to be a dialectical relationship of influence and adaptation between the two perspectives. Local religious practices and ideologies, often maintained by ecclesial authorities as well as the laity, work to form—as well as conform to—wider, institutional parameters.[5]

This switching of terms from "popular" to "local" does have its shortcomings, however. Because themes and practices among majority traditions are often widespread in nature, there are times when the term "local" signifies a misleading geographic or demographic limitedness, thus making the term "popular," in this respect, more appropriate. Although this chapter demonstrates how themes in "local" devotion cross geographic and religious boundaries, I nonetheless maintain my preference for the term because, from the standpoint of the devotee, each shrine is unique. Attributes and efficacies of a certain holy site are often known only to that particular place. So, regardless of the broad patterns identified between different shrines and their practices, I feel it important not to diminish the ways in which, from a devotional point of view, physically enshrined saints and deities speak uniquely to the particular needs of a particular people. As proof of these particularities, common themes found at different shrines often are disrupted by local nuances. Such subtleties act as a reminder that these sacred sites and the activities connected to them are, after a closer look, indeed local.

Another reason I prefer to use the terms "local" or "regional" religion when referring to the majority and their devotions, especially among Kerala's Catholics, follows from Christian's (1981) definition of local religion as something practiced, in contrast with that which is prescribed. Where practiced "local" religion may be conspicuously Keralite (that is, domestic), prescribed, nonlocal religion that originates, for instance, in the Vatican can be somewhat removed from the realities of regional traditions and embedded understandings. The breach between localized practice and universalizing precept thus has to do not only with differing theologies but also with geographical and cultural contingencies. Although members of the Syrian Christian traditions, particularly Orthodox Syrians with their religious leadership in Kerala itself, may not experience the same pull of foreign religious authority as, say, Roman Catholics, there nonetheless remain institutional prescriptions, formed by their leadership and meant for all practitioners. The term "local" might therefore be applicable to some "unorthodox" Orthodox Syrian shrine practices, but general tensions between such traditions and institutional prescription will tend not to be as striking.

William Christian's distinction between particular "local" practice and universalized "institutional" prescription is echoed in Talal Asad's (1993, 1996) discussion of a shift in the way the category "religion" has been constructed: from centering around bodily practices to internalized abstracted beliefs. At one end of the spectrum, Asad discusses "religion" as understood through the performance of correct and therefore effective practices. This is contrasted with "religion" as viewed by post-Enlightenment European Christianity, in which prescribed beliefs are meant to be internalized and privatized to the extent that they have no connection to bodily practice or behavior. Commenting during a 1996 interview on this distinction, Asad maintains that

> the important contrast to bear in mind is the difference between this kind of intellectualized abstracted system of doctrines that has no direct bearing on or relationship to forms of embodied practices, and lives that are organized around gradually learning and perfecting correct moral and religious practices. The former kind of religiosity is much more a feature of modern religion in Europe and, indeed a part of what religion is defined to be: a set of belief-statements that makes it possible to compare one religion to another and to judge the validity—even the sense—of such abstract statements. This state of affairs is radically opposed to one in which correct practice is essential to the development of religious virtues and is itself an essential religious virtue. (1996: n.p.)

What I refer to in Kerala as local and institutionally authoritative understandings of religion, although in some ways similar to Asad's distinctions, differ in that both are concerned to varying degrees with bodily practice. The institutionally authoritative perspective, which promotes the virtues and emulation of saintly asceticism, reflects a category similar to Asad's, in which expressly stated "religious values" or "correct moral(s)" are often honed and articulated through embodied forms. Local practices, on the other hand, often encourage similar ascetic behavior, but not because such behavior seems to be valued exclusively as an end in itself. Rather, these performances are tools meant to aid devotees in reaching a material (and perhaps, secondarily, a moral) goal. The primary authoritative "power" that drives local practices is not therefore a temporal mandate promoting religious values but, somewhat indirectly, the efficacy of the saint herself to grant favors.[6] I must quickly add, however, that local religion, although more overtly driven by concerns for material gain than by publicly expressed "religious values," is not devoid of ethical or moral impetus. The implicit moral foundation that, I argue, drives local practice (referred to as an "ethic of equity") will be discussed in more detail later in this chapter.

In spite of the fact that the lines I draw between Kerala's local and institutionally prescribed traditions do not fit tidily into Asad's system, there is some interesting overlap when we discuss saints rather than humans. Mirroring Asad's distinction between abstract and embodied religion, Kerala Christian saints and their powers tend to be portrayed institutionally as spiritualized disembodied figures, whereas local devotional practices emphasize to a much greater degree their material accessibility and activity on earth. Keralite Christian devotees themselves may express bodily their religious values—whether institutionally or locally informed—but these values reflect a split in emphasis between otherworldly and this-worldly sacrality and concern. It is this divide which, for the purpose of this chapter's arguments, marks much of the difference between practices within Kerala's local and institutionally authoritative systems and the saints who emerge from these systems.

It is important to emphasize the extent to which perspectives like mine, formed by and currently holding sway within Euro-American academia, are far removed from widely represented "local" understandings of sacrality.[7] William Christian argues this point by noting the vast popularity and notoriety of sixteenth-century monastics, Erasmians, and mystics like Teresa of Avila—elite figures who have shaped our understanding of Christianity.

> These are precisely the people, because they were least local, because they were idea makers, literary as well as literate, who controlled the written culture and whose religiousness we know most about. After all, they are most like the translocal idea makers who write history. Our biases conforming with theirs, we systematically exclude information about the local, or look at it, from their view, as superstitious whereas in fact the local-minded are by far in the majority in our culture as well as theirs. (1981: 179)

Contemporary European and North American scholars may not share many of the biases and understandings of religion held by sixteenth-century adepts—no matter how elite and literary they may have been. Nonetheless, the value of Christian's statement is that late twentieth-century religion scholars' thinking about religion (although not perhaps their practice, or lack thereof) has been formed primarily through the traditions and writings of elite, nonlocal saints and scholars. Removed, as most of us are, from the bodily informed religion of these literate monks and mystics, we are that much further afield from locally performed understandings reflected through materially based, nonelite traditions.

This division between a local-minded majority and an institutionally minded few, as played out today in south Indian Christian contexts calls for a final point of clarification. In Kerala, tensions between local and institutional religion often reflect a gap between different interpretations of practices rather than different practices themselves. By comparison, European priests working on behalf of authoritative precepts have spent centuries, especially since the Reformation, actively trying to "modernize" their flock by ridding them altogether of their "superstitious" public and materially oriented traditions.[8] As a result, the level of European anticlericalism during different historical periods tends to be far more dramatic than the apparent tensions in Kerala between the institutional- and the local-minded. Furthermore, when looking at the various approaches to religion that many Kerala clergy and laity take, it is difficult to argue that they are necessarily or widely divergent.

Because some clergy do interpret religious practices in a way clearly unlike the majority, however, there are occasions when their beliefs are regarded with suspicion by the laity. Such suspicions can surface, for instance, when the resolutely held perception of Alphonsa as sufferer who relieves suffering is confronted by conflicting institutional nuance. During Sr. Josephina's "warning" to me that nine out of ten people come to Sr. Alphonsa's shrine for healing and consolation, she was interrupted by a middle-aged gentleman from Kochi who was also a part of our conversation. Laughing out loud about the 10 percent who claim Alphonsa as a model for sanctity, he argued, "When pilgrims come here saying that they are trying to learn more about and improve their sense of holiness or purity, it is most likely a lie. These poor and innocent people, they are the ones who come and tell the truth—that they have come for favors. What bishops are really saintly after all?"

The Management of Calamity and Sacred Ambivalence

Like Sr. Alphonsa, the majority of Christian saints in Kerala are not primarily understood as models of sanctity but, rather, as sources of sacred power acting to solve earthly problems. Yet in contrast to Sr. Alphonsa, whom devotees generally call upon to treat a wide spectrum of ailments and issues, the roles that other Kerala saints play are often more specialized. For instance, in Kottayam district Keralites usually associate three of their most popular saints, St. George, St. Gregorius, and St. Sebastian, with the eradication of particular types of calamity.[9]

St. George, as mentioned before, is portrayed iconographically as a European-looking armored soldier on horseback, thrusting his lance down the throat of a dragon; many Malayalis attribute to him the power to protect his devotees from poisonous snakes—a legitimate concern in Kerala's tropical terrain. St. Gregorius of Parumala, depicted in paintings and prints in the Orthodox Syrian bishop's garb, gray-bearded and holding his staff, was a Keralite from the mid-nineteenth century. Malayalis routinely consider him to be the most popular saint from the Orthodox Syrian and Jacobite traditions. St. Gregorius's powers are more all-purpose than those of St. George and St. Sebastian, but devotees nonetheless often associate him with a particular calamity, the *yakṣī*.[10] Although the *yakṣī* throughout South Asian history has taken on a variety of forms, often with benevolent powers, today's Keralite *yakṣī* is most commonly depicted as a female vampire who makes her home in sweet-smelling, night-blooming *pālā* trees. She can, at will, transform herself into a beautiful woman who, at night, lures unsuspecting men (and occasionally women) up into her tree. From here, she sucks her victim's blood, killing him before he gets a chance to run away. St. Gregorius's association with the *yakṣī* comes from one of his most commonly described exploits, in which he chases a menacing *yakṣī* out of Parumala, a village located near a forested area. As a result, he releases the local people from their perpetual terror. Finally, St. Sebastian was a fourth-century Roman said to be martyred by Diocletian for his faith. Iconography commonly depicts him as a young European-looking man tied to a tree with arrows pierced into his side. Invoked throughout Europe for protection from the plague, this saint tradition was brought to Kerala by the Portuguese, and he has, until recently, been called upon to guard against smallpox—now chickenpox and other epidemic diseases.[11]

Within Kerala's Hindu traditions, the sacred powers acting to manage these same calamities—snakes, *yakṣīkaḷ* (plural of *yakṣī*), and smallpox—often emerge as symbolic embodiments of the calamity itself. Commonly visible on the outskirts of many temple grounds are the *yakṣī* stone and *sarpa* stone (see Figure 14).[12] Acting as a representation of the *yakṣī* and the snake, respectively, and of their powers, these stones frequently sit side-by-side in the temple compound, where they receive offerings from visitors. As for smallpox, the Tamilian goddess Māriyammān—referred to as "Mariyamma" in Kerala—whom devotees believe to be present in or embodied by the disease itself, enjoys a certain popularity among Malayalis, as well.[13] Although

Figure 14. *Sarpa* stone outside Bhadrakali temple near Puthupally.

these three physical representations of calamity—the *yakṣī* stone, the *sarpa* stone, and Māriyamma—may function to solve a variety of problems, nonetheless they represent an effective means for reigning in the particular calamity they symbolically embody.[14]

At first glance, an obvious pattern emerges when comparing these two traditions of crisis management. On one hand, the Christian saint as conduit for sacred power acts as an enemy against the calamity with which he or she is associated: St. George in all his regalia saves people from snakes, St. Gregorius banishes the *yakṣī*, and St. Sebastian wipes out smallpox. By placing these saints and their powers in direct opposition to a particular "evil," they are—by contrast—associated with pure, unmitigated goodness and strength. On the other hand, the Hindu representation of the problem itself as a means for devotees to have control over it through supplication or appeasement discloses an ambivalent power. When I described this juxtaposition of Christian/Hindu crisis management to Swami Suprabhananda, the current director of the Sri Ramakrishna Sanskrit College outside Kottayam, he nodded his head knowingly, and said, "Even evil things are made by God, so we should not try to reject them but rather try to make them godly. Sometimes, when it looks as though crowds of people are getting out of control, the government will employ a rowdy to help settle things down. There are times when it is good to have rowdies working for us."

This idea that evil is a part of divine responsibility and thus should not be rejected or done away with presents a challenge to official Christian understandings of good and evil. For instance, Vatican II documents argue that everything has been made by God and therefore is, by nature, good. Evil only enters the scene because of free will—also given by God. And then, of course, there are demons; "the devil and the other demons were created by God good according to their nature, but they made themselves evil by their own doing. As for man, his sin was at the prompting of the devil" (Flannery 1981: 463).

In her discussion of the problem of evil within the Hindu tradition, Wendy Doniger O'Flaherty notes that Vedantists likewise try to find ways to rescue God from some of the responsibility for evil. For instance, blame has on occasion been put on *līlā*, the imminent and playful aspect of God's nature; thus the resignation: "Who after all can blame a child for acts done in joy and playful exuberance?" (1976: 3). As Zimmer observed, this kind of philosophical tactic which helps to explain away evil—of which there are a variety within the Hindu tradition—tends to become dogmatic, thus flattening and obscuring the ambivalences and ambiguities of life (1946: 179, quoted in O'Flaherty 1976: 8). According to O'Flaherty, the treatment of the problem of evil within Hindu mythology, on the other hand, "discards the more elaborate solutions of the Vedantins and seeks a more direct answer, an answer illuminated by the 'coarse' ritual imagery which philosophy scorns. . . . It is the moment when people normally caught up in everyday banalities are suddenly confronted with problems that they have hitherto left to the bickerings of the philosophers" (9).

From the perspective of Hindu mythology, O'Flaherty finds that responsibility for evil is shared by a variety of factors—humanity, fate, devils, and gods—largely depending upon the branch of mythology one consults (378). In spite of this diversity, the perspective that deities themselves are to blame for evil—both moral evil and misfortune—is one preferred by Hindu purāṇic literature and by most Hindus themselves (13, 372–73).

In contrast to what O'Flaherty refers to as Hinduism's mixing of a monistic with a dualistic understanding of good and evil, she comes to the conclusion that "Western theology cannot bear to blame God" for evil; it consistently puts the burden on an evil "other," most commonly the devil (373). Helping to bring this cross-cultural comparison of theodicy onto common ground, O'Flaherty cites the work of Paul Ricoeur and his collection of a variety of Jewish and Christian myths (and some Greek and Babylonian, as well). O'Flaherty notes that these myths reflect an array of perspectives on the problem of theodicy, offering alternatives to the "master myth" of Adam and Eve's Fall. In spite of this diversity, however, responsibility for evil within these mythologies rests most consistently upon humanity's sinfulness or on an

Evil Other—the former conspicuously absent in Hindu mythology and the latter playing only a small role (O'Flaherty 372–73). The clear distinction between good and evil so prevalent in Jewish and Christian thought thus seems to emerge, as well, through its mythologies. This pattern is especially striking when compared with Hindu mythological systems.

As viewed by institutionally authoritative Christian theology, this need to understand God as diametrically opposed to evil and thus blameless for its existence can be extended to perceptions of sainthood, as well.[15] Fundamentally important as this dichotomy seems to be for Christian orthodoxy, saint devotion, when translated to the local or "practical" level, regularly challenges such one-dimensional ideas of sacred power. By paying attention to the ritually based "mythology" of sainthood rather than official, theologically driven constructions, we find a different outlook or, as O'Flaherty puts it when speaking of Hindu mythology, "a commonsense logic which discards the more elaborate solutions" (9). The "elaborate solutions" discarded, in this case, are the abstracted, dualistic answers to the problem of saintly justice. Although I speak of saints and not gods, it is my hope that their mythological and ritual disruption of institutional ideas of good and evil help to make what appear to be easy distinctions between Hindu and Christian approaches to theodicy a little less easy.[16]

The saint who most consistently and conspicuously rebels against orthodox standards in Kerala's Kottayam district is St. George. As expressed through the intricacies of local devotion, this saint regularly defies his own official depictions in that he does not always behave in a wholly benign manner. As we learn through shrine practices and stories, St. George's powers are potentially dangerous and in need of appeasement. For instance, although he is known to offer protection from snakes, devotees also describe him as sending snakes after community members. I heard a number of tales that portray an otherwise upstanding family who, through innocent oversight, neglects to give its requisite chicken or rooster offering (most commonly rooster) to the local St. George church during the saint's annual festival celebration.[17] After failing to carry out this yearly duty, so the story often goes, a hapless family member is terrorized to find a large snake in or near the house the next day. Even a Mar Thomite neighbor of ours who, according to tradition, does not take part in saint devotion told my husband and me one such anecdote. Apparently, many years back, his mother, who was normally quite scrupulous, forgot to send one of their roosters to the nearby St. George church in Puthupally. The next day, everything seemed perfectly normal until his sister opened up the door to go outside and nearly stepped on a large snake resting on their front steps. The gentleman laughingly added, "Needless to say, she never forgot that duty again!" His wife, seated next to him, also laughing at the story, added that, although she and her husband are not in the habit of giving a rooster to the church, she sees to it that they give money every year. As she put it, "You can never be too sure."[18]

Vengeful snake stories aside, the idea that Kerala's St. George is not unconditionally valiant toward his devotees emerges plainly enough through his insistence upon fowl offerings.[19] This caped crusader does not offer his services unreservedly but, rather, in expectation that he will get something in return. Although some kind of exchange is expected in most saint/devotee shrine transactions, some clergy members, nuns, and lay people attribute St. George's more overtly destructive insistence on exchange to influences from the surrounding Hindu culture. Susan Bayly, whose work gives much attention to popular devotion in Kerala and Tamil Nadu from the late eighteenth through early nineteenth centuries, comes to a similar conclusion about St. Thomas as portrayed at that time by local Keralite devotion. Because local legends depicted him as wielding powers not only for curing diseases but for punishing the unjust, as well, Bayly implies that a Hinduization of the apostle had taken place. In her words, he "has come to be regarded as a figure of vengeance and all-devouring wrath much like the goddess herself" (1989: 277). The examples Bayly uses to illustrate her point certainly reflect St. Thomas's potentially destructive power—such as turning a would-be temptress to stone—but seem far too mild to merit a comparison with the goddess's "all-devouring wrath." Because the saint's powers call into question a strict separation of good and evil, so atypical of the Christian figures with which Bayly is likely to be familiar, she is willing to stretch the comparison as far as she does.[20]

Rather than immediately connect local Kerala Christian traditions of ambivalent or potentially destructive sacred powers with things Hindu, it is important to question the extent to which such local traditions are necessarily due to "outside" influences. In other words, in spite of the Vatican's official and decidedly non-Hindu perspectives on the nature of good and evil, is the belief in an ambivalent sacred power necessarily foreign to the Christian tradition? It appears that in Europe—far from the influences of Hinduism—local Catholic traditions have and often still do portray saintly heroes as wielding ambivalent powers similar to those of St. George in Kerala. William Christian describes communities in sixteenth-century Spain as interpreting local disasters (such as hail, fire, floods, earthquakes, and epidemics) as either punishments by particular saints or as a message to the public that they should start offering the saint his or her due public respect. Most commonly, the mishap experienced by the community was thought to be caused by the very saint who was the locally designated guardian against that particular calamity (1981: 34–35). Michael Carroll's (1992) study of local madonna traditions in Italy unearths a multitude of local stories that describe manifestations of Mary who physically harm those who ignore their wishes. In Judith Devlin's detailed description of a widespread belief in the irascible nature of saints in nineteenth-century France, she quotes an old woman's remark to her neighbor in church, overheard by the parish priest during a saint festival procession: "You can still bother the good God every day, but those miserable saints, they're so vindictive that you can only chance disturbing them on the day they allow" (1987: 16).

Sacred Materiality

Another distinction related (through Plato and others) to the institutionally promoted rift between good and evil is the configuration of the spiritual realm as separate from and superior to that of the material. This officially recognized hierarchical split between spirit and matter is directly challenged by local European and Kerala Christian saint traditions and, more specifically, by the ways devotees gain access to saintly powers. Beyond the fact that the expected exchange of vows and miracles between holy figures and corporeal humanity underscores the potential earthiness of heavenly power, the belief that the saint's efficacy is present in his or her statue, picture, or relic also bridges the material world and that of the spiritual. This meeting of realms in Kerala Christianity emerges again and again through local understandings that many (although certainly not all) saints' statues and paintings wield particular powers. In such cases, these tangible images and remains—anchoring the saint's forces to a particular place—are responsible for healing and miracles that occur within the shrine (see Figure 15).

During festival occasions this perspective is reflected in the fact that, for many, the most important and emotionally charged moment of the multiday event is the unveiling of the saint's picture or the removal of the statue or relic from its customary dwelling place at the start of the procession. As we have seen, images have the capacity to play pranks, lop off the arms of other images, offer furtive glances, pay

Figure 15. Offering prayers and flowers to miraculous St. George statue near Kollam.

respects to a family member, or push an angry sister into the drink (but not before sweating and straining himself). And, in many cases, because the image not only embodies sacred powers but also represents communal identity, the results of such material antics can be either curses or blessings that tangibly affect constituent human communities.

Because Hindu traditions commonly understand the power of a local deity to be physically embodied by his or her temple representation, some people assume, perhaps understandably, that this mixing of the material with the spiritual in Kerala's saint cults can be traced to Hindu influences.[21] Susan Bayly seems to imply this when she notes that "the power which comes to be vested in stone crosses, statues, relics and other sacred items is one of the most notable features of south Indian Christian religious culture" (1989: 278). Although Bayly does not explicitly discount the possibility that similar physical embodiments of sacred power occur within Christian traditions beyond south India, I think it bears mentioning that this challenge to the spirit/matter split has been and continues to be a "notable feature" outside the sphere of Hindu cultural influence. Michael Carroll argues that wonder-working images are so tenaciously central to Italian Catholic devotion that the logic behind such practices represents "one of the most important constraints to which the institutional Church in Italy has had to adapt over the centuries" (1992: xi). In Nolan and Nolan's study of contemporary pilgrimage shrines throughout Western Europe, they found that 96 percent of the sites in continental Europe were centered around the reputation of a miraculous image or relic associated with a holy figure (1989: 162).

Instances in which saints' powers are manifest through their physical representations is a theme that European devotees commonly weave into their stories of miracles. For instance, William Christian describes anecdotes in which Spanish statues exert their influence over where their shrines ought to be built. They make known their wishes by escaping from the churches where they were being kept—apparently against their will—and repeatedly returning to the desired location of a future shrine (1981: 75). Further demonstrating the existing desires and needs of a saint's material representation, a contemporary Greek villager argues that there are definite ways to care for an icon in order that it, in return, properly watch over the household. He thus reasons, "It is a guest in your house. It should have a place to sit down; it should never be hung from the wall" (Danforth 1989: 27). This tangibly located power of a saint, commonly embodied by a very human-like representation, is expressed as well in the many present-day accounts of weeping, bleeding, and moving statues.[22] In reference to nineteenth-century France, Emile Sevrin aptly describes this cross-cultural phenomenon that still occurs today: "the saint was both a mysterious and a familiar being, both immobile and active, confined to his alcove and to his chapel, one with his statue. . . . The saint of history, the saint glorified in heaven was not thought about (quoted in Devlin 1987: 14).[23]

The tendency for a saint cult to be regionalized—that is, made in many ways unique through local shrine-practice traditions—is the logical byproduct of this phenomenon whereby sacred powers are anchored to a particular location and animated through a particular image rather than to the "saint of history." Along these lines, William Christian describes Marian shrines in New Castile during the sixteenth century up to the present: "The saints of these shrines were considered resident patrons of their communities. Our Lady of This-Place, located by this particular spring, tree, or castle, with that particular view, was different from any other Mary (1981: 124–25).[24]

Similarly, in Kerala, many of the popular miracle-working saints—linked with particular shrines and inhabiting powerful statues or paintings—are given a unique identity based upon these images and shrines. St. George of one place, for example, although having features similar to St. George in a different location, may be understood as an entirely different figure due to variations in such things as ritual expectations, sibling ties, local legends, and—above all—potency.[25]

Vow as Material and Bodily Exchange

Whereas saints' statues, relics, or pictures act as material conduits for heavenly powers, tangible transactions between devotees and saints are necessary to further ensure the accessibility of these powers. Such material or corporeal interchange between saint and devotee are central not only to the deity's or saint's function as calamity manager in Hindu and non-Protestant Christian practices but also to local depictions of sacred ambivalence.

This exchange of goods and promises holds such a pivotal place within European Catholicism that Sanchiz (1983) argues that pilgrimage sites in all their diversity can be characterized, above all, by the vow, "a distinguishing feature not only of the festival but of popular religion generally" (266). Although vows are often carried out through bodily practices, such as crawling to the shrines, fasting, and so on, monetary vows are arguably a sustaining part of the life of the Spanish Church. According to William Christian, cash offerings have "largely built and almost completely maintained most shrines and chapels and still do" (1981: 31). In spite of the importance of vowed currency and the centrality of vows in general to local traditions, Dubisch and Christian note that historians of Christianity commonly ignore this aspect of religious practice (Dubisch 1990: 126; Christian, 1981: 31). Christian goes on to speculate that the importance of the vow has been underestimated because of its private nature. It typically represents an agreement made solely between the devotee and saint, eliminating any need for public—that is, clerical and therefore "noteworthy"—intervention (32).

Within Hindu devotional traditions, the practice of making and keeping material and/or corporeal vows bears striking resemblances to both European and Indian Christian vow practices. In rural Rajasthan, as described by Ann Gold, one of the most important functions of the *jātrā* (the most commonly performed type of pilgrimage, from which tangible goals rather than spiritual aims are sought) is the offering of a *bolari* or *votana*—translated as "pledge" or "vow" (1994: 142; 1987: 92). When making a pledge, devotees often carry out physical acts such as circumambulation around the shrine or hard labor without compensation as a sign of their faith. After the deity has successfully carried out the desires of the devotee, the latter will commonly offer "tangible signs of success that all these regional deities apparently covet," such as buildings, sacks of sugar, or cash for the shrine-priest's coffers (1987: 186; see also 1994: 91–92).

In Christian and Hindu places of worship in Kerala, devotees from both traditions offer vows in a similar fashion and in a variety of forms. Bodily vows commonly include any of a variety of "acts of humiliation" (as put by Sr. Josephina), in which a devotee performs such feats as crawling to the shrine with a cured baby on his or her back, rolling on the grounds surrounding the shrine or temple, or shaving his or her head.[26] Material vows can include the offering of the "first fruits" of agriculture or industry, ornate umbrellas for annual festivals, or money for church or temple funds.

A particularly interesting interreligious "overlap" incorporating both material and bodily vows to saints and deities in Kerala is the practice of offering *āḷrūpangaḷ*, small silver or gold pieces (although people commonly claim that today's vendors are selling counterfeits) molded in the shape of body parts symbolizing the area of the anatomy that has experienced or needs healing. Devotees offer them to the saint or deity as a means of expressing thanksgiving or as a plea for help. Aside from the more commonly seen legs, arms, heads, and eyes, *āḷrūpangaḷ* also come in the shape of babies, snakes, or houses. Selling their wares on the side of the road or shrine entrance way, *āḷrūpangaḷ* vendors typically set up display tables outside major pilgrimage sites, most commonly when business is sure to be brisk: on saint or deity festival days or, at Christian pilgrimage sites, on the first Friday of the month (see Figure 16).

Although *āḷrūpangaḷ* are equally popular at Christian and Hindu pilgrimage centers in Kottayam district, people seem universally to understand them as having indigenous roots, passed from the Hindu community to the Christians after their

Figure 16. Manarkad St. Mary's Church office during festival time, where devotees buy *āḷrūpangaḷ* and oil offerings and sponsor prayers and masses.

arrival in Kerala. But, contrary to popular opinion, I propose that the tradition of offering *āḷrūpaṅgaḷ* to a saint or deity is Christian in origin. Nolan and Nolan (1989) describe the offering of replicas of afflicted or healed body parts as a long-standing European tradition; similar artifacts were left at Mediterranean healing sites as early as the first century B.C.E. Commonly found today in Italian, Spanish, and Portuguese Catholic shrines, this practice was at one time popular in Switzerland, as well. Although these figures are most often made from metal, in Spain they are more customarily fashioned out of wax (Nolan and Nolan 1989: 71; see also Christian 1981: 96).[27] Greek Orthodox pilgrims also offers these figures, referred to as *tamata* or *simadia*, to their saint shrines (Dubisch 1990: 120; Danforth 1989: 11). Further supporting the likelihood that this practice in Kerala was Christian before it was Hindu is its virtual nonexistence in the northern part of India. Because of its popularity in eastern as well as western Christianity, it is entirely plausible that the tradition of offering *āḷrūpaṅgaḷ* was initially brought by the early Syrian community and later reinforced by the Portuguese.

The dogged insistence that Kerala's *āḷrūpaṅgaḷ* tradition stems from early Indian (and thus Hindu) culture in spite of evidence to the contrary is similar to the common (mis)identification of material devotion solely with Hindu practice and not with Christianity. Such mistaken identifications are probably a natural consequence of ignorance about Christian, especially Catholic, practices of the "local-minded." As discussed above, this information gap is due in part to the fact that certain segments of society have limited access to local traditions, both in their daily life and in their libraries.[28] The fact that materials written about Indian Christianity largely sidestep local practice—whether passively out of disinterest and/or ignorance, or actively through a conscious preference for institutional models—simultaneously reflects and perpetuates this phenomenon. Information available in India about religion from Europe and North America likewise appears to be limited mostly to institutional perspectives or literature—similar to what is available to European or American audiences—that deals mainly with nonlocal issues. Consequently, few Keralite Christians seem to be aware of the many similarities between their local traditions and those of European Catholicism and Orthodoxy, the practice of offering *āḷrūpaṅgaḷ* being a prime example.[29] This lack of awareness is further complicated by a cross-culturally held institutional disdain for the "excesses" of material religious expressions, of which many Malayali Christians apparently feel they are the sole perpetrators.[30]

In spite of institutional suspicions and reservations, the importance of the vow as a human tool for forging a working relationship with the spirit world and vice versa should not be underestimated. Key to this importance, as we have seen, is that saintly and divine dependence upon material relationships with devotees assumes in them certain human-like qualities, especially that of vulnerability. Susan Wadley describes this "reciprocal arrangement" between equally vulnerable devotee and deity as typical of north Indian Hindu traditions, as well. As voiced in *kathā*, or devotional folk songs, a devotee ideally offers either faith or service to a deity in return for mercy or boons, respectively. On the other hand, if the devotee fails to uphold his or her end of the bargain, the deity whose "needs" have not been met will respond by inflicting anger or revenge upon the guilty party (1975: 81–82).

As argued by Jane Schneider in her discussion of testy spirits (who require similar relationships with humans as do saints), the ambivalence of his or her power—an outgrowth of vulnerability and reliance upon proper treatment—is an intrinsic part of the spirit figure's character, inasmuch as human transaction is necessary or even desirable. In other words, you cannot have one (supernatural power based on human exchange) without the other (supernatural capriciousness). Schneider notes that when devotion to an ambivalent power is replaced by a dualistic system—in which spirits are either entirely benevolent or entirely nasty—the need for reciprocal exchange vanishes. Under these circumstances, "the good spirits selflessly promote the prosperity and morality of the people they protect to the neglect of their own well-being, whereas the bad ones are gratuitously unpredictable or mean, hence unworthy of a relationship" (1990: 32).

As described above, devotees engaged in relationships of mutual exchange with a sacred entity, whether Christian or Hindu, will suffer consequences if they fail to maintain their end of the deal. The spiteful side of these "rowdy" figures (as proposed by Swami Suprabhananda) is both constructed and ensured by the give-and-take between the human and the sacred realms. Tales describing St. George as unleashing the biggest and most poisonous snakes on neglectful devotees thus ring an important note of caution: refuge from dangerous vermin is not an easy "given" but depends upon a system of mutual loyalty and exchange. Even among those of little faith this loyalty remains since, in the words of our Mar Thomite neighbor, who is not normally accustomed to giving offerings to saints but who makes an exception for St. George, "You can never be too sure."

St. George and the Symbolic Embodiment of Calamity

To push further this discussion of uneven-tempered saints and deities, let us take a closer look at St. George's Keralite "*avatār*," characterized by his feisty demand for roosters in return for his services. These "services," which involve the capricious handling of snakes, effects a management, not banishment, of their threat—which helps bridge the divide between the saint and his local Hindu counterpart, the *sarpa* stone. A clear difference remains, nonetheless: unlike the *sarpa* stone, St. George is not portrayed as the symbolic embodiment of the calamity itself. Although admittedly ambivalent, the saint's power seems to be, to a large degree, separate from and (most of the time) in opposition to the snake as calamity. As a result, St. George escapes the ultimate ambiguity and ambivalence of representing both the calamity and its cure.

An event regularly taking place at the Puthupally St. George Church during festival time, however, adds an interesting twist to the saint's profile. During this period, church officials make available for devotees a large snake image, its gaping mouth meant to be a depository for cash offerings. As described by Meena, a young Christian woman who cooked for my family, putting money into the snake's mouth was just as important as offering a chicken or rooster. Furthermore, as she put it, "if anyone makes fun of this they will get terrible diseases." So persistent is this practice that people often place money in wide-mouthed images of serpents or dragons in churches other than those of St. George. In St. Mary's Church in Bharananganam, the Clarist

Sisters seemed to be continuously removing money from the mouth of a wooden dragon figure carved into the side of a chariot designed to carry the statue of the Virgin Mary during processions. The first time I was with Sr. Josephina when she fished some coins out of the dragon's mouth, she clucked annoyedly, saying, "It's the Hindus; they always do these kind of things."

A similar blurring of St. George's power with that of the snake is through interpretations of fowl offerings. I asked a number of people why the rooster was the agreed-upon offering for the saint, as opposed to other animals or items (a common offering to Mary is a sweet dish called *pāyasam*, and St. Sebastian is offered small arrows or *kalūnu*).31 As there does not seem to be any set tradition within memory that connects St. George with the rooster, this question was difficult to answer. People who were most sure of themselves and their rationale, however, told me that roosters and chickens were actually an offering to the *snake*—to satisfy its hunger—since it was the number-one enemy of domestic fowl.

Given this interpretation of rooster sacrifice, along with the presence of a snake image at Puthupally St. George's festival, it appears that we have incidents within the Christian tradition in which calamity acts as a means for its own cure. If the snake image and rooster sacrifice at St. George festivals indeed allow or invoke contact with the reptile and subsequently offer a ritual means for its management—similar to the *sarpa* stone, *yakṣī* stone, and Māriyamma—what then can be said about the role of St. George himself in the management of snakes? From this vantage point, it appears that his tricky antics become overshadowed by the powers of the snake, and thus the saint's importance and strength seem diminished. Such issues aside, the remaining question is whether or not the fair-skinned saint could act, as the snake does, as an embodiment of calamity as well as its cure.

This recalls a lively conversation I had with a literature professor at a college in Kottayam town. A committed Marxist, Dr. Thomas was very interested in speaking, when I met with him in a bustling faculty room, about such things as economics, political oppression, and liberation theology. When I told him I was interested in (among other things) the cult of St. George, he animatedly described to me his interpretation of the saint as a symbol of colonial power. The colonized, he explained, were represented by the snake—thus they are dehumanized and seen as dangerous. The lance St. George thrusts past the jaws of the snake expresses the view that, as he earnestly put it, "If they can't be saved, then they must be killed." I dutifully jotted down the professor's interpretation in my notebook, doubting whether this kind of analogy, although interesting, would ever be of any serious use to me in my efforts to understand mainstream local devotion.32

Nonetheless, the same train of thought that leads me to construe St. George as a cultural hybrid compels me to take seriously Prof. Thomas's proposal that a saint, so revered throughout Kerala, could represent or symbolically embody the brutalizing and terrifying powers of the colonizer. To begin with, although St. George devotion probably thrived in Kerala before the arrival of colonial Portugal or Britain, the fact that both colonizing countries regarded the saint as their patron must have had an impact upon domestic culture. The possibility that St. George acted, on some levels, as a kind of embodiment of these foreigners and of their powers is further suggested in the prevalence of an iconographically depicted fair-skinned and fair-haired saint.

As argued by Bishop Paolos Mar Gregorios from his office at the Orthodox Syrian Seminary, the old-style Syrian iconography of St. George no longer exists because "the British laughed at it." The fickle natives, "only interested in the latest," wholeheartedly adopted the colonial European image.

Furthermore, we have seen that local shrine stories portray a saint who, like the *sarpa* stone, offers a way to manage "himself"—the foreign colonizer—and the religious traditions associated with his cult. It was during the high points of Portuguese and English rule in Kerala—the sixteenth and nineteenth centuries, respectively—that a number of churches previously dedicated to other saints were refurbished or torn down and rededicated to St. George. These refashioned St. George churches include a conspicuously un-Anglican one in Puthupally during the British period and another in Aruvithura which—in spite of its conversion to Roman Catholicism during the Portuguese era—centered around a miraculous Syrian statue. Timely endorsement of the virulent St. George by Keralites thus appears to have been a means for harnessing and subsequently "protecting" devotees from the colonial powers he represented. In short, he became a symbolic embodiment of a calamity for which he simultaneously offered a "cure."

Local Interpretations of the Cult of Sr. Alphonsa

Now to return, in greater detail, to the more recently established cult of Sr. Alphonsa. Although her character and cult are in many ways dramatically different than St. George's we discover here some similarities, particularly in her role as a materially accessible saint who defies authoritative Christian "rules" that she remain spiritualized and benign.

As to be expected, Alphonsa's power to heal and bless often manifests itself through physical objects including, so far only to a limited extent, statues cast in her image. In contrast with some of Kerala's older saint traditions, it seems that the powers attributed to her tomb and a few of her personal possessions reduce the need for miracle-working painted or carved images. As a result, Alphonsa's Bharananganam shrine and birthplace hold something of a monopoly on tangibly accessible miraculous power. Despite the fact that they are not often considered miraculous, statues do play a prominent role on special occasions such as her feast day or birthday. The image of Sr. Alphonsa used in festival procession is often garlanded and set up next to a basket of edible *nērcca* (essentially the same as Hindu *prasādam* and often referred to as such) (see Figure 17).[33] Devotees form a line and take turns touching the feet of the image as a way of honoring the saint, afterward receiving *nērcca* as a form of tangible blessings from her.

Another means of gaining earthly access to Alphonsa's power (largely absent in stories about St. George) was related to me with surprising frequency: dreams and visions. Although Alphonsa's appearance in dreams and visions is not tangible in the same way her relics and statues are, its healing power—usually involving human touch or contact—tends to be concrete. An elderly man, Alphonsa's third cousin, describes such a vision whose perceptible touch cured him during an illness.

> In the middle of the night I was fully unconscious, but I was found sitting upright in the bed by my wife. I was praying. In that stage, I had a vision of Alphonsa and the

Figure 17. Volunteers distribute *nērcca* during Alphonsa's birthday festival, Kudamaloor.

Virgin Mary. They were saying something to me, but I could not make it out clearly. They were stroking me. I was feeling uneasy because no other woman except my wife herself had entered my bedroom. I just turned my back to them in my bed. In that position also I found that they continued to stroke me. In the morning, I was really soaked with sweat and my fever had vanished. I was completely all right. My wife was surprised and asked me what I was doing all night. I narrated the whole incident to her but she didn't believe it. In the dream, the Virgin Mary was seen standing on a globe and Sr. Alphonsa was standing beside her.

Although this dream vision apparently jolted this gentleman's sense of propriety—and portrayed Alphonsa in a somewhat disturbing light—the following tale tells of an apparition that apparently terrorized the woman who unwittingly found herself in its presence. As described by a group of nuns in northern Kerala near Thalassery, this Hindu woman to whom Alphonsa paid a nerve-rattling visit was notorious for her hatred of Christianity. She was, at the time of the vision, particularly upset over the impending installation of Alphonsa's statue directly across the street from her house.

> On the day before the placing of Alphonsa's statue in the roadside grotto, the lady's daughter got a sudden fever. At midnight, the child suddenly got up and began to cry. The woman jumped up from her bed and went over to her daughter, but she found that her daughter was not there on her bed. The lady began to cry out. Just then, a bright light pierced the darkness of the room. In the bright light the lady saw Alphonsa with her child. The woman, terrified, cried out, "Give me back my child!" Sister said, "I'll give you your child back, but what will you give me in return?" The woman said, "I'll give you anything you ask for. Tell me who you are." But the Sister didn't say who she was. The Sister gave the child back. After that, she vanished. After she was gone, the lady experienced some kind of a feeling all over her body. The next day, in the morning, the lady jumped up in great happiness, spreading the news that, "Yesterday Sr. Alphonsa came to me; she spoke to me and made my child all right." The next day, when the lady saw Alphonsa's statue on the grotto, she was very happy and became a believer.[34] Ever since then, the woman has been lighting a candle in the grotto every day.

Sr. Alphonsa's question, "what will you give me in return?" implies a kind of sacred vulnerability that goes hand-in-hand with saintly capriciousness. By displaying the capacity to bestow blessings along with a hot-headed insistence upon devotion, Alphonsa seems, in this case, a bit like St. George when he sends snakes or diseases after the negligent or doubtful among his flock. In the following well-circulated anecdote related by a Clarist nun in Kudamalur, Alphonsa's birthplace, the long-suffering nun appears to have little patience with some greedy relatives. This time she metes out an appropriate punishment by infusing her ambivalent powers into a material object.

> The church decided to build a convent there, near Alphonsa's house, in memory of her. They discussed this with Alphonsa's relatives. They gave consent, and the church gave them some money. The relatives, one after another, came back and took the things of the house for themselves. They came and took away the cot but nobody could sleep on the cot. If they tried to do so, they would be found lying on the floor the next morning. Recognizing their mistake, they returned the cot to the convent. Now the cot is here in Alphonsa Bhavan. Every year, thousands are coming and kissing it, even people with wheezing are lying down on the cot to get rid of their illness.

Alphonsa's personal belongings from her days as a nun—relics of historic interest as well as vessels of sacred power—have been carefully preserved by the Clarist Sisters. Items such as her Roman habit, books, umbrella, and toilet articles sit on display, available to the general public, in what used to be the "parlor" in the Bharananganam convent.[35] Adjacent to the parlor museum is the room where Alphonsa spent many of her years in confinement and where she finally died. Today, centrally located in this room and considered most sacred of all her possessions is her cot, continuously in use during her seemingly interminable span of illnesses. It is significant that Alphonsa's wooden-framed rattan-woven cots, in both Kudamalur and in the Bharananganam convent—the actual *sites* of her sufferings—are so heavily imbued with the power to admonish and particularly with the capacity to heal (see Figure 18).

Sr. Alphonsa as Symbolic Embodiment of Calamity

Beyond the potential ambivalence of Sr. Alphonsa's powers—seen through her roles as both helpmate and (occasionally) disciplinarian—a more basic contradiction intrinsic to her nature comes from her function as an embodiment of calamity (that is, suffering) as well as its cure. As we have seen, the vast majority of Alphonsa's devotees view her as a personification of suffering and self-deprivation who likewise provides a means for alleviating the same. From this viewpoint, her association with and the subsequent enshrinement of this suffering could be compared with the Hindu enshrinement of snakes, *yakṣīgaḷ*, and (once upon a time) smallpox, in

Figure 18. Alphonsa's childhood cot, memorialized in her original home, Kudamaloor.

that it represents the power of a "rowdy" which can be at once undesirable and invaluable. Made accessible through her image in dream visions as well as through her cots, Alphonsa's power, generated from her lifetime of pain, is encapsulated through representations of that suffering: her body as its vessel and her cots as its site.

A more specific means by which Alphonsa acts as an efficacious sufferer is through her role as a "specialty saint" for her devotees (as St. George "specializes" in warding off poisonous snakes, St. Sebastian in epidemic diseases, and so on). Although it was not initially obvious to me, the possibility that Alphonsa could be perceived as a specialty saint became clear during a conversation with a group of elderly Malayali nuns while we were seated around a table at their convent outside Bharananganam. After finishing interviews with some of the Sisters who had known Alphonsa personally, a group of us, including Sr. Josephina, lingered for a while longer as our discussion about Alphonsa and her miracles continued. During the course of our conversation, the miracle of healing clubbed feet kept surfacing. Of all her miraculous cures, the Sisters agreed that this particular kind of healing was uniquely potent in Alphonsa—it indeed was her "specialty." I asked Sr. Josephina why she thought this was so. She quickly responded, "Oh, that's easy!" (As I was continuously haranguing her with obscure and probably irrelevant—and maybe irreverent—questions, she seemed relieved that she could, without hesitation, answer this one.) "She heals clubbed feet because she damaged her own legs when they were burned in the fire." The fire episode, described in more detail in the following chapter, is probably one of the most well-circulated events of Alphonsa's life story. It is an incident that, more than any other, lends specificity and potency to her life of suffering.[36]

As mentioned earlier, devotion to Alphonsa promoted by institutionally authoritative channels does not focus on her capacity for curing suffering but, rather, on her stellar performance of asceticism and self-denial meant as an example for her devotees to follow. This latter portrayal clearly contrasts good and evil and applauds Alphonsa's lifelong endurance of suffering as a dramatically successful banishment of, or victory over, evil—particularly in a context where the body, especially the female body, signifies sinfulness. Although local devotees also recognize the value of suffering—and understand Alphonsa as having earned her powers through life's tribulations—their desire to use this power (through tangible exchange) to gain material and bodily well-being for themselves represents a framework quite different from this institutionally prescribed asceticism. The disparity between these two approaches again seems to lie in local devotion's tenacious rejection of divides that strictly separate and prioritize good over evil as well as spirit over body. Local expressions of saintly ambivalence that fly in the face of established dichotomies reflect ideas of good and evil—or, in this case, suffering and its relief—not entirely at odds but, in many respects, interconnected and even interdependent.

The question arises again of whether this Keralite phenomenon, the symbolic embodiment of calamity as its cure—seen in Christian as well as in local Hindu traditions—is necessarily alien to non-Indian Christian practice. In other words, is Alphonsa's role as sufferer who takes away suffering similar to roles played by the

European Christian saints who are likewise known for their ascetic practices? Assuming that local approaches to sainthood commonly operate to solve mundane rather than spiritual problems, symbolic embodiments of calamity as cure may not be as "foreign" as they appear—or at least not as foreign as the *sarpa* and *yakṣī* stones appeared to me when I first discovered them in Kerala.

Examples of Christian saints who represent a particular type of calamity and who have been called upon by their devotees for the eradication or healing of the same are not difficult to find. The tradition of St. Agatha, a martyr from Sicily, portrays the saint as being tortured by rods, racks, and fire, culminating in the ultimate torment of having her breasts lopped off (or in some versions, twisted off) before she was killed. Her iconographical emblem is that of two breasts on a platter lying in a pool of blood (often mistaken for loaves of bread), and she is invoked against diseases of the breasts as well as against fire, especially eruptions of Mt. Etna (seemingly combining the motifs of breast and fire) (Farmer 1981: 6). Hagiographical accounts of St. Apollonia, deaconess of Alexandria, depict her as being seized by pagan enemies who break all her teeth with blows to her jaws. After refusing to recite the blasphemous prayers of her captors, Apollonia leaps into a fire that ultimately consumes her. Religious art most commonly depicts her as a young woman (although earliest accounts portray her as elderly) holding a tooth in a pair of pincers or having her teeth extracted by an elaborate machine. As to be expected, she has been invoked by people with tooth pain (28).[37] St. Jude (popular in Kerala as well as in North America), who is commonly referred to as the "patron of hopeless causes," originally acquired his reputation because he is, as a saint, a hopeless cause. According to tradition, his name is so similar to Judas, the betrayer of Jesus, that no one (until recently) invoked him for anything (271).[38]

The Hair of the Dog: Some Thoughts and Interpretations

Christianity and Hinduism are not the only religious traditions that manage specific calamities through sacred representations of the same. In *The Buddhist Saints of the Forest and the Cult of Amulets*, Stanley Tambiah describes a similar dynamic in the wearing of amulets, currently popular in Thailand, especially among businessmen. People typically wear these medallions—shaped in or stamped with a wide array of forms and holy figures—around their necks for their protection as well as for a host of other benefits. Of particular interest are the amulets imprinted with specific symbols of asceticism: the begging bowl, the umbrella, and the kettle. When he asked people in Thailand about the meaning of these symbols popularly worn as amulets, Tambiah learned that "These same objects signified quite another world-affirming prosperity when stamped on the medallion and carried as an amulet by the layman. The begging bowl signified . . . that the amulet owner will acquire material goods and prosperity; the umbrella would offer a peaceful life . . . the kettle means that there will be sufficient water to go with the food" (1984: 278).

In Loring Danforth's study of Maine's New Age firewalking movement, he notes that the rationale behind the act of walking on fiery coals is that "fire heals," referring most specifically to the healing of fear. As described by a leader in the American firewalking movement, the healing principle of firewalking is a bit like homeopathy: if great quantities of disease—or in this case, fire—can harm a person, a little bit of the same should be able to heal (1989: 223).

Just as Alphonsa provides for her devotees a model of tribulation as well as a model for its eradication, the amulet and fire operate as mimetic models *of* poverty and fear, respectively, as well as efficacious models *for* overcoming them. Following Geertz, these symbolic embodiments of calamity can be understood as religious symbols that provide both a "parallel with the pre-established non-symbolic system" (model of) and a "manipulation of the nonsymbolic systems in terms of relationships expressed in the symbolic" (model for) (1973a: 93–94). Models of calamity offer a way for devotees to come in contact with a particular affliction through tangible transactions in order that a type of material transformation (that is, manipulation) take place.[39]

The nature of such symbols is also at the root of the Greek medical term *pharmakon*, which carries the meaning of both "poison" and "remedy." Because *pharmakon* is commonly translated into English simply as "remedy," Derrida argues that this interpretation "erases, in going outside the Greek language, the other pole reserved in the word pharmakon. It cancels out the resources of ambiguity and makes more difficult, if not impossible, an understanding of context" (1981: 97). By the same token, to understand sacred representations of calamity simply as remedies for the troubles of their devotees is to ignore the "poison" inherent in their efficacy and, ultimately, to misunderstand the nature of their power. As suggested by New Age members of the firewalking movement, participants must physically engage with a "little bit" (just a dog's hair) of the calamity by walking over a bed of coals (or swallowing a pill, wearing an amulet, or giving material offerings to a symbol of pain). By thus coming into contact with a manageable representation of the larger, otherwise unwieldy, original, its power is contained and subsequently harnessed.

As for an explanation of these fundamentally ambivalent symbols of sacred power, I suggest that they stem from what Jane Schneider describes as an "ethic of reciprocity," associated with local devotional traditions and their surrounding cultures. Schneider argues against interpretations of such local (particularly animistic) practices that view these traditions as being performed solely for material ends, to the exclusion of ethical and spiritual concerns. She thus questions the assumption that ethical concerns are largely the domain of institutionally promoted forms of religious expression. Such biases are not hard to understand when we consider, for instance, contrasting perceptions of Sr. Alphonsa. Reflected in church-sponsored hagiographic accounts, she is a model for ascetic practice or simple, holy living, whereas locally she is revered for her ability to offer mundane benefits such as health and material gain. Schneider argues, however, that beneath local devotion's apparent preoccupation with personal benefit lies loftier concerns for equity and reciprocity. At different moments in history, most conspicuously during the Protestant Reformation and the concurrent rise of capitalist economy, Schneider posits that this ethic of equity has been pushed to the side, replaced with the notion of "brotherly love and a belief in providence [which] de-emphasized personal accountability in these regards" (1990: 25).

Taking her cue from Max Weber's essay, "The Social Psychology of World

Religions," Schneider argues that in animistic societies which largely base their actions upon underlying concerns for equity, "good fortune . . . wants to be legitimate" (Weber 1946: 271). To build her case, she discusses traditions that involve guarding against the evil eye and staging threshold rituals for new houses or businesses. These practices reflect the idea that an ethic of reciprocity does not necessarily prevent people from trying to get ahead in life but, rather, "we see them trying to look over their shoulders as they seek health and good fortune" (Schneider 1990: 28). Schneider also refers to rites of propitiation for dead ancestors and other spirits as being performed with the same concern for equilibrium, in that "such acts show concern that the dead might resent the living, particularly those who died before their time" (30).

Although not directly mentioned by Schneider, an obvious example of this distributive justice between humans and spirits may be found in the rituals of exchange between devotee and local saint or Hindu deity. The transactions and expectations that flow in both directions are often of a material and self-serving nature, but the "rules" of transaction are clearly based upon a system that values equity and reciprocity. People who come to shrines or temples with practical and material concerns hope for their resolution by way of making fair "deals" through vowed exchanges.

Furthermore, as I have described above, the tangible contact required of such ritual transactions becomes a mechanism by which the devotee, by necessity, must come face to face with the calamity itself, inasmuch as the object of devotion or potency is a model or symbolic embodiment of the same. This balance of equity achieved through contact and exchange does not therefore work to level or annihilate the undesirable (yet needed) force but, rather, offers it—as a partner in ritual transaction—a certain validation. Calamity is thus not actually conquered but, instead, undergoes a reconfiguration in which the original symbol of threat or debilitation becomes transformed, and subsequently transformative. The devotee might therefore be considered to pay his or her "dues" through a ritual relationship of equalization with a particular affliction, ultimately hoping that limited contact will allow the human participant to escape its totalizing grip. As we have heard so many times (hinting, once again, that this mindset may not be so foreign after all), "No pain, no gain!"

In support of my argument is an observation Michael Taussig makes of what he calls the "transgressive" aspect of ritual: that which involves a necessary "return of the repressed" or taboo fraught with danger that "exists in order to be broken, so transgression fortifies the taboo" (1993: 126). The result of breaking a taboo (or ritual contact with calamity's symbolic embodiment) is a kind of "equilibrium" that differs from the "great [Western] classical tradition" which, on the other hand, "yearns for harmony, narrative closure and structural integrity" (125).[40] This capricious equilibrium, as described by Taussig, "is the precariously contained explosion of the transgressive moment that allows for and indeed creates the 'mimetic slippage' whereby reproduction jumps into metamorphosis, whereby the duplicating power of spirit (image) is also a self-transforming power—and hence a power for healing and for evil, transforming Being itself " (126).

This mimetic model *of* which is ritually transposed into an efficacious model *for* represents an interdependent relationship between sickness and healing, deprivation and abundance: between calamity and its resolution. As suggested by both Schneider and Taussig, this ritualization of equity/equilibrium is rendered useless by the kind of bifurcated or dualistic spiritualization that is supported by institutionally authoritative ideologies. The designated goal of this latter system is the obliteration of proverbial "rowdies," resulting in a kind of "narrative closure."[41]

Far from desiring that the mimetic undesirable be wiped out, on the other hand, "fearful" firewalkers will eagerly continue to venture onto the coal bed, aspiring Thai businessmen will bedeck themselves with begging-bowl amulets, and needy devotees of Alphonsa will pay homage to her as a model of deprivation. Such ritual activity will continue as long as life's contingencies create the need and as long as devotees' transactions of physical exchange or contact are successful in engaging these models of calamity in such a way that they become models for addressing the same—as long as sacred symbols of ambivalence continue to keep up their end of the "deal."

4

The Life and Cult of Sr. Alphonsa

A Celebration of Complexity and Paradox

Stories and Patterns

Catholic Saint and Hindu "Saint": Problems with a Category

As we turn to Alphonsa's official hagiography as a way of exploring themes in both Hindu and Christian patterns of female sanctity, we need to be aware of one of the potential hazards of attempting to compare categories across cultural and religious divides: the conundrum of using terms appropriate to one religious tradition as a means to investigate roughly similar phenomena within another tradition. More specifically, the label "saint," which is attached to individuals recognized as spiritually or morally exceptional, although it is an interreligiously accepted association, is in some ways an imposition of a Christian category rife with misleading Christian connotations.[1] To begin with, nothing remotely similar to the systematic, centralized, juridical, Catholic Christian process of sanctioning holiness can be found within Hindu traditions. Furthermore—and more pertinent to the task at hand—an attempt to lump Hindu and Christian female ascetics into the same "saintly" category overlooks fundamental differences between the ways idealized holy women are meant to behave within their respective traditions. Whereas a renunciative, ascetic lifestyle most often stands squarely within the bounds of institutional expectations for Catholic women saints (Weinstein and Bell 1982: 223), the same path strays considerably from normative Hindu standards.

Today's highly centralized, time-consuming, and costly process that leads to an official Roman stamp of approval could not be more unlike the identification of a Hindu holy figure, which is established, by and large, by popular consent.[2] Although the understanding of holiness in India might be formulaic to a certain degree— involving certain overarching religious and social expectations—there are nonetheless regional differences, as well as a variety of lifestyles that claim their own traditions for recognizing holiness. The Vatican identifies the ultimate mode of being a Catholic Christian through the highly organized process of canonization, but Hindus recognize exemplary holiness through a variety of roles loosely defined and categorized. Such categories might include, for instance, the lifestyle of sannyasi or sannyasini, yogi or yogini, tantric ascetic, guru, or god-man (or woman); these categories, although often identifiable, can overlap or even be subject to debate.[3] With the absence of an agreed-upon process of "saint-making," an exceptionally adept Hindu may represent extraordinary human holiness in the eyes of some people, the god(dess) incarnate to others, and brazen charlatan to yet others; such classifications, in the end, largely depend upon one's perspective.

Further complicating the possibility of a "sainthood" category for Hindu females— something that could be comparable, that is, to Christian sainthood—is the fact that the valorized role for women within Brahmanical Hinduism is the *pativratā*, the devoted wife and mother—a far cry from the Hindu non-householder renunciate roles.[4] Indeed, Hindu women who have been singled out for their extraordinary sanctity—labeled by some as "saints"—are not usually *pativratās* but, in effect, have rejected this socially acceptable path for acquiring sanctity.[5] In direct contrast to this, religious authorities have tirelessly promoted virginal asceticism for Christian women, which is also the most common means to gain official recognition for extraordinary sanctity (Newman 1990; Schulenburg 1978). In essence, whereas (currently non-Protestant) Christianity has historically glorified women who forgo their sexuality—those who avoid marriage and motherhood and, ideally, live in convents—Hindu women who similarly renounce their sexuality in exchange for a spiritually fervent lifestyle stand outside the realm of proper behavior.[6] Because the *pativratā* role of wife and mother is the conventionally approved lifestyle for Hindu women, and because this role, in a normative context, is not meant to be left behind at any time or mixed with that of extreme renunciation, the relative "deviance" of a female renunciative ascetic who strikes out on her own makes it a rare choice for women—but one certainly not unheard of.[7]

This section's exploration of themes in Alphonsa's hagiography and the ways they correspond with Hindu and Christian notions of female sanctity thus represents a comparison of two very different entities: a highly formulaic, institutionally sanctioned mode of Christian living, on one hand, and a variety of somewhat specified aberrant Hindu roles, on the other. It is not my hope—nor is it really possible— to dredge up a tidy "saint" category for Alphonsa from within a Hindu context. To label her as a sannyasini, yogini, guru, or goddess would be a contrived endeavor, not only because of the multivalence and relativity of these terms but also because it would entail a superimposition of a kind of Hindu female "deviance" upon a figure who is anything but deviant in the eyes of the tradition claiming her as their "own."

Alphonsa's Hagiography

What follows is a hagiographical sketch of Alphonsa's life that reflects a number of themes which commonly run through the telling of her story, both written and oral.[8] Because the pilgrims' understanding of Alphonsa most often has to do with her healing powers and, to some extent, with her life of suffering, the finer details of her life story seem, to most people, of little consequence. Nonetheless, the devotee who happens to have a penchant for Alphonsa's published hagiographies, widely distributed and available in nearly a dozen languages and in differing lengths and genres (including comic books), will probably be familiar with many of the themes recounted here.[9] The extended quotes below, most attributed to Alphonsa in the first person, are primarily from K. C. Chacko's *Sr. Alphonsa* (1948), the most detailed of Alphonsa's written hagiographies, which has been translated into several Indian and European languages.

In the year 1910, in the small village of Kudamalur outside the town of Kottayam, Mary and Joseph Muttathupadathu were expecting their fourth child. One particularly hot and balmy evening in August, Mary and her sister, Annamma, lay on a mat in Mary's courtyard in an effort to get a cool night's rest. As she was drifting off to sleep, Mary awoke suddenly, startled to find a huge snake wrapped around her neck. The pregnant woman was not bitten but, because of her shock, went into premature labor and died soon afterward. The child born of the incident, who in later cloistered life took the name Alphonsa, was christened Anna and called Annakutty (literally "Annachild") by friends and family.

Through her early school years, Annakutty lived at home in Kudamalur with her father and siblings. During this period, people who met her found her to be an extremely pious, kind, and intelligent child. Her physical sufferings, which later became the hallmark of her existence, began at the age of four with a nearly fatal case of eczema. After she finished the school's second standard in Kudamalur, Annakutty was moved to Muttuchira at the insistence of her aunt, Annamma, who took on the role of foster mother for the young girl.

Although she enjoyed physical health and comfort while in Muttuchira, Annakutty's trials began in earnest, due to her foster mother's strict code of discipline, her youngest cousin's cruelty, and the jeers of the other schoolchildren. Later in her life, Sr. Alphonsa reportedly described the psychological tumult of this period:

> Even for the slightest shortcomings my mother used to chide me severely. I was not allowed even to justify myself. Having cultivated such dumb endurance it has become impossible for me now to retort even in jest. My mother never let me enjoy any freedom whatever. I had to talk always in very low tones. Many times have I paced to and fro in the kitchen. There my knowledge of the world ended. I was not allowed— but for one or two exceptions—to talk to anybody in school or to look around me on my way there. Nor did I talk to anybody. The children nicknamed me the dumb girl. I hardly knew anything. Mother got angry with me frequently, and it grieved me much. I used to tremble with fear. Maybe it was because I had lost my own mother that I was so afraid. If I tried to excuse or justify myself when my mother scolded me, that was considered criminal on my part. If I held my peace, she would accuse me of stubbornness—"See, she hasn't a word to say to all this," she would say. If I tried to speak, she would burst out: "And you, have you the cheek to answer me back?" When the storm had passed and she was free from her household duties, she would sweep the tiled floor and lie down on it. She would invite me to her side and embrace me and cover me with kisses; innumerable kisses she would bestow on me, and that would console me. When next she had to attend to something or other, off she would go and then start all over again. (Chacko 1990: 31)[10]

In spite of the severity with which Annamma treated her foster child, Annakutty seemed to understand it as being a part of her aunt's intense love for her sister's child. As she was the only "daughter" in Annamma's care, the elder woman was merely fulfilling her duty by providing the discipline needed to mold the young girl into a good and capable woman. Annamma also enjoyed dressing her only girl in fashionable clothing and costly jewelry—to the extent that Annakutty's classmates laughed at her, calling her a dressed-up bride. Unbeknownst to her foster mother, Annakutty used to remove her jewels and change into simple clothes before walking onto the school grounds.

Also setting herself apart from her peers in Muttuchira was Annakutty's growing dedication to her spiritual development. About this stage, Alphonsa later recounted,

> In my early days I made more progress in my spiritual life than at present. I loved God more ardently. I took great care to avoid all faults. I had nothing special to mention in my First Confession. I zealously aspired to become a saint.[11] I felt that desire while I was reading the biography of Saint Thérèse of Lisieux. Whenever I visited a Carmelite nun who was a relative of mine, she used to tell me, "My child, you must become a saint." Her words redoubled my desires. (Chacko 1990: 32)

It was during this period that Annakutty first took up small ascetic practices. Without anyone knowing, she would seize every available opportunity to fast and abstain from fish and buttermilk. What she did not eat, she gave to the servants.

As the years passed, Annakutty became increasingly determined to emulate the life of St. Thérèse of Lisieux. One day, while walking on the grounds of her Muttuchira home, she met a Carmelite nun who spoke to her about the grandeur of religious life, encouraging her to join. Later, when Annakutty recalled that nuns were not allowed to wander beyond the confines of their convent alone, she suspected that her conversation with this anonymous Carmelite must actually have been a vision of Thérèse of Lisieux herself. This experience further strengthened her resolve to enter a religious order.

By the time she entered adolescence, in spite of Annakutty's determination to enter the convent, her foster mother enthusiastically embarked on a search for a suitable husband for her only daughter. Realizing this, Annakutty increased her fasting. Adding other mortifications to her daily routine such as kneeling on gravel and praying with her arms outstretched, she pleaded with God to change her foster mother's mind. Her actions prompted the other children to laugh at her, but she offered this humiliation up as further sacrifice to God. In spite of her prayers and mortifications, as well as her direct pleas to Annamma to allow her to enter the convent, her foster mother stood firm in her opinion that Annakutty should be married. In her desperation to put an end to her aunt's efforts, Annakutty conjured up a dramatic solution to her problems. As described in later life to some of the Sisters in the convent,

> I prayed all night. An idea then struck me. If my body was somehow disfigured, then nobody would like me. There was a huge hollow in the ground close to the house— a hollow into which was shoveled all the chaff and grain husks at the end of harvest time. Fire was applied to it to burn it away. Early in the morning I walked up to the pit and put one foot into the fire. I slipped and jumped into it. To get out, I had to climb up more than my own height. I was not accustomed to climbing even two feet. I ran to and fro in the fire in my efforts to climb out. The clothes caught fire. My hair, which I had forgotten to tie up, was also burnt at the ends. I might well have

sunk in right up to the neck and been burnt away. I do not know how, finally, I climbed out and escaped from the pit. (Chacko 1990: 34)

Annakutty's first impulse was to hide her burns from Annamma by putting on new clothes. When Annamma saw her condition, however, she screamed, and Annakutty fainted from the pain. Soon afterward,

> A goldsmith was procured to remove the bangles from my feet. A doctor was summoned to attend on me. Pus had begun to ooze out of both my legs. The doctor came daily, scraped off the pus and renewed the cotton bandages. My toes had been so badly burnt that they were just one mass. The doctor separated them and dressed each one separately. How much I suffered. And all of it I offered up for my one great intention. (Chacko 1990: 34)

In answer to her excruciating pain, Annakutty's "one great intention" became a reality. About a year afterward, she was accepted by Bharananganam's Clarist nuns to enter their convent school's seventh standard. She joined the convent's high school for two years of higher studies and, in February 1928, received the veil of postulancy. Entering the order on the feast day of St. Alphonsus, she took the name Alphonsa. Two years later, on May 19, 1930, Alphonsa entered the novitiate. As was the custom, she wore a wedding dress for the ceremony, and was lavished with the many wedding ornaments her family had earlier bought for her marriage. After the ceremony, Alphonsa, along with the other new novices, shaved their heads and exchanged their wedding finery for coarse religious habits.[12]

A few months after her vestition, Alphonsa fell ill and was hospitalized in Ernakulam. Although she was well enough to teach for a year following this affliction, it was the first episode in a chain of agonizing illnesses that kept Alphonsa bedridden for virtually her entire career as a nun, until her death in 1946. During one bout of particularly debilitating ill health while she was still in the novitiate at Changanassery, Alphonsa regretted that it kept herself, as well as the others who had to wait on her, from community life. At the suggestion of her spiritual director, she conducted a novena to Fr. Elias Chavara (one of the other Malayalis currently being considered for canonization) in order that she be healed. At one point during this nine-day period, the novice mistress heard the sound of talking coming from Alphonsa's room around midnight. Because it was meant to be a time when novices observed a strict rule of silence, she angrily entered the room and found Alphonsa talking and gesturing in her sleep. Upon waking the sleeping nun, the novice mistress learned that Fr. Chavara had appeared to Alphonsa in a dream, telling her that she was completely healed of this particular ailment—which she was—but would have to endure more suffering at a later date.

After returning to Bharananganam in 1936 from the year-long novitiate in Changanassery, Alphonsa contracted a high fever, which was suspected to be tuberculosis. Not wanting to be removed from the convent, Alphonsa again made a novena—this time to Thérèse of Lisieux as well as to Fr. Chavara. Visited by both of these people in a dream, Alphonsa was cured once again. After a short period of stable health, Sr. Alphonsa experienced a number of other ailments that again relegated her to her bed. As she continued to be bedridden, some of the nuns suspected that she was faking her illnesses in order to gain special attention from the authorities.

For this reason, some of the Sisters spoke sharply to her, criticizing her behavior. As she had done in response to the teasing children of Muttuchira, Alphonsa made an offering of every tribulation, physical as well as emotional, as a sacrifice to God. She also took every opportunity to offer acts of charity to the nuns who were unkind to her, and eventually won the favor and friendship of most of them.

To add a further dimension to her sufferings at this time, a thief broke into Alphonsa's room, terrifying her and triggering a period of mental instability that lasted for many months. Chacko describes the scene that occurred while she was lying in bed, praying:

> she raised the crucifix that she was holding and asked him, in the name of Jesus Christ, not to harm her. As the thief made his escape, Alphonsa was able to crawl out of bed and out onto the verandah and attract the attention of some of the other nuns. In her already weakened condition, the shock of this encounter caused her to lose her mind. For many months she lost her memory, was unable to recognize those who were not constant companions, and had difficulty eating and sleeping. When she had nearly recovered from the shock, she was beset by a painful swelling in her legs—so painful that she could scarcely eat or even breathe. (Chacko 1990: 45)

After Alphonsa's complete recovery from her shock, a full year after her encounter with the thief, she was given the power to read Tamil as well as Malayalam. It was also during this latter period of Alphonsa's life that she became fairly well known for her abilities to read the minds of others and to predict future events. All of these things she confidently performed for those desiring such services.

Convinced as always of the merits of suffering, Alphonsa spent much of her energy praying for and receiving a continuous stream of ailments that helped quench her overwhelming desire to unite herself more closely with the suffering Jesus. In 1945, however, she was given a new and particularly agonizing suffering that threw her into fits of violent convulsions every Friday. These furious attacks, weekly marking the occasion of Jesus' Passion, lasted from three to seven hours and were so unbearable to watch that many who tried attending to her were forced to leave the room. After it seemed that Alphonsa was close to dying, she would recover and have no recollection of the actual details of her pain, except that it was very intense.

In spite of the various scheduled and unscheduled agonies Alphonsa suffered, she was known throughout the convent for her charming disposition, her charity toward others, and her gifts of prophecy and mind reading. Through her prayers and extreme dedication to God she was often able to endure much of her pain with such courage and fortitude that she—to the astonishment and admiration of those who knew her—no longer considered it to be suffering.

As the end of her life neared, however, the level of Alphonsa's physical distress had increased to such a degree that she entered a period of spiritual desolation reflected in her letters to her confessor, Fr. Romulus. She therefore requested from him permission to pray for her death, which he eventually granted. On Sunday, July 28, 1946, she entered yet another bout of agonies, normally reserved for Fridays. This time, instead of keeping silent as she normally did, Alphonsa stated, "I can't stand the pain. Pray for me." She pulled the blanket over her head to cover the tears that had begun rolling down her face. Minutes later, after calling out to Mary, the mother of Jesus, she smiled a radiant and peaceful smile and then seemed to be getting ready to go somewhere. She called on those who stood around her bed, "Get me my dress. Let me go." They told her that she was already dressed. She insisted, "Give me a good habit and a good toque and let me go." In a final flash of consciousness Alphonsa cried out, "Jesus, Mary, and Joseph," and, soon afterward, breathed her last (Chacko 1990: 86).

Saintly Scripts: Thérèse and Alphonsa Revisited

> Oh Mother, thy life that went unnoticed by any
> Has now become world famous.
> The Bharananganam that was fortunate to be your grave
> Has become sanctified: The Lisieux of India.
> Fr. Kavyan Chengalam

One of the saintly roles hagiographers and others carve out for Alphonsa is that of antidote to material excess and scientific skepticism—a role similar to that which Thérèse of Lisieux also assumed for devotees in late nineteenth- and early twentieth-century France. Whether their subject is Alphonsa's life as Kerala's remedy for modernism or her small deeds of kindness and suffering—central also to the life of St. Thérèse—songs, sermons, and hagiographies repeatedly draw comparisons between the Keralite nun and the French saint.

A theme that permeates both of these women's hagiographical (and, in the case of Thérèse, autobiographical) accounts, and that forms the main basis for their comparison, is that of physical and emotional suffering. Both Alphonsa and Thérèse are described as taking on austerities at a tender age and, for this reason as well as others, they are portrayed as being misunderstood and mistreated by their childhood peers. Each woman entered religious life only after overcoming seemingly insurmountable obstacles—from the religious authorities in Thérèse's case (because she was too young) and from family (especially her foster mother) in Alphonsa's case. Although Thérèse did not have the opportunity—or the reason—to disfigure herself, her equally brazen act was to bring her request to enter the Carmelite convent personally to the pope. When other religious authorities barred her entrance, her bold appeal to the top—in spite of explicit instructions not to speak before the pontiff—ultimately won her success. Convent living meant additional physical and mental trials for both women, yet provided for each a context in which their desire for suffering increased and in which such desires were eagerly fulfilled. Thérèse's passionate longing for suffering was reinforced by the expectation that Jesus had many "crosses" in store, designed especially for her (Lisieux 1957: 53). In a similar way, Alphonsa's hagiography depicts her as yearning constantly for discomforts, reveling in them as gifts from Jesus.

The parallels many Malayali Catholics draw between Alphonsa and Thérèse—in light of the fact that the Little Flower is one of the better known European saints throughout Kerala—offers an important alliance with saintly eminence recognized around the globe. Although this kind of notoriety undoubtedly spurs on the making of cross-cultural connections, it is also important to consider how Alphonsa herself may have struggled during her lifetime to emulate the French saint and, consequently, provided much of the fodder for her devotees' posthumous associations. According to George Alackappally in his article in the February 1987 edition of *The Passion Flower*, a quarterly devoted to the cause of Blessed Alphonsa, Thérèse's autobiography, *The Story of a Soul*, was available in Malayalam translation by the time Alphonsa was a young schoolgirl. Judging from Alphonsa's (Annakutty's) alleged vision of St. Thérèse in her Muttuchira compound, as well as references to her reading of *The Story of a Soul*, it is indeed possible that the life of the French nun was influential from a young age. In one of her interviews with *The Passion Flower*, Sr. Sales, one of Alphonsa's closest convent companions, recalled that the aspiring saint seemed to always be reading Thérèse's autobiography, and kept a copy of it on her window sill. Apparently, although the book in her possession was not old, it eventually became worn out from constant use.

Although Alphonsa's hagiographers undoubtedly had in mind the religious and cultural expectations of, or scripts for, female sanctity when they wrote about her, Alphonsa seemed to have her own ideas of sanctity in mind and thus her own script to follow—modeled in part, though it may have been, on someone else's script. As we attempt to untangle some of the many ways Alphonsa conformed and subtly did not conform to Hindu and Christian notions of female sanctity, we must allow for the possibility that these conformities are not all necessarily a part of hagiographic strategy. It is also conceivable that they are tied to Alphonsa's own "strategies" for becoming that which she seems to have deeply desired: a saint.

Hindu and Christian Patterns of Female Sanctity

Regardless of whether familiar hagiographical themes were consciously lived out by Alphonsa or embellished after her death, the similarities between her life story and personal philosophies and those of St. Thérèse are indeed worthy of note. Yet, if we place these shared themes within a larger framework of Christian female sanctity, the parallels between the two women's life stories begin to look a lot less particular. Furthermore, when compared with Hindu patterns of sanctity for women renunciate-ascetics, what seems to be a widely held Christian theme can, on occasion, look less uniquely Christian. By focusing on several of the key motifs found in Alphonsa's story—important to hagiographers as well as devotees—I intend here to complicate some of the easy distinctions sometimes made between Hindu and Christian notions of female sanctity and asceticism, while not erasing the important differences that exist between the two traditions.

Precocious Beginnings and Parental Prohibition Two commonly described aspects of Alphonsa's early life, her extraordinary piety during her youth and her (foster) parents' resistance to her desires for pursuing it through celibate living, are prominent themes in the lives of Hindu as well as Christian holy women.

Among Christian saints, Weinstein and Bell's extensive study shows that men are far more likely than women to undergo conversion experiences during adolescence. Female saints, on the other hand, often commit themselves to a holy life before the age of seven (Weinstein and Bell 1982: 235). Within Hinduism's anti-orthodox *bhakti* movement A. K. Ramanujan notes a similar trend. He reasons that, given *bhakti*'s ideology of societal reversal, women's low status prevents a need for any kind of dramatic conversion. As a result, a female *bhakta*'s extraordinary devotion often originates in early childhood and remains fairly constant throughout her life (Ramanujan 1983: 316, 320). For male *bhaktas*, particularly for those belonging to higher castes, a personal crisis during adolescence or later—and subsequent conversion— are necessary for them to embody their challenge to the dominant order (323).

The struggle between Alphonsa and her foster mother after the young woman pledges herself to a life of unmarried virginity also reflects a theme typically found in the lives of female renunciates, both Hindu and Christian. Women's struggles with parents (or in-laws) over their desire to escape domesticity makes particular sense within a Hindu context in which the *pativratā* role of a devoted wife and (ideally) mother is the expected norm. Ramanujan notes that female *bhaktas* who avoid human marriage in order to form a type of matrimonial union with the divine almost always meet resistance from family members on this account (Ramanujan 1983: 320).[13] Although a Christian woman's determination to live a cloistered life, often vowed during childhood, does not defy societal norm in the same way, such designs are not typically received with enthusiasm or acceptance by members of her family, particularly parents. Stories abound of Christian women saints who refuse to wear ornaments, give their fine clothing to the poor, and disfigure themselves in order to stave off marriage. Also popular are tales of young women who are forced by relentless parental pressure to abandon their personal vows to Jesus for the sake of an earthly marriage (Weinstein and Bell 1982: 234; Goodich 1981: 23).

In the case of Alphonsa, relentless pressure does not succeed in joining her to a human husband but, rather, pushes the young woman into taking drastic measures to ensure that she steer her own course in life. The decisive turning point marked by her fire episode can be viewed as a kind of rite of passage in Annakutty's life. Here she makes the transition from being a dependent, spiritually precocious child to an adult who asserts her right to arrange her own "marriage" and her own future.

The Power of Burning   Although a holy woman's avoidance of marriage through self-disfigurement is not unheard of in Christian hagiography, the fiery way Alphonsa carries this out is a richly symbolic act from an Indian perspective. In the formal Hindu rite that readies a person for the role of sannyasi(ni), an aspiring renouncer often ritualizes the casting off of his or her householder status through the burning of a grass effigy, which signifies symbolic death to the world (Denton 1991: 219). In a similar manner, Alphonsa's disfigurement through burning establishes—according to most hagiographical accounts—a final liberation from the worldly responsibilities planned for her by her foster mother, and makes it possible to enter into a life of convent renunciation.

An interesting Christian parallel to the sannyasini initiation ceremony of ritual death/cremation is a kind of symbolic burial recounted in the life stories of many early ascetics. Here, hagiographies describe saints (usually male saints) as spending time in a tomb or cave underground before beginning the final phase of their life. Based on her study of a wide variety of early Christian ascetics, Alison Goddard Elliot deduces that this motif of burial is meant to be an enactment of a kind of death, which enables the ascetic to achieve a certain "transcendental purity" (Elliot

1987: 110). She writes, "This emblematic death prefigures his real death and resurrection into Paradise, but even more it serves as a *rite de passage*, a purificatory ritual in which the saint sheds his cultural existence in preparation for a new way of life. It marks or confirms his step across the division between the cooked and the raw" (110).

In India, the motif of fire (evoked also in Elliot's culinary language) in folk epics of deified heroines told from Rajasthan to Kerala often include the theme of self-sacrifice through burning (Blackburn 1985: 261). Related to the more familiar *satīmātā* who joins her deceased husband on his funeral pyre, the epic heroine is a virgin (although commonly married) who often mounts a burning pyre alone. In either case, it is this act of self-immolation that earns for the woman her heroic status and is the main reason for her posthumous deification. The epic heroine's male counterpart, on the other hand, does not burn himself but typically earns his hero status through death in battle (Narayana Rao 1986: 134). Complicating these distinctions a bit, in Narayana Rao's study of south Indian folk traditions he distinguishes between two types of epics: the sacrificial and the martial.[14] Echoing themes from Alphonsa's hagiography, the sacrificial epic features a young female protagonist who must defend her virginity through burning (and death). This normally takes place in the form of willful defiance against an authoritarian figure. Whereas martial epics end on a tragic note—the death of the male protagonist being mourned by his followers—sacrificial epics are not normally perceived as tragic. The denouement of the latter speaks of the "magical powers of ritual sacrifice," and views it a victory rather than a tragedy; the woman's self-immolation brings prosperity and security for those to whom the story belongs (Narayana Rao 1986: 140–41; see also Kothari 1989).

Other motifs running through Alphonsa's hagiographies as well as through many folk epics are a miraculous birth and a premature death involving great suffering (Kothari 1989).[15] Blackburn notes that devotees of deified heroes and heroines give much attention to the fact that his or her death was violent, and was preceded by great tribulation and torment. This emphasis on suffering is so insistent that it seems to overshadow completely the importance of the hero or heroine's morally upright character. Finally, like the Catholic process of apotheosis, cult recognition of an epic hero or heroine happens only after his or her posthumous spirit can be successfully invoked to shower blessings upon those who offer devotion (Blackburn 1989).

The two events in Alphonsa's hagiography that are also found in folk epics—her unusual birth and the fire incident—seem to be of particular importance to her devotees and hagiographers alike. In a typical answer to my questions about Alphonsa's life story, Jaya, a teenage Christian pilgrim visiting the Bharananganam shrine with her Christian and Hindu friends, replies (with nodding consent from her companions),

> Alphonsa was born in the Kottayam district. She lost her mother as soon as she was born. She had her education in Bharananganam as well as in Muttuchira and was later taken to her aunt's house. There, the aunt decided to give her in marriage but she wanted to join the convent. Alphonsa refused to get married, so she jumped into an ash pit. Later her aunt consented. In the convent, she was liked by all. She used to perform so many miracles for the people who went to her. All the sufferings which were given to her by God were accepted by her with a happy heart.

The importance to devotees of the birth and burning event is further witnessed by the fact that although many official and unofficial accounts of Alphonsa's story highlight these moments, her relatives consistently refute them. Regarding the snake incident, according to most of Alphonsa's relatives who were available for comment, Alphonsa's birth and her mother's death had little to do with a frightening snake. Furthermore, family members insist that her mother died months after Alphonsa (Annakutty) was born rather than immediately afterward.

Although family members rarely bring up the subject of the snake event unless asked (suggesting perhaps that it is of little consequence for them), they commonly address the "problem" of her jumping into the burning ash pit. Recent interviews with family members as well as earlier accounts by relatives who are since deceased show consistent efforts to set the record straight about Alphonsa's burning event. From their point of view, the young woman entered into the fire by mistake; her aim was simply to perform the routine chore of going to the edge of the pit to collect ashes used for cleaning teeth. Through a loss of balance or carelessness, she ended up falling into the center of the pit and burning herself. In the 1986 "Beatification Special" of *The Passion Flower*, Murickal Pilo Luka, Alphonsa's cousin who also lived in the Muttuchira house, addressed the controversy:

> It was the desire of my mother to marry her off to some educated and fairly rich young man and she soon was on the lookout for a bridegroom for "the bride of the Murickal family." But she [Alphonsa] chose to espouse herself to Christ and at last my parents bowed to her desire. I don't believe that the incident of Annakutty burning her feet was in any way connected with her desire to forestall a marriage. More than anything else, it was the persuasion of Fr. Jacob Murickan, my paternal uncle, who prevailed with my parents to let her join the convent.

In answer to questions raised by Alphonsa's relatives' accounts—sometimes expressed publicly—those who are of the opinion that the young woman jumped into the fire on purpose argue that she carefully planned the deed and carried it out in great secrecy. The fact that the family believes otherwise merely proves that Alphonsa was successful in hiding her motives from those around her. According to Chacko, it was not until her entry into the convent, after her novitiate, that she admitted to the Clarist convent chaplain, Fr. Aloysius, that her burning was deliberate (Chacko 1990: 35). It does stand to reason that family authorities would consider an adolescent's conscious disfiguration as a means for steering her own course in life to be a brazen, punishable offense. Furthermore, such an act probably would have acted as a deterrent for acceptance into a religious order. It is therefore entirely understandable that, if disfiguration and resistance to her foster mother's wishes were Alphonsa's motives for burning herself, she would have reason to try to keep such things to herself.

In any case, regardless of her actual intentions, the culturally resonant theme of Alphonsa's deliberate and defiant self-immolation is indeed central to all types of hagiographical accounts, unlikely to be dimmed by family members' refutations.

Union/Identification with the Divine   Despite differing opinions as to why Alphonsa entered the fire pit, her motivation for entering the convent—to not be bound to a life with a human spouse but, rather, to be a kind of *patīvratā* for Christ—is something on which most hagiographers, devotees, and family members agree. A prayer attributed to Alphonsa, printed on the reverse of her holy cards, underscores this desire for union, and its connection to pain and burning.

> Humiliate me until I am almost nothing—until I become a spark in the fire of the love burning in "Thy Divine Heart." My sweet Jesus, sweet beyond all description, transform all my worldly consolations into bitterness. Jesus, Sun of Justice, by Thine divine rays clarify my thoughts, illumine my mind, purify my heart, consume me in the fire of Thy love and thus unite me with Thee.

Alphonsa's fire incident aside, hagiographers and devotees understand her life of suffering to have provided daily opportunities for sacrifice that brought her ever closer to her God. More specifically, in many of Alphonsa's own writings as well as in the words attributed to her, she interprets her daily sacrifices of pain as an opportunity to share in the agonies of Jesus, which ultimately allows her to unite with him. Chacko attributes to Alphonsa the use of marital imagery in a description of the richness of shared pain and deprivation that enable her to join with a divine spouse: "When the king marries a little shepherd girl and she as queen is entitled to share the king's possessions, does she complain or grieve over them? Does she not accept them with pleasure? Would she not consider it a grave misfortune if she were denied her share of the king's riches? But we are averse to accepting the possessions of Our Divine Spouse. We even go so far as to complain of our share. Does that become a bride? Should we not rather be happy over it?" (Chacko 1990: 62).

In written accounts of Alphonsa's life, depictions of her union with Jesus which tend to surface more often than bridal imagery are those that focus intensely on her extreme self-mortification and illness. From this perspective, her life emerges as an imitation of the suffering Jesus, in which her agony provides the common link. This union culminates, in a sense, in Alphonsa's capacity to *become* Jesus through her pain. Although generic penitential asceticism is a common mode for expressing Christian sanctity, particularly in the lives of female saints (Weinstein and Bell 1982: 229; Bynum, 1987: 25), imitatio christi, achieved through suffering and often mixed with erotic or marital imagery, is a form of asceticism typically taken on most literally by women, particularly during the late Middle Ages (Bynum 1991: 131). In one of the entries in which Chacko describes Alphonsa's imitatio christi, where imitation of Jesus' agony is combined with spousal union, she is depicted as speaking from the throes of one of her more excruciatingly painful episodes:

> I am stretched on the Cross now. Our Lord could not move His limbs or turn to the side while He was on the Cross. He had no bed or pillow. Those who stood by the Cross only mocked Him in his agony. Our Lord had no consolation whatever. As for me, how many are crowding round to sympathize with and to console me by attending to my needs. Our Lord was not served as I am. I am His bride, but how trifling indeed are my sufferings when compared to the agonies of my Spouse. I would willingly drain to the very dregs of the chalice which the Lord has presented to me. (Chacko 1990: 43)

In addition to the words attributed to Alphonsa in which she identifies herself with Christ through suffering, her endurance of what became known as her "Friday agonies" bodily express her imitatio christi through weekly reenactments of Jesus' Friday Passion.

Also typical of medieval Christian women's ascetic practices (Bynum 1991: 119–50), the physicality of Alphonsa's union with Jesus was supplemented by receiving his body through the eucharist—either physically through eating it or spiritually by meditating upon it. A note written by Alphonsa, found after her death, includes the phrase, "I will spend all the time I can manage to find before the Blessed Sacrament." Commenting on her frequent vigils in front of the convent chapel's tabernacle, one of her superiors purportedly noted that "Sr. Alphonsa seemed to become one with Jesus during her meditations before the Blessed Sacrament" (Chacko 1990: 65).

Although penitential asceticism has continued to be an important theme in the live of Christian holy women throughout the centuries (Weinstein and Bell 1982: 233–34; Mooney 1990: 75–76), suffering meant as a form of imitatio christi seems to have faded in popularity after the sixteenth century.[16] In Thérèse of Lisieux's writings, brief references to her eager reception of the cross of Jesus through her sufferings infer a more subtle type of imitatio christi. Suffering as a way to identify with Christ seems to have been less meaningful than her strategy for emulating Jesus through works of charity in the form of small acts of kindness and self-sacrifice. In the case of mental and physical sufferings, Thérèse's writings tend to portray them as further opportunities to offer something of herself to God rather than as a tool for imitation or union. Although Alphonsa likewise refers to her suffering as a sacrifice, the frequency with which themes of imitation and union with Christ appear in her hagiographical accounts demands attention.

In light of the fact that the performance of literal bodily imitatio christi has not lately been a prominent theme in the lives of female (or male) saints, it is interesting to note that the life of Mother Mariam Thresia (1876–1926), one of the six other candidates for sainthood in Kerala, also highlights this theme.[17] Whereas Alphonsa's union with Jesus through her imitation of his Passion on the cross seems, in some ways, to be a natural extension and sanctification of her many bodily illnesses, Mariam Thresia's imitation appears to have been supernaturally- and self-imposed. Like Alphonsa yet much more extreme in her ways, Mother Mariam Thresia performed self-mortifications in her youth. From the age of four and five onward, she reportedly made it a habit to deny herself physical comforts by regularly lying on gravel, rolling on thorny bushes, and lashing her body with spiked twigs. She purportedly told her confessor later in life that she did not wish to receive anything in return for these deeds except for the satisfaction of pain shared with Jesus (Chacko 1992: 31). As she grew older, Mariam Thresia's childhood austerities were exchanged for more sophisticated ones, such as lashing her body with whips, wearing spikes around her waist, and sleeping on mats spread with pebbles. Consistent with her dramatic style, she regularly received supernatural visions that were both holy and demonic in nature and, during these occasions, entities—holy and otherwise—spoke out from within her (71–73).

Although hagiographical accounts never say that Jesus spoke through Mariam Thresia, they describe her union with him through painful Friday episodes in ways somewhat similar to Alphonsa's (although with a sensationalism quite unlike Alphonsa's more subdued suffering). During Mariam Thresia's Friday events an unseen force would pin her to the wall while she bled from her hands, feet, and side as well as from small punctures around her head. As hard as people tried—and Mariam Thresia at times challenged them to do so—her hands could not be pried away from their crucified position on the wall. Rumors of this weekly bleeding with/as Jesus on the cross brought crowds of people clamoring to see Mother Mariam Thresia on Fridays or, if this was not possible (she preferred to endure her passion with/as Jesus alone), to catch a glimpse of the wounds that marked her body throughout the rest of the week (Chacko 1992: 78).

Aside from the drama that sets Mariam Thresia's suffering apart from Alphonsa's, the two nuns differ in their interpretation of their Friday episodes. Mariam Thresia, who lived an extremely active life caring for the poor and infirm, purportedly viewed her reenactment of the Passion as an extension of her life's work of easing the suffering of others. The pain that united her with (and as) Jesus did not function solely as a glorious end in itself (as Alphonsa might have it) but also as a salvific means to alleviate the misery of others. This latter function furthermore served as an additional means to unite Mariam Thresia with Jesus during her Friday Passion events—so potent is her Christlike ability to offer relief that Jesus himself comes to her for consolation. She writes, "Having consoled me, Our Lord came suffering, in pain, carrying the cross and asking me to relieve him of his sufferings. He embraced me and passed the cross on to my shoulders and told me not to be afraid of anything." In spite of variations in interpretation and sensationalism, which reflect basic differences in these women's approaches to life, Alphonsa and Mariam Thresia's reenactments of Jesus' Passion demonstrate a shared understanding that holiness can be attained most strikingly during moments in which one emulates and, in a sense, becomes the divine.

Although it would be impossible to neatly fit all the details of Alphonsa's and Mariam Thresia's experiences into particular categories of Hindu practice, there are ways in which they challenge some of the distinctions traditionally made between Christian and Hindu mysticisms. W. T. Stace has expressed what he believes to be practitioners' different understandings of Hindu and Christian mystical experiences, which, he argues, masks the singularity of experience itself: "The Christian mystic *usually says* that what he experiences is 'union with God.' The Hindu mystic *says* that his experience is one in which his individual self is identical with Brahman or the Universal Self. The Christian *says* that his experience supports theism and is not an experience of actual identity with God, and *he understands* 'union' as not involving identity but some other relationship such as resemblance" (Stace 1961: 34).[18]

Conspicuously overlooked in this assessment of mysticism are the experiences of Hindu *bhakti* adepts who most commonly describe their mystical union not as an identification with but, rather, as a relationship to the divine, commonly in the capacity of lover. Absorption into the divine, or *samādhi*, is typically a state reserved for the moment when the *bhakti* practitioner's earthly life has ended.[19] By contrast, the yogic adept (the term *yoga* is often construed as "union")[20] commonly identifies *samādhi* as the highest goal, ideally achieved periodically through such practices as bodily postures, breath control, and meditation. *Samādhi*—the experience of "union of person with God, of the individual with the universal reality" (Chattopadhyay 1987: 249)—is thus approached differently by different Hindu practitioners, depending on one's tradition and perspective.[21]

Offering an interesting juxtaposition of these religious perspectives—devotion to and identification with the Divine—is a segment of a published hagiography of a Keralite god(dess)-woman, Mata Amritanandamayi, whom devotees honor as a contemporary manifestation of Kṛṣṇa and Devī. Her hagiographer describes a period in her life when she becomes permanently absorbed in Kṛṣṇa's identity, leaving behind her ability to relate to him in a devotional manner.

> Sudhamani [later referred to as Mata Amritanandamayi], who was fully established in the consciousness of Krishna, still had an unquenchable thirst to enjoy the bliss of Supreme Devotion—*Para Bhakti*. But her complete identification with Lord Krishna made it impossible for her either to meditate on His Form or get immersed in His thought. Then and there her prayers stopped flowing to Krishna and her Krishna *sadhana* [devotion] came to an end. (Amritaswarupananda 1993: 96)

Although it is doubtful that Sr. Alphonsa and Mother Mariam Thresia would go so far as to claim a permanent identification with God, as does Mata Amritanandamayi, there appear to be moments in their lives when they move beyond a *bhakti* type of relationship of love and devotion for Jesus and toward a more direct identification. Particularly in the enactment of their Passion Friday episodes, their standard position as individuals who are separate from and in relationship to the Divine becomes, for the time being, transfigured.

From the point of view of Alphonsa's devotees, some people, particularly nuns at the convent, explicitly identify her with Jesus in a manner somewhat similar to Mariam Thresia's apparent identification and self understanding. On such occasions, Alphonsa's sufferings are interpreted as having salvific powers; as Jesus' suffering serves the purpose of healing souls, so Alphonsa's suffering heals bodies and spirits. A devotional song "This Chalice," written by a Catholic priest, Michael Panachicken, which was recorded commercially on cassette tape, offers an example of such a perspective. Alphonsa is identified with Jesus through her powerful suffering; this association is so complete that the listener cannot be sure whether the song is meant to describe Jesus or Alphonsa until the last stanza, when reference is made to an unresurrected body buried in a tomb:

> This chalice is full of bitter drink.
> I shall drink it
> According to Thy holy will, my Father.
> I shall become the Lord of Life to this people.
>
> I shall struggle upon the cross
> Raised on the peak of Calvary.
> My blood, falling drop by drop,
> Will remit their sins.
>
> My soul, having been entrusted into Thy hands,
> I shall remain buried in the tomb
> So that they may be arrayed on the right side
> At the second glorious coming on the clouds
>
> Fr. Michael Panachicken
> "This Chalice"
> (*Ī Kāsa*)

Although a Hindu context probably helped to form Alphonsa's and Mariam Thresia's understandings of their relationship with/as God—as well as the interpretations of their Indian devotees and hagiographers—identification with the divine within European Christianity may have set some precedent as well. Caroline Walker Bynum, in her study of medieval woman mystics, notes that during the middle of the twelfth century, imitatio christi as an avenue for holiness was taken up in an increasingly literal sense.

> Whereas Bernard of Clairvaux taught that we identify with Christ by extending our compassion to his humanity through pitying the suffering humanity of our neighbors, Francis and Mary of Oignies became Christ on the cross while a seraph looked on. Indeed some male descriptions of holy women explicitly stress that *imitatio* is fact, not memory or imagination. We are told, for example, that Margaret of Cordona and Lukardis of Oberweimer became one with the Crucifixion rather than simply remembering or pitying Christ's suffering. . . . Beatrice of Nazareth . . . spoke of three grades of moving toward Christ: turning toward grace; growing in the memory of Christ's passion; and, finally, inhering in Jesus. (Bynum 1991: 145–46)

Female Asceticism in Cultural Context   Literal bodily union with the suffering Jesus was a path most typically taken—especially during the thirteenth through the fifteenth centuries—by women. Why asceticism, in general, was a mode of sanctity more central to the lives of women than of men seems to have been related to societal limitations on a woman's lifestyle. Although the Church could recognize male sanctity through the public roles of pope, bishop, priest, or preacher, it largely limited women's roles to the private sector (Mooney 1990: 27).[22] McNamara notes that by the middle of the twelfth century and with the rise of primogeniture, women patrons who had earlier been recognized by the Church for giving money to the poor were replaced by women who took on roles of voluntary poverty and care for the needy. By the thirteenth century, the trend toward suffering in isolation came as a result of institutional restrictions on women's voluntary poverty and works outside the convent. Earlier holy lifestyles that involved charitable works were thus replaced by spiritual almsgiving through voluntary and involuntary suffering (McNamara 1991: 206–7; see also Goodich 1981: 23).

The narrowly defined ascetic lifestyle for late medieval women saints—particularly in the form of imitatio christi—was also more prevalent because this was an era, as Bynum puts it, of "fierce world denial" (Bynum 1991: 176).[23] As part of this trend, religious movements commonly denounced worldly values and secular power, whereas qualities that were previously belittled—femininity, poverty, weakness, emotionality, and so on—were exalted. As a result, people from within these world-denying movements viewed women as having special access to holiness, and men's conversions involved taking on "feminine" attributes of poverty, irrationality, and powerlessness (176).[24] As an extension of this trend, Jesus' humanity and bodily nature were given greater emphasis than his divinity, providing further opportunity for women, who were traditionally linked with materiality, to meld themselves with the carnal Christ (148–50; see also Robertson 1991).

Given that this reversal prompted a significant number of medieval European women to identify themselves bodily with Christ, it is worth noting that Alphonsa and Mariam Thresia's lives and recorded hagiographies coincide with the height of

India's Independence movement. As such, these women and their hagiographers were probably influenced by publicly held ideas about the troubling bombardment of Western values. The cult of Alphonsa as antidote to the comforts, technologies, and values associated with colonial and postcolonial Europe and the United States, as I have argued, represents its own kind of domestic reversal and justified critique of dominant structures. An extension of this formula is the valorization of the "feminine" attributes of the "East" (that is, emotionality, simplicity, and tradition) as against the denigration of the "masculine" qualities of the "West" (that is, rationality, scientific/ technological prowess, and modernity). This gendered dimension of colonialist representations of East and West, although originally imposed, thus becomes transposed (with the rest of the orientalist package) through domestic interpretations.[25] As a result, the Indian "essence" of advanced spirituality, when merged with an idealized femininity, offers a framework from which Indian women of this period potentially gain access to godliness not available to men. As a result, the cultural and political stage seems to have been set for Alphonsa's and Mariam Thresia's "uncharacteristic" (for twentieth-century Christian saints) bodily identification with Jesus.[26]

As is to be expected, the four male candidates for sainthood in Kerala lived lives radically different from those of the three female candidates; the women's hagiographies all emphasize, to a much greater extent, private suffering and self-denial.[27] The four men (two bishops and two priests), on the other hand, involved themselves in public deeds of great institutional import such as fighting Church schisms, single-handedly founding new religious orders, and converting the masses. In spite of their unswerving faith and seemingly superhuman (that is, Christlike) abilities, however, none even remotely identified himself or appears to be identified by his devotees with Jesus in the literal, bodily way that Alphonsa and Mariam Thresia are.

Hegemonic Habits and Their Reappropriations:
The Paradox of Female Renunciative Asceticism

As we keep in mind the above comparisons of Sr. Alphonsa's hagiographical themes with patterns of female sacrality within Hindu and European Christian traditions, let us now look at the way these traditions view the *problem* of female renunciation as an antifeminine lifestyle or as a contradiction in terms. Here we also explore the fraught, paradoxical formula within both Hindu and Christian ascetic traditions, in which pain and powerlessness beget ecstasy and power. I earlier explored Kerala Christian reconfigurations of colonizers' cults and ideologies; the following approaches this hybrid relationship from the perspective of gender dynamics. Like the weighing in of colonial power over the colonized, the extent to which patriarchal authority is partial or totalizing is, once again, perspectival, situational and, most of all, ambiguous.

Female Renunciative Asceticism: Vocation or Contradiction?

Early Christian writers, particularly Jerome in the late fourth and early fifth centuries, promoted a type of holiness for women meant to be achieved through a transcendence and rejection of their natural state of femaleness. Women were advised to conquer this goal of "female virility" through the state of virginity, which absolved them from their connection with Eve and the guilt of original sin and, as a result, made them spiritual equals with men (Schulenburg 1978: 117–18; Ruether 1974: 150–83). As we saw above, the writings of a number of female ascetics (and some of their confessors) during the late Middle Ages tell a very different story.[28] These later writings make use of traditional associations connecting women with the material realm as a means of offering them special access to a mystical union with the bodily Christ (Bynum, 1991: 119–50, 181–238). Yet the earlier thinking that women should defy their femininity was not abandoned completely as the centuries wore on, and gained in popularity at different moments throughout history (Newman 1990: 115–17; Robertson 1991: 271). In such cases, this lifestyle of virginity was urged for women in spite of its being "unnatural." Its most extreme form, expressed by Jerome, was the recommendation that women abandon their household responsibilities as well as the care of their children (Ruether 1974: 176).

Brahmanical Hindu views of the female celibate lifestyle, as we have seen, stands in sharp contrast to Catholic Christianity's historical encouragement of it. Within normative Hinduism, perpetual virginity is typically perceived as aberrant and, moreover, as a dishonorable abandonment of a woman's "natural" duty or *strī dharma*. An elaboration upon this interreligious difference can be found in Frederique Marglin's analysis of gender and sexuality in Hindu puranic literature. In her discussion of the fierce single goddess (that is, one without a consort) with highly ambivalent powers, Marglin takes to task the usual scholarly conclusions that attribute her ambivalence to the danger of unharnessed sexuality. According to Marglin, this debasement of sexuality per se is the result of a hasty overidentification with Jewish and Christian notions that view female sexuality as negative and prevents a more nuanced interpretation of the single goddess. A more appropriate understanding, she insists, would be to link the single goddess's ambivalent, potentially dangerous powers to the problem of female celibacy, not sexuality. To argue her case that these myths do not reflect the idea that sexuality itself is negative, Marglin notes that women's (and men's) marital sexuality (that is, fertility) may be polluting, but is always auspicious because of its potential to be regenerative. Within the framework of the world (*samsāra*), male and female celibacy—the latter imaged in the goddess without a male consort—is therefore dangerous or ambivalent at best. Only for the renunciate who chooses to leave *samsāra* behind—a path traditionally prescribed only for men and not for women—is celibacy an acceptable means for gaining benign spiritual power (1985: 39–47).

Although Brahmanical norms traditionally work against the idea of female renunciation—or as Lindsey Harlan puts it, deem it a contradiction since women cannot renounce what they do not have: male duty (Harlan 1992: 217)—women do assume renunciative roles on occasion. Moreover, when they do, the conventionally minded often hold such unconventional women in high esteem. Rajput women's perceptions of Mira Bai, a famous *bhakta* poet from Rajasthan, reflect such mixed sentiments. It appears that although these upper-caste women do not view Mira as someone to emulate, they nonetheless honor her memory, and commonly list her as one of the two women they most admire (206, 216).[29]

As Catherine Ojha notes in her study of Hindu female renunciates, their precarious status within Indian society also emerges in the breach existing between what they practice and what they preach—between their radical lifestyle and the general conservatism of their spoken and written words. Most commonly, for instance, women renunciates who assume the role of guru instruct their female disciples to take the path of *strī dharma* rather than renunciation (Ojha 1981: 280; Khandelwal 1996: 117, 19; Mukerji 1989: 392).[30] By personally rejecting but verbally prescribing the message of normative Hinduism, Ojha reasons that the "deviant" ascetic woman forges for herself an acceptable reputation within the wider community (Ojha 1981: 280).

The Hindu female renunciate, navigating in many ways a life of tricky contradictions, thus appears to adopt a normative "male" mode of behavior somewhat like the "female virility" promoted in Christianity. The key difference is, of course, that for most Hindu women—unlike their Christian counterparts—this is not a lifestyle towards which they are traditionally encouraged, even by female renunciates themselves. This discrepancy between a tradition openly advocating a celibate, nonfeminine ideal for women and another in which such roles are often taboo makes sense on the basis of different values ascribed to female sexuality: it is viewed with suspicion within Christianity and granted a more nuanced understanding within Brahmanical Hinduism as polluting but auspicious.

The Hindu *bhakti* traditions, which represent a different system altogether, characterized by world-denying, tradition-defying impulses, can be viewed, particularly by orthodox outsiders, to be "deviant" in itself. As such, it presents a framework in which normally debased attributes such as femininity offer a valuable means for approaching the divine. For example, as A. K. Ramanujan describes it, the "feminine" nature of the *bhakti* movement is typically expressed through an erotic mood, seen almost entirely from the woman's perspective. As a result, *bhakti* practitioners, whether male or female, commonly take on the role of the female in relation to the deity (Ramanujan 1983: 316). As in forms of renunciation outside the *bhakti* movement, however, Ramanujan notes that male practitioners— and not female—are most commonly the spokespeople for societal critique. A woman's challenge to society lies mainly in her aberrant lifestyle rather than in her words. Another tendency within the *bhakti* movement that further echoes mainstream expectations is that a male authority figure normally tests and approves the female *bhakta*'s lifestyle, ultimately giving her the necessary consent for her anomalous behavior (321).[31]

In the context of world denial and reversal found in the perspectives of both *bhakti* movements and aspects of European medieval piety, as well as in Independence-era Kerala Christianity, the rationale of the saintly paradox in which the last becomes first and the meek inherit the earth makes sense.[32] The idea of world denial is certainly nothing new to religious movements to the extent that they are critical of, or work to undermine, dominant structures. From this scenario, lives of exemplary holiness are perceived as such inasmuch as they stand in opposition to a perceived dominant order. What complicates and adds tension to this framework is the fact that such defiance is seldom total but must exist in and, to some degree, adhere to the dominant order.

The Power of Suffering and the Paradox of Asceticism

> Alphonsa used to tell me that we should suffer our pains without complaining to others. Nobody should know about our pains. We should pray to God and seek strength to bear the pain. If we speak about our pain, it would be like a hen laying her eggs and making noise after that. If we were to hear the hen making noise someone would come and take away the egg. In that way, if we speak about our pain, Satan would come and take away our merit (*nanma*).
>
> Sr. Xavier, aged 84

The question of the ecstasy and efficacy of suffering provides a framework for viewing an ascetic's uneasy position in a context of reversal not entirely reversed. The circularity of thinking that stems from this paradoxical position in which self-denial becomes a tentative kind of dominance is, as might be expected, reflected in Alphonsa's hagiography as well as in her own writings.

A similar paradoxical tension emerges in nonrenunciate roles for Hindu women, in which self-restraint and suffering offer a similar type of spiritual benefit. For even within Brahmanical Hinduism, the nonrenunciative householder role of the good wife, or *pativratā*, provides a norm for female asceticism. Like Christian patterns of asceticism as well as Hindu renunciative asceticism, religiously prescribed behavior for the *pativratā* involves levels of ritual adherence, discipline, and self-restraint that could be considered ascetic. Proper attention to the demands of the *pativratā* role furthermore earns for a woman a measure of sacred power (*śakti*). In her extensive study of women's traditions of vows or *vrats* in Banaras, Anne Pearson argues from a variety of angles that the performance of *vrats* by householder women, which requires self-denial and discipline through fasting and ritual adherence, win for them a measure of spiritual power and personal control over their lives. She asserts that scholars have neglected the ways in which householder women, "traditionally denied access to formal asceticism, have found a way to tap into this powerful realm for their own benefit through the performance of *vrats*" (1996: 11).[33]

Adding geographical and historical scope to our view of this "informal" householder asceticism, George Hart notes, on the basis of his readings of first- and second-century Tamil poetry, that south Indian ideas of female chastity (*karpu*) involve a type of asceticism related to modern understandings of the *pativratā*. As discussed by Hart, *karpu* consists in a woman's faithfulness to her husband and, in relation to this, restraint and modesty in speech and in conduct. Early Tamil poets describe women with these attributes as having benevolent and efficacious sacred powers (Hart 1973: 234). Extending this notion a bit, Margaret Egnor (1991) suggests, on the basis of ethnographic work in Tamil Nadu, that the self-restraint and chastity that men and women currently associate with a married woman's *karpu* often signifies, more explicitly, a life of suffering—both voluntary and involuntary. Because of this suffering, which stems in part from a compromised position in society and which is bolstered by acts of self-denial, Tamilians (men and women) commonly consider women to have more *śakti* than men.[34]

Egnor notes that the allied—and ambiguous—reversal of the gender hierarchy emerges from the "strong anti-authoritarian populist streak in Tamil culture," as it is reflected in Tamil literary genres such as *bhakti* poetry (1991: 15). Basic to this system of reversal is a tangle of contradictions, however, in which a suffering woman's potential challenge to the dominant patriarchal structure will never entirely—or perhaps even remotely—dismantle it. As Egnor puts it, when suffering is successful in bringing about the power expected of it, then "the underdog ceases to be the underdog, ceases to suffer, and loses the moral power inherent in his or her previous subordinate position" (16–17). Owing to the fact that women themselves claim greater amounts of *śakti* based, in part, on their subservient status in relation to men, Egnor notes that they are often the staunchest supporters of the gender hierarchy (15).

To return to portions of Alphonsa's hagiography as well as some of her own writings, we find a similar kind of circular reasoning. For example, in answer to those who express astonishment at her ability to endure excruciating pain, Alphonsa purportedly describes the bliss of union that she connects with her misery. This joy is so all-pervasive that it ultimately cancels out the profound suffering of her Friday agonies.

> It is indeed true that I am so frightened that I cannot even bear to think of my agonies. I know also that it is difficult for others to watch me suffer. But when I think of the bliss that is mine on the nights following my struggles, I even wish my pains to recur more frequently. I have never before enjoyed such divine happiness and the intensity of my happiness varies with the acuteness of my pains. . . . I fall into some kind of trance on the nights following the convulsion. I can not describe the visions I see during the trance. It appears to me that Our Divine Lord comes to me, caresses me and pours out upon me all the affectionate sweetness of His Sacred Heart. . . . The happiness of the moment is unbounded and limitless. (Chacko 1990: 53)

Salomi P. L. describes Alphonsa's ecstatic suffering in more general terms, and assures us of its Christian legacy: "It is the beauty of Franciscan suffering, that the more you suffer, the more you experience ecstatic joy" (1992: 87). Yet in a letter to her confessor—one of the few available samples of Alphonsa's writings (she unfortunately asked her Mother Superior to burn the rest)—she seems troubled by the contradiction of her joyous suffering. Expressing concern as to whether or not the happiness derived from her suffering and insignificance cancels out some of the benefits, she writes on November 30, 1943, during a period of emotional turmoil:

> If it were not for this nervous affliction I suppose I might have been too proud, but now, when I come to myself after these attacks, I realize my littleness and rejoice at it. Now, I wonder whether this rejoicing might lose for me some of the merits of suffering. I think I ought to rejoice in these sufferings since I am sustained in everything by Divine Providence. "Sweetest Jesus," I keep saying, "turn all the world's joys into bitterness for me." If, after that, bitterness comes, I have no cause for grief. (Chacko 1990: 75)

As we dig further into the paradox of Alphonsa's path of self-denial, we see her ardent desire to become a saint—with all the trappings of spiritual and earthly power implied by this—amid a life of self-abnegation and subservience. This longing to achieve sainthood, mentioned briefly at different points in her hagiographical accounts, is directly addressed by Alphonsa in a letter to her confessor. Writing three months before her death, she boldly pleads, "Father, make me a saint. I am doing all in my power, but my weaknesses are many" (Chacko 1990: 82). Bold though this desire may be, it is nonetheless strategically couched in a request—an assertion that if she could achieve sainthood by her own volition, it might negate her subservience and therefore (paradoxically) her power.

This apparent determination to be certifiably holy also emerges in the way Alphonsa followed a particular script—commonly cast for Christian (and Hindu) women through a life of self-denial—to the letter. The dog-eared copy of Thérèse of Lisieux's *The Story of a Soul* speaks to this determination, and so does her early disfigurement (if it was indeed premeditated), as well as her unflinching response to the excruciating illnesses throughout her later life. For better or for worse, Sr. Alphonsa took on with a fiery vengeance the narrowly defined cultural script which asked that she embrace silent suffering in order that she later become memorialized.

Although there do not seem to be many traces of struggle in Alphonsa's writings, such as hints of disdain for the narrow constraints of the ascetic path, Thérèse of Lisieux's autobiography has moments (brief ones) when she seems to question the rigidity of culturally ordained scripts for sanctity. If we keep in mind her desire for greatness, similar to aspirations expressed by Alphonsa and by Alphonsa's hagiographers on her behalf, it stands to reason that Thérèse might yearn for a lifestyle that would more readily—and perhaps more publicly—put to use her spiritual gifts.

> It should be enough for me, Jesus, to be Your spouse, to be a Carmelite and, by union with You, to be the mother of souls. Yet I long for other vocations: I want to be a warrior, a priest, an apostle, a doctor of the Church, a martyr. . . . I would like to perform the most heroic deeds. I feel I have the courage of a Crusader. I should like to die on the battle field in defense of the Church. If only I were a priest! Yet though I long to be a priest, I admire and envy the humility of St. Francis of Assisi. . . . But above all, I long to be a martyr. From my childhood I have dreamt of martyrdom, and it is a dream which has grown more and more real in my little cell in Carmel. But I don't want to suffer just one torment, I should have to suffer them all to be satisfied. (Lisieux: 1957: 153–54)

After Thérèse briefly allows her longings to trespass beyond the more normative—and readily available—roles for women, she thus returns to the acceptable and attainable life of the (figurative) suffering martyr. Yet, in typically excessive saintly style, she wants to be a martyr who supersedes all others. Similarly, as if Alphonsa's series of excruciating illnesses were not enough for her, she purportedly prayed that her sufferings increase and, furthermore, that she take on the debilitating illnesses of others. When she learns that the bishop of Changanassery and a nun in her convent are suffering from malaria, she reportedly reasons, "How numerous are the duties to which His Lordship has to attend. Also our Sister here has to attend to the work in the school. I am, in any case, idling in bed. In this way the Lord has purposely set me aside to endure all suffering. So I shall pray to my Lord, if it is His will, to let me suffer from fever on their behalf" (Chacko 1990: 52).

Although Alphonsa's life remains a portrait of one whose path to power was traveled by way of subservience and sacrifice, her determination to follow this difficult route to sainthood paradoxically reflects a courageous heroism comparable to the heroism of a warrior-saint—someone more like, say, Joan of Arc. Alphonsa's life in some ways lies in stark contrast to this (anomalous) publicly aggressive female figure, but their hagiographies nonetheless include parallel themes of superhuman perseverance. The difference between these two women's lives that cannot be diminished, however, lies in Joan's complete transgression of normative female roles, and Alphonsa's somewhat strict adherence to them. But some minor transgressions or, at least, saintly audacities are also a part of Alphonsa's story.

The Fruits of Asceticism: Audacious Alphonsa

> *Thēyil kurutthal vāttukayillā* (The sprout which comes up in fire will not wither)
>
> Malayalam proverb, a favorite of Alphonsa

Sr. Alphonsa reportedly reaped some tangible benefits as a result of her asceticism. Underlying the different extraordinary talents she displayed while in the convent (such as prophesy, telepathy, and an ability to read foreign languages) was the exceptional confidence she needed in order to perform them. According to a variety of sources, Alphonsa regularly spoke with considerable assurance of her capacity to communicate with God. For instance, Chacko describes a period of extreme economic deprivation in the convent, in which Alphonsa assures the Mother Superior of the effectiveness of her prayers: "One day when the Mother Superior expressed that she was particularly distraught about the convent's dwindling money supply to buy food, Alphonsa assured her, 'Tomorrow, by the time you want the money, you will get it from somewhere. Have no fear; trust fully in Divine Providence. I shall see to it, please don't worry'" (Chacko 1990: 54).

In a letter dated January 20, 1944, responding to a priest's request for prayers, Alphonsa states a similar confidence in her abilities, and uses the opportunity to sermonize about the benefits of suffering, as well. "I have already told you that, if I pray, the response will be more and more crosses. When crosses cease to appear, you may conclude my prayers are growing less. I believe that love and fortitude increase in direct proportion to the number of crosses" (Chacko 1990: 49).

Regarding her gift of prophecy, many of the nuns who knew Alphonsa described to me during interviews her ability to predict boldly the day and the hour of different people's deaths. In a Keralite story-art form, *caritrakattā prasangam*, commercially recorded on audiocassette, a Hindu artist, A. N. R. Pillai (n.d.) describes one such occasion that was also mentioned (without details of Sisterly skepticism) by some of the elderly convent nuns:

> Alphonsa had the gift of prophecy—the miraculous power to know in advance the sorrows and death of others. She gained knowledge from afar about the death of Fr. Joseph Pundikulam. At eleven on the night of the 23rd of July 1943, Alphonsa roused up all the other Sisters: "Sisters, let us pray. Fr. Pundikulam is dead. Don't you hear the sound of the death knell?" The Sisters stared at her. "She must be delirious due to the worsening illness," they thought. They could not believe that Fr. Joseph Pundikulam was dead. "Hearing the death knell miles away," sneered the Sisters. They chuckled, unnoticed by Alphonsa. "Poor Alphonsa," they sympathized with her. "Come, let us pray for the repose of the dead one," they said. In response to Alphonsa's

invitation, some looked upon Alphonsa with contempt. The next day, to the utter dismay of all, the message of Fr. Pundikulam's death arrived. Fr. Pundikulam's soul had left for the other world at the exact time indicated by Alphonsa. How did she get this miraculous power? Maybe through prayer.

Alphonsa's record for having prayers answered as well as her tendency to prophesy dauntlessly and accurately became well known not just in the convent but throughout the surrounding community, as well, especially during the final years of her life. Sr. Pius, a middle-aged Clarist nun who was an adolescent when Alphonsa died, remembers that her mother, who lived in Bharananganam at the time, sought help from Alphonsa during a difficult period.

> Once, my brother, eager to join the army, went out of the house without asking anybody's permission. My mother became upset about this and went straight to Alphonsa and informed her about the sudden disappearance. Alphonsa prayed and said, "Your son will be back within three days." My brother, in the meantime, reached the place and, during his enrollment, he decided not to tell anyone about his honorable family or mention the name of his family to anyone [as this would probably deter them from enlisting him]. Somehow, his family name and background became known to the person sitting there and he advised my brother not to be in the army, and to go home. Thus, my brother got back home on the same day as Alphonsa predicted and, as she also predicted, he had a dog with him.

A period in Alphonsa's life when she appeared to have particularly bold exchanges with authority figures (that is, God and priests) was during the time of mental instability set off by the fright she received from her encounter with the thief. Because of this upheaval, Alphonsa was suddenly struck by an inability to read as well as by a loss of memory, the latter which she gradually regained over a period of several months. In her interview with *The Passion Flower* in 1987, Sr. Sales remembers this span of mental imbalance as one in which Alphonsa occasionally delivered moralizing sermons to priests. She also spoke to God in more familiar terms, often demanding favors on behalf of others. In Chacko's elaboration upon this phenomenon, he reconstructs Alphonsa at prayer.

> My Lord of Love, hast Thou not promised a reward to those who renounce everything for Thy sake? Have I not despised my own will in all things? And shouldst Thou not grant me my desires and prayers when I have always sought to do only Thy will? Art Thou not bound by Thy promises to reward those who endure hardships for love of Thee? Therefore shouldst Thou not grant me these my prayers? I will not move away from here until they are realized. Do I not reason well? Didst Thou not tell St. Catherine of Siena, "If you take care of my interests always, I shall not fail to take care of yours?" (1990: 45–46)

Eleven months after the thief incident, on the feast day of St. Thérèse of Lisieux (September 30, 1941), Alphonsa's ability to read returned, as she herself had predicted. As some of the Sisters who lived in the convent at the time told me, she suddenly was able to read Tamil as well, a talent that apparently made Alphonsa a handy resource for a number of people in the convent as well as in the surrounding community.

Alphonsa's growing reputation as having spiritual gifts and sound insights caused an increasing number of Clarist Sisters and community members to regard her as a type of guru figure to be sought out for prophetic advice and prayers. Most important to Alphonsa's interpersonal appeal throughout her life, however, was her basic human charm, remembered fondly by many who knew her. Sr. Stephen, a seventy-year-old nun who was a junior teacher at the convent school during the time when Alphonsa briefly taught, reminisced: "We [teachers] didn't have that much freedom to talk to others. When we got the chance, we rushed to Alphonsa for the opportunity to talk to her. My chats with Alphonsa gave me great joy. She used to inquire about our health, our life in the convent, etc. Everybody waited for the opportunity to talk with Alphonsa. Everyone wished that Alphonsa would love her the most. Her behavior was so sweet and captivating." Referring to the period when Alphonsa was no longer able to teach and was confined to the convent due to her illnesses, Sr. Stephen continues, "Whenever people from the outside came to visit her she used to talk to them. If there were any children, she used to give them presents. Everybody called her 'the loving nun.'"

The people who were the most ardently devoted to Alphonsa and who regularly flocked to speak with her from the window outside her room were the children of the nearby schools. Village members, priests, and nuns who knew Sr. Alphonsa when they were children fondly recall the beauty and loving charisma that drew them to her. Sr. Demetrius, a sixty-seven-year-old nun, remembers the occasion when, as a young boarder at the convent school, she first met Alphonsa:

> I first saw Alphonsa in Bharananganam when I was studying there in boarding. It was in 1943. One of my friends took me to her room and told Alphonsa that I was a new student in the boarding. Alphonsa came to me and talked to me a lot. It seemed to me that some kind of light was radiating from her face—she was that pretty. She had some kind of bruise in her mouth and she showed me that. I was fascinated by her beauty, so I did not even think that she was suffering from such terrible pain. After talking with her for some time I thought that if every nun were like Alphonsa, I would also join the convent. That was my first experience of her.

Although the force that attracted children to Alphonsa's garden window and bedside had much to do with the allure of her kindness and beauty, it also stemmed from the children's firm belief in the sick nun's miraculous ability to help them with their exams. In her recollection of one of Sr. Alphonsa's characteristically bold and prophetic statements, Sr. Pius relates, "During one of our public examinations, we wrote our center, 'Bharananganam,' on it. Everybody told us that our papers would not be valued, and that we all would fail. We went straight to Alphonsa and told her about this. She just looked up and prayed and then told us, 'You all will pass the exam.' It came true."

Aesthetic License of Asceticism: A Hidden Transcript?

In looking at female asceticism—and, more particularly, Alphonsa's asceticism—from the perspective of the power imbalances basic to gender relations, the theoretical framework laid out in the first chapter in the discussion of theories of colonial hybridity and hidden transcripts is, for the most part, useful here, as well. Alphonsa's life of suffering and self-abnegation in relation to certain Hindu and

Christian expectations would be incomplete if I did not examine Alphonsa's own part in shaping her life. By viewing female asceticism as including a hidden transcript or legitimate aesthetic expression into which an individual might infuse her own, perhaps contentious, position, we make room for the creativity and particularity of one who assumes this role, which in itself rests within the narrow confines of institutionally recognized female sanctity.

A similar view of gender dynamics in north India is taken by Ann Gold in her description of women who make use of culturally prescribed practices as a means for creative expression as well as a way to extend the bounds of normativity. Gold describes the wrap or shawl that a Rajasthani woman uses to cover her head and face at appropriate moments; Rajasthanis generally understand this use of the shawl as a means for maintaining a woman's modesty as well as shielding her from the unwanted gaze of male nonfamily members. However, from the perspective of the songs and stories related by Rajasthani women themselves, the wrap also becomes an aid for enacting or hiding transgressive and irreverent behavior (Raheja and Gold 1994: 47–72; 164–81).[35]

Within the realm of Christian saint traditions, Robert Orsi (1996) finds that St. Jude's cult in the United States feeds women the "poisonous" concept that they are held responsible for their families' woes (thus it is their job to seek St. Jude's help) yet are entirely unable to effect change on their own (thus they must pray rather than act). Although this serves to support traditional Catholic notions of women's self-abnegation and subservient devotion to St. Jude—as reflected in women's interpretations of the saint and his actions—it also allows them a sense of autonomy, courage, and power. Orsi speaks to this irony by asserting that

> the analysis must be dialectical: through the power of their desire and need, awakened by and in response to the new challenges and possibilities of their American lives, and with the flexible media of devotional culture—the images they could take away with them into their rooms and beds, the water and oil they could touch to their pains in gestures and rituals of their own improvising—the immigrants' daughters could do much with what they inherited. (Orsi 1996: 210)

Returning more specifically to the notion of aesthetic license within asceticism and its availability to women, Bynum describes a rather extreme example in which ascetic traditions in medieval Christian Europe provided an avenue from which women could criticize and subvert the authority of male clergy members. For instance, Bynum describes the thirteenth-century mystic Mechtild of Magdeburg, whose ascetic practices involved an identification with Christ through loneliness and persecution (1991: 132). Yet Bynum identifies Mechtild, because of her lifestyle, as an abundantly confident woman, someone "who did not scruple to hurl abusive epithets at local canons and friars, saw visions in which hell and the lower circles of purgatory were populated entirely by men," and so on (136). By the same token, Alphonsa's self-assured intimacy with Jesus as well as her audacious and boldly expressed prophetic statements suggest a perceived privilege similar to that reflected in the writings of Mechtild and other medieval female mystics, although less dramatic.

In her elaboration of the privileged position enjoyed by medieval female mystics, Bynum insists that these women did not buy into the framework of Christian hierarchical dualisms in which spirit is esteemed over matter and, by extension, men are valued over women. Rather, these women interpreted the world in a radically different way, giving importance to suffering not because it reflected rejection of a potentially defiled and defiling female body but because it provided a holy conduit from which they might achieve intimacy with Christ. Bynum (1987) repeatedly argues that the extravagant austerities and mortifications performed by these women were not therefore a cooptation of patriarchal expectations so much as they were creative self-expressions based upon a radical reinterpretation of patriarchal values.

Not surprisingly, Bynum has come under fire by feminist scholars for her position that medieval female mystics' particularly assiduous ascetic practices have such unquestionably positive implications for women and are disengaged so completely from traditional patriarchal expectations. In a review of *Holy Feast and Holy Fast*, Amanda Porterfield argues that by meeting these female mystics on their own terms, Bynum's emergent "argument that self-inflicted pain was life-affirming for medieval women is, in its own way, as tortured as the experiences cultivated by female saints" (1990: 187). Because Bynum avoids questions about the social and psychological assumptions underlying these women's representations of God and their desire for suffering, Porterfield charges her with "over-interpreting" medieval women's experience, leading to some "peculiar feminist conclusions" (188).

Although I laud Bynum for her efforts to take seriously the self-proclaimed understanding of medieval women's experiences, I nonetheless share with Porterfield a suspicion that this understanding may not be as completely divorced from normative (that is, patriarchal) medieval prescriptions and perceptions as Bynum argues. Rather than dismissing such performances of suffering as being indelibly contaminated by the conditions of patriarchal society, however, I take on a "hybrid" interpretation somewhere between Bynum's and Porterfield's. Although Christian ascetic women in medieval and modern times cannot entirely sequester themselves from their cultural context and its worldview, neither can they be passive empty vessels into which patriarchy simply places its goods.[36]

This "middle ground" may seem to be a rather obvious position, but it is important to note that European and North American feminist scholarship has traditionally taken a different stand. In Chandra Mohanty's review of Western feminist scholars' perceptions of non-Western women, she critiques their perspective in much the same way as Said, who derides the half-imperialist stance commonly taken by Western liberals.[37] Within the realm of feminist scholarship, Mohanty identifies a tendency to construct an "average third-world woman" who "leads an essentially truncated life based on her feminine gender (read: sexually constrained) and her being 'third world'" (1994: 199). This re-presentation—one which, to me, appears quite similar to understandings of premodern non-"third-world" women—is entirely different from the "self-representation of [contemporary] western women as educated, modern, as having control over their own bodies and sexualities, and the 'freedom' to make their own decisions" (199–200). Ultimately, Mohanty critiques this rigid image of "the third-world woman" on the grounds that she is narrowly understood in terms of her object status. As victim of religious and colonial structures and male violence, she is construed as someone who is affected by but does not affect certain institutions and systems (201).

Although Mohanty draws on a wealth of evidence to support her critique, the notion that "third-world" (and other) women are inescapably influenced by, yet have an influence upon (or, at least, express resistance to), certain institutions and systems is also argued by a number of contemporary feminist scholars trained in the United States and Europe.[38] For instance, as noted by Raheja and Gold, "Though the women we know in Uttar Pradesh and Rajasthan do in many ways assent to the dominant ideologies of gender and kinship, they also sing of their resistance to these ideologies" (1994: 25). In the introduction to her book about the lives of Bedouin women, Abu-Lughod warns that "things are and are not what they seem. The Awlad 'Ali are patrilineal, but reckoning descent, tribal affiliation, and inheritance through the male line does not foreclose women's opportunities or desires to shape their own lives or those of their sons and daughters, or to oppose the decisions of their fathers" (1993: 19).[39]

Similarly, as I have been arguing in light of Christian female asceticism, things are and are not, to differing degrees, what they seem. Alphonsa's life of suffering was, in many ways, carved out for her by surrounding religious and cultural forces. Yet, it was from within this space, endorsed by normative expectations, that she was given—and safely took on—the license to become a kind of hybrid, fused with cultural and societal contradictions. Ironically, if she had not embraced so fully and successfully her ascetic role of subservience and self-denial, there might not have emerged a space from which she could (co-)create what eventually became her powerful and prestigious position. Admittedly uneasy with her possession of power, yet desiring wholeheartedly to become a saint, Alphonsa's "conundrum" reflects the idea not only that calamity and cure are interconnected but that they can be inverted and confused, as well.

The Miracle(s) of Fame:
Origins of Alphonsa's Posthumous Cult

In keeping with the theme of paradox, the conclusion of this chapter traces the continuation of Alphonsa's cult after her death—the events that propelled a nun in a small village from relative obscurity into a position of national fame. Alphonsa's posthumous cult is a "continuation" in that it appears to have been an extension of a prior, more modest, "cult" following begun by those—primarily children—who loved and revered her while she was living, and who had faith in her miraculous powers. Many of Alphonsa's convent Sisters acknowledged her sanctity during her life, yet at first were hesitant to view her as a saint, that is, deserving of posthumous devotion. As we have seen, this reticence had much to do with their impressions that canonized sainthood was synonymous with Europeanness. For the children who knew Sr. Alphonsa, and for whom saintly precedent seemed to carry little weight, qualifications for sainthood were an entirely different matter. What is notable—and for some, miraculous—about Alphonsa's cult, therefore, is that it not only emerges from a life of relative insignificance but that it was formed by resolute children who ignored Church tradition and adult chiding and who, in their determination, hopped fences and braved punishment to be by her graveside.[40]

Furthermore, it is from these humble beginnings that Alphonsa became an object of cult veneration unprecedented in popularity by any other Keralite Christian figure in recent history.

Alphonsa's Death and Funeral: The Might of Meager Beginnings

As she was telling me her story of Alphonsa's demise, 87-year-old Annapennu, a woman who was a young domestic worker in 1946, used this opportunity to impress upon me Alphonsa's relative obscurity during her lifetime, even within the local community. From her sick bed in her small quarters behind her employer's house, the elderly Annapennu described being struck by a sudden premonition of Alphonsa's death the morning she expired. Startled by the tolling of the nearby chapel bells, she remembered dashing from her house toward the convent and, upon meeting a male convent worker heading her direction, she stopped him and asked why the bells were being rung at this hour. Demonstrating to her his belief that Alphonsa was nothing out of the ordinary, the young man answered flippantly, "One of the eggheads died." (The term "egghead" was an irreverent nickname for nuns of that era because of their shaved heads.) Knowing at once that the bells must be tolling for Alphonsa, Annapennu continued to run as fast as she could in the direction of the convent.

On the morning that Alphonsa died, news of her failing health quickly spread among the entourage who knew and revered her, especially the children of the convent boarding school. Describing the scene from her girlhood memories, Sr. Pius, who is now a Clarist nun herself, makes use of an opportunity to compare the children's zeal for Alphonsa's sanctity with the lagging faith of the Sisters.

> One Sunday morning, after our Sunday school, somebody came to us and said that Alphonsa was seriously ill. We rushed to her, but the Mother [Superior] told us to go away. Disappointed, we turned back to go but, at that moment, we heard someone saying that Alphonsa was dead. A priest who was in the convent at that time spoke out that Alphonsa was a saint. Nobody wanted to believe that Alphonsa was dead. They all tried their best to believe strongly that it was someone else who had died. Her body was later taken to the chapel. On the way, during the procession, people from the shops commented that the Sisters put makeup on Alphonsa for her burial.[41] She was that pretty. She seemed like an angel on her death cot. One of my friends, Marykutty, was able to obtain Alphonsa's mat on which she was lying. She cut off pieces from it and then distributed it among all of us, telling us that this was something sacred. Children began to proclaim, "Alphonsa is a saint! Alphonsa is a saint!" But the elders, mostly nuns, did not like that.

A neighbor of ours in Vadavathur, Mrs. Joseph, happened to have been a teacher at the Bharananganam convent school at the time of Alphonsa's death. A Mar Thomite who does not typically believe in saints, she nonetheless was drawn to Alphonsa because of the holy brightness of her face, which she described as being "like the sun." Although the two women had only exchanged glances and smiles, Mrs. Joseph (then in her early twenties) felt compelled to stand outside Alphonsa's window while she died, watching nuns and some outsiders pay their last respects— the more faithful among them touching personal items to her body for blessings.

Mrs. Joseph had never gone to any of the other nuns' funerals but found herself at Alphonsa's because of this attraction. She remembered that at the ceremony Fr. Romulus, Sr. Alphonsa's confessor, delivered a sermon which proclaimed a holiness in Alphonsa that he had never seen before in anyone else. Mrs. Joseph also recalled the priest's description of the crowds of important people who ought to have flocked to Bharananganam to be at her graveside, if only they had been aware of her extraordinary holiness. In response to this sermon, which confirmed for her something she already intuited, Mrs. Joseph remembers being startled and impressed: "These words convinced me of what I had suspected all along: she really *was* a holy woman. It was at that point that I knew. After that, I could be seen among the children, visiting her grave to pray and place flowers. It really was not for another couple of months that her devotion took off and people started coming from all around."

Although it was primarily children who acknowledged Alphonsa's posthumous sanctity from the beginning, there were also a few adults. Aside from Mrs. Joseph, other notable anomalies included Fr. Romulus, who regularly visited Alphonsa before her death and corresponded with her for many years, and Fr. Vadakil, the convent chaplain (the priest who, in Sr. Pius's account, announced when she died that she was a saint). In his foreword to *Sr. Alphonsa*, K. C. Chacko offers a quote from Fr. Romulus's "prophetic" eulogy, delivered at Sr. Alphonsa's funeral.

> With the most profound conviction in my heart and as one who has known this religious [i.e., nun] very intimately, I affirm that we are now participating in the last rites of a saintly person. If the world had realised her intrinsic worth, unprecedented crowds including hundreds of priests and bishops from all over India would have assembled here. They would have rushed and clamoured for even a glimpse of this body and for some precious relic or token of this person. (Chacko 1990: 13)

Bold and inspiring though the eulogy may have been, the reality was that Alphonsa's funeral was very sparsely attended. Because very few family or community members showed up, Fr. Romulus was, for the most part, preaching to a select audience of nuns and school children.[42] As a result, the difficult decision as to who would carry her body in procession, a task normally performed by male family or community members, was solved in a rather unconventional manner: it was assigned to a group of Clarist nuns. According to some sources, these nuns tried to convince nearby laborers to take up the task, but Fr. Vadakil scolded them, saying that the women should carry her themselves.

During my conversations with two out of the eight female pallbearers still living today, these women offered me their own rendition of the event. They denied charges that they refused Alphonsa's casket (an aspect of the story of which they are well aware) and insisted, instead, that they were fully prepared to carry it in procession. They felt that the mix-up is based upon the expectation (in those days) that carrying funeral caskets would be relegated to male laborers because of the fear of catching tuberculosis from corpses. In any case, these two elderly nuns expressed great pride in having been a part of the funeral procession of a saint, and recalled with smiles the joking and laughter aimed at their motley group. Adding further comedy to this scenario, they described the female kitchen workers who led the funeral procession, followed by the eight nuns carrying the casket. Bearing the typical funeral paraphernalia—the wooden cross, the thurible with incense, the candlesticks, and at least one black umbrella—these convent laborers also usurped tasks traditionally reserved for males (in this case, clergy). Consistent with the theme of paradox running through Alphonsa's hagiography, the Sisters who conjured up images of this all-female funeral procession portrayed it not only in terms of the ridiculous appearance it seems to have had in the eyes of most onlookers but also as a sacred event from which Alphonsa had the last laugh (see Figure 19).

This portrait of the sparsely attended funeral, juxtaposed with the current hordes who flock to Bharananganam to celebrate her death anniversary, is indeed a favorite means for devotees to depict the irony of Alphonsa's fame born of obscurity. In spite of the account insisted upon by the elderly pallbearers, many people who wish to

Figure 19. Celebrating her sickness and death in statue form, this wooden likeness lies as Alphonsa did in her coffin, with a wreath of flowers around her head. Statue donated in thanksgiving by a devotee. Alphonsa Museum, Bharananganam.

drive home this paradox continue to tell stories of laborers carrying the coffin, and thus draw a more vivid contrast between the nun who had no friends to (literally) support her and the now-famous Alphonsa. During Bharananganam's week-long death anniversary celebration in 1994, a young priest elaborated on this point in a speech delivered to a chapel overflowing with devotees, in which he compared their plenteous presence with the meagerly attended event forty-eight years prior.

> God did many great and wondrous things through Alphonsa. In 1946, July 29, on a wet day during the rainy season, the rain came down like tears. A funeral was taking place in the Bharananganam church—the funeral of a humble nun. There were not any festivities or the presence of great people. Also there was not any fame. Alphonsa, in her day, was looked down upon by the authorities and the people living in the convent. She had a terrible time, but God held out His helping hand and lifted her up from her tribulations. Yet there were only four rickshaw drivers there for lifting her dead body. But God worked miraculously and the small group which came to her funeral was transformed into a great many devotees. Do you wonder how a few drops of rainwater can be transformed into a big ocean? The work which God did in the life of Alphonsa that surprises us is that her meager reputation was transformed into something great.

Alphonsa's transformation from a nearly anonymous nun to a holy figure well known throughout the region did not take place overnight. Contributing to this was the fact that the charter members of Alphonsa's cult were small not only in number but in stature, as well.

Daily Devotion and Feisty Miracles: Small (Yet Audacious) Beginnings

> With a smile on flowery lips
> And with flowers in their tender hands
> Like the flame of burning candles, little darlings prayed.
> Embracing the tomb, they prayed:
> "Oh Mother! Hear our prayers and give us success in our exams."
>
> At whose prattlings did the village awake?
> By their prattlings did the village awake.
> People of all castes and creeds by the tomb
> Sat in prayer and called,
> "Blessed Alphonsa, pray for us, relieve us of our pain."
>
> They burned candles.
> Miracles in large numbers occurred.
> The ecstasy of the pilgrims
> In the form of prayer resounded there.
> "Blessed Alphonsa, pray for us, shower upon us your heavenly flowers."
>
> Fr. Michael Panachicken (n.d.),
> *"Pūmṛudu Chundil"*
> "Nectar from Their Lips"

Consistent with the theme that runs throughout Alphonsa's life story, the small and meek ironically possessed the powers of discrimination unavailable to the older and mightier. Furthermore, not only are grown-ups portrayed as having been unable to grasp the true nature of Alphonsa's holiness but they actively discouraged the little ones' devotion, as well. In her description of the first few months after Alphonsa's death, Sr. Agnus, a young girl at the time, recalls the children's general disregard for adult admonishment in an anecdote that demonstrates the superiority of the children's faith over that of the convent nuns.

> After Alphonsa's death, we children used to go to her tomb in groups with baskets of flowers with us. After Alphonsa's death, the cemetery was a lonely place except when there was a funeral procession. The children were thus afraid and went in groups for each other's company. We used to put flowers on her grave and pray, then return home. After one or two days, the watchman of the cemetery told us not to enter the cemetery, and we were denied the ability to go there. One day, when new kinds of white flowers grew in our garden, my brother and I plucked them, put them into small baskets and spread them on her grave. One of the Sisters complained about this to my father, saying that we should not be picking the beautiful flowers of the garden, but he didn't mind at all. Once we plucked flowers from coffee bushes. The elder ones scolded us for that, saying that now we wouldn't get coffee seeds. We ignored them, however, and carried on with that. But, surprisingly, a large amount of coffee seeds grew on the bushes that year.

Sr. Pius, also a young girl at the time, gives an account of her daily pilgrimage to Alphonsa's tomb, and suggests that the grounds keeper eventually had to relent his stern position for the sake of the safety of the insistent children. In this rendition, like Sr. Agnus's above, adults and older children appear to lack the faith of their juniors—a faith that, in the final analysis, proves to be fruitful.

> We children, after her burial, used to go and put flowers on her tomb. We would go in groups because we had to go through dangerous roads where there can be serpents. We used to climb on the cemetery walls and jump onto Alphonsa's grave. After offering the flowers we had brought, we would kneel down before the tomb and pray for our future career and everything. It brought us great mental peace. Once, we were discovered by the caretaker of the cemetery. He scolded us because we were jumping onto the grave. He advised us not to because, when jumping, we children might hurt ourselves. So, for the children, he opened the gate to the cemetery. It became a practice to go and meet Alphonsa every day after classes.
>
> The children used to take things from the cemetery, considering them to be sacred. But their parents and elders scolded them, telling them to stop bringing the remnants of ghosts. Our brothers used to make fun of us. Eventually, elders started to come with us. Favors began to be received by the people, and thus there was a great rush to the place.

To the playful accusations of my research collaborator, Sr. Josephina, that Sr. Pius must have been "the ringleader," the latter woman went on to describe an incident in which some of the children took it upon themselves—since the adults seemed to be indifferent—to assess Alphonsa's sanctity. On the basis of rumors and stories that saints' bodies do not decompose, they plotted to carry out a task normally reserved for Vatican officials and appointees: "I, with my friends, decided to look and see if Alphonsa's body was already decayed. We decided to dig into the soil.

When we reached half way down, the other children began to get frightened and, one by one, they retreated. At last, I too retreated. But there wasn't any bad smell there. We were sure that Alphonsa's body was not yet decayed" (see Figure 20).

Although disbelieving adults are portrayed by most accounts as eventually finding faith in Alphonsa's powers through news of miracles, a number of stories describe the early stages of cult devotion in which nonbelievers are jolted into believing (or, at least, performing right action) by Alphonsa herself. Sr. Josephina relates such an incident in a widely circulated story about a Hindu man who was duly corrected after making fun of Alphonsa's newly blossoming cult.

> This man remarked to some of his family members that pilgrims were coming from miles around to pay homage to "a dead body which does not decompose." The next day, his entire family, except for his son-in-law, got a bad case of diarrhea. Their neighbor advised them that they should not despise that in which they do not have

Figure 20. Alphonsa's garlanded marble tomb, currently located in Alphonsa Chapel, Bharananganam.

faith, and that they had better go and make amends with Alphonsa by going and visiting her shrine. The Hindu man agreed that he would do this, and the following morning they were all well enough to visit the shrine.

Another incident in which devotees understand Alphonsa's somewhat capricious powers as having directly readied the path for devotion happened on the Monday morning of her funeral. Recollecting that Fr. Romulus, the funeral eulogist, was harried and nearly late for Alphonsa's funeral mass, Sr. Agnus relates, with laughter, the commonly told story of a wily bus, understood as being guided by Alphonsa's invisible hand:

> Fr. Romulus, who was running late for the funeral, was also running late to catch the bus to Bharananganam. He nearly made it to the bus stop and waved, signaling for the bus driver to stop, but the driver refused to stop for him. So Fr. Romulus started walking. After going some distance, the bus just stopped—it just could not move. As he walked along, Father eventually saw the bus on the road. When he approached the bus he boarded it and it immediately started up again. Thus he was able to make it to the funeral on time.

It is by Alphonsa's insistence that she be honored, supplementing the children's (equally insistent) display of honor and devotion, that devotees understand her cult as eventually taking on a life of its own. Through a gradual increase in adult devotion and reports of miracles seemingly more dramatic than the children's success in their exams, local church officials began to take notice of Alphonsa. Although today's devotion is fully supported by the diocese and ecclesial hierarchy, nuns at the convent consistently express pride in the fact that she is the people's saint and hails from humble beginnings. Unlike most of the other Keralite candidates for canonization, people of faith started receiving favors from Alphonsa in great numbers long before the official church took notice. As Sr. Josephina enjoyed reminding me from time to time in reference to her canonization campaign, "We know that, in the end, Alphonsa is her own best advocate."

Official Recognition and the Politics of Canonization

> Sometime after Alphonsa's death, the Changanassery bishop came to meet me [at the Changanassery novitiate]. He inquired about the events taking place in Bharananganam after her death. I told him that many people were coming to her tomb and praying for favors. With great bliss, the bishop told me that he earlier thought she would really become a saint. After hearing all this, he wished to go to Bharananganam himself. It was wartime then and no petrol was available. On his way, someone stopped his car and gave him three liters of petrol, saying that he would not get petrol further down the road. He did not know the man. With the petrol, he went to Bharananganam and came back proudly.
>
> Sr. Alberta, Clarist nun, aged 67

Although the Clarist Sisters of Bharananganam gradually came to realize that Alphonsa's posthumous efficacy and popular appeal were not just a passing phase, official Vatican recognition was not possible until the local diocese (that is, the local bishop) recognized her cult's potential, as well. Although it is typical for a saint candidate's religious order to promote his or her campaign for canonization, Kerala's Clarist Sisters were, at the time of Alphonsa's death, a noncanonical organization. Because of their unofficial status, they had to rely upon the diocese to take up and promote Alphonsa's cause. Later, when the Clarist congregation gained canonical recognition, the diocese refused to hand over Alphonsa's campaign because, as Sr. Josephina put it, with a twinkle in her eye, "they want the money." In any case, she asserted, "It is better this way. With money comes additional responsibilities and besides," she added, cryptically hinting at the disputes that often erupt at wealthy shrines, "things can happen." Because Sr. Josephina sees Alphonsa's simplicity as central to who she is, she feels that the convent's remove from such financial concerns allows the Sisters to emulate more easily Alphonsa's lifestyle. Instead of a business relationship, Sr. Josephina and her colleagues say they are content to maintain a "spiritual relationship" with their potential saint.

More typical of recent historical trends, the campaigns for five of the other six Malayali candidates for sainthood have been promoted primarily by institutional organizations rather than by popular appeal.[43] Sr. Mariam Thresia was the founder of the Holy Family convents, so the Sisters from this order run her campaign. Sr. Euphrasia was the Mother Superior of a Carmelite convent whose members promote her canonization process. The founder of the Sacred Heart Sisters in Kerala, Fr. Matthew Kadalikattu, has his campaign run by a female religious order, as well. Likewise, the cause of Bishop Thomas Kurialassery, who founded the Adoration Sister's Convent in Kerala, is being supported by them. Finally, Fr. Kuriakose Elias Chavara's campaign is being supported by the Carmelites of Mary Immaculate (C.M.I.), a men's order he founded. The fact that these cults were not initiated by popular appeal is apparent not only from the inner administrative workings of their campaigns but also by the flow of pilgrims who regularly visit their shrines. None of the six other candidates for sainthood, including Kunyachan, a priest whose cult is also driven primarily by popular appeal, can claim a following nearly as vital and consistent as Alphonsa's. Not surprisingly however, Kunyachan's popular cult is relatively healthy— a result of his tireless advocacy and care for thousands of poor people.[44] This popularity ensures, to some degree, that his campaign is moving more quickly than that of some of the other candidates, though not as quickly as Alphonsa's and Chavara's.

Although organized support and popular appeal are important for the progression of a saint's campaign, this—along with sanctioned miracles and proof of virtuous living—is not always sufficient. What is often needed in order that an individual's cause continues to progress through what is normally a very time-consuming process is a certain amount of political clout from within the Vatican. During my stay in Kerala, only two of the seven candidates, Fr. Chavara and Sr. Alphonsa, had made the transition from the first stage of canonization, "Servant of God," to the second complete step, beatification. At this second stage, which directly precedes full canonization, the candidate is given the title, "Blessed." This unprecedented promotion of two Indians from the status of Servant of God to Blessed was officially performed by Pope John Paul II in front of vast crowds in Kottayam town on February 8, 1986. Although Alphonsa's recognition by the Vatican was not entirely unexpected because of her popularity, many people claim (although guardedly) that Fr. Chavara's rise to fame had much to do with the C.M.I. Fathers' notable presence in Rome. Their persistent championing of his cause within close range of the main power source appeared to have had its desired effect. In spite of their cynicism about the process, many of these same people believed Fr. Chavara to have been a man of many great accomplishments, but one whose popular cult following pales in comparison to Alphonsa's.[45]

Conspicuously absent among Kerala's candidates for sainthood are representatives from the Latin rite, a group consisting mainly of coastal fishing communities converted by the Portuguese in the sixteenth century. All seven Malayali candidates, along with Bishop Mathew Kavukattu, who is rumored to be about to earn the status of Servant of God, are Syrian Catholics. Although Syrian Catholicism, an eastern rite within the Roman Catholic Church, represents a nonmainstream and even slightly contentious tradition in the eyes of the Vatican, it is found among the segment of the Kerala Catholic population that possesses economic and social clout typically not available to followers of its Latin counterpart. As a result, the vast majority of Keralite Catholics who reside at the Vatican—potentially able to persuade those who make decisions about canonization—are from the Syrian community (Dougal 1971: 59; Koilparampil 1982: 9–10). Providing somewhat of an exception to this pattern of canonization among Kerala Catholics are the three Servants of God associated with the Latin community: Fr. Zachareus, Fr. Aurelias, and Bishop Benzigar—all priests who, significantly, were foreigners who lived in Kerala. The former two are from Spain and the latter from Belgium. A thriving campaign was recently started for a Malayali Latin priest, Fr. Theophan, however, complete with its own magazine, *Manuṣya Snēhi*, put out by the Franciscan Capuchins. Supporters of his cause are hoping he will soon be recognized by the Vatican as a Servant of God.

Among Malayalis, Latin and Syrian Catholic alike, with whom I had conversations on the subject, most felt that Syrian Catholic affluence and representation in the Vatican directly contributed to their success in promoting candidates for sainthood. Knowing this to be potentially a sore subject, I nonetheless hoped to somehow bring it up during a postinterview lunch I was invited to share with the Latin Catholic archbishop of Thiruvananthapuram. Perceiving this young and engaging archbishop to be an amiable and open-minded person, I finally broached the subject to the people at our lunch table (who included a number of young priests and seminarians) by blurting out rather abruptly, "So, when do you think we'll be getting some Latin Catholic saints?" I was relieved when the question was received with a burst of laughter from the small group of men. With a wry smile, the archbishop quickly responded, "We have plenty of saints up in heaven, we just don't have the money to canonize them [more laughter]."

Alphonsa as Her Own Best Advocate

Although the importance of political clout and all its trimmings (affluence, social standing, and so on) are not to be underestimated when managing a campaign for a person's canonization, the worldly stature of a cult figure may also work against her or him when it comes to popular appeal. Suresh, a Hindu devotee of Alphonsa in his early twenties, offered this idea to me metaphorically when he described praying to Sr. Alphonsa as somewhat like appealing to the secretary of the prime minister.

Whereas the prime minister (God) is far too busy and important to listen to people's problems, the job of a good secretary (saint) is to mediate between the inaccessible figurehead and the public, making sure people's wishes are heard. Furthermore, Suresh reasoned, the portrayal of Alphonsa as having led a suffering, unhurried lifestyle (that is, she was not able to take on any extra tasks because of her continuing illnesses) makes her seem readily available, at any moment, to listen to and pray for people's woes. Indeed, this image of the woman who received small devotees at her sick bed and garden window produces a notion of a saintly power particularly accessible to those without worldly clout, one which stands in contrast to the more worldly wise, politically prominent saints and saint-candidates. This latter style is best exemplified by Fr. Chavara, known for starting both women's and men's religious orders, feeding and clothing the poor, educating the masses, establishing the first Catholic printing press, and stopping a statewide schism for the sake of the larger Roman Catholic Church. In spite of—and in some ways related to—his order's clout within the Vatican, his perceived availability to wait upon potential devotees cannot compare with Alphonsa's.[46]

As reflected in the discussion of Renuka, a Hindu medium for Alphonsa, accessibility to Alphonsa's powers extends well beyond the boundaries of the Christian community. Renuka expressed this with particular clarity when she unabashedly announced to me, "I am here as an instrument for carrying out Alphonsa's work here on earth." In addition to the fact that it is not unusual for Keralite Hindus to pay homage to powerful Christian saints, the themes in Alphonsa's life that lend themselves to Hindu expectations for holy women probably give further grounds for her interreligious appeal. Also contributing to this appeal is a fairly well-known aspect of Alphonsa's young life, related by Renuka and other Hindu devotees: she was, from an early age, inseparable from her Hindu best friend, Lakshmikutty, until she went to live in Muttuchira. According to local stories, the two girls regularly ate together, defying the strict injunctions of their time—followed by both Christians and Hindus—which forbade intercaste and, therefore, interreligious dining.[47] It is likely that from such stories of conscious nonexclusivity, Hindu devotees feel a validation of their choice to ignore religious distinction.

Beyond the nonexclusive aspects of Alphonsa's character, the most important contribution to her cult's popularity is her reputation for performing healing miracles—which has an interfaith dimension, as well. We have seen that in the case of the Thalassery Hindu woman whose daughter was cured (and abducted) by Alphonsa, and the Bharananganam Hindu man whose family contracted diarrhea, the restoration of health—and child—were not contingent upon conversion to Christianity. Rather, the daughter was returned and health regained when cynicism was replaced with belief in Alphonsa's efficacy, not her religion. This is likewise the case in one of Alphonsa's most widely told miracle stories involving the healing of a Muslim boy in northern Kerala.

Although I had heard several abbreviated versions of this miracle tale from Clarist nuns in Bharananganam, the retired Bishop Vallopilly, an ardent devotee of Alphonsa, told me a slightly more detailed rendition as a result of his own involvement in the case.[48] He related this story to me, my husband, and our two sons as we sat in his northern Kerala office in Thalassery—watching two birds nesting in his overhead light as he spoke:

About ten years ago, when I was in a small village in Wayanad outside Manatavady, I saw a boy walking with some difficulty, using a stick. As he approached me I noted that both of his feet were turned upside down [clubbed feet]. I had a stack of holy cards in my pocket with Alphonsa's picture on them, so I pulled one of them out and gave it to the boy. When I told the boy that he should pray to this woman for the cure of his feet, the boy—he was quite smart for a ten-year-old boy—replied, "But I'm a Muslim and, besides, I was born this way." I replied that God is very powerful, so let's pray. A few months later, a boy and a gentleman appeared at the house here. I didn't recognize them at first, but soon learned that it was the Muslim boy with his father, here to tell me that his feet had been cured through their prayers to Sr. Alphonsa. They showed me the calluses on the tops of his feet, and you could see the marks that had been made from the years of his walking with his feet turned under. Before they left, the three of us had our pictures taken.

The two visitors explained to the bishop that the boy had taken the holy card in his hands and "simply asked Alphonsa, that if she could help him, could she please fix his feet." Several days later, one of boy's feet turned around. He and some members of his family then took up praying in earnest for the healing of his other foot. According to the bishop, it eventually turned around, as well.[49]

When the bishop had finished his story, although I should have known better, I felt compelled to ask if "the Muslim boy" had become a Christian as a result of his miraculous cure. Responding as though I had not heard him correctly during his recital, the bishop responded, "No, he's *Muslim*." Apparently, for the bishop, conversion to Christianity was not a foreseeable or even a desirable result of the boy's healing. For this man who is well known for championing the cause of struggling Muslims and Hindus as well as Christians in the Malabar frontier, what was worth celebrating was that the miracle, in effect, spread the news of Alphonsa—not Christianity—throughout the region.[50]

Within the Christian community, closer to Bharananganam, the first incident in which Alphonsa dramatically acted as her own best advocate was in the curing of another boy, Thomas Attuvyayil, of his clubbed feet.[51] Occurring January 30, 1947, less than one year after Alphonsa's death, this cure, attributed to the intercessory powers of Alphonsa, advanced her cult like none other before. As described by Salomi P. L., after the healing of the boy, "the news spread like wildfire. The neighbors flocked to have a look at him. Thomas became a celebrity at school. People came to see him even from distant places. A busload of people from Ponkunnam under the leaderhsip of Fr. George Mulangattil visited Bharananganam to thank the holy Sister. Fr. George celebrated mass at the mortuary chapel. After the mass, the Father lifted Tom in his arms and showed his feet to the people" (1992: 106).

In light of Alphonsa's gradual posthumous rise to fame, which had much to do with the faith of local children and an ever-increasing number of outsiders, the Bharananganam community, for the most part, had radically changed its view of the convent-bound nun by the time of her first death anniversary. Locals decided that they should hold a *śrāddham* feast—a Hindu custom also performed by Kerala's non-Protestant Christians to commemorate a family member's death anniversary—as a way of honoring Alphonsa. According to Sr. Josephina, local community members had become so penitent about their earlier dismissal of Alphonsa's powers and their mockery of the faithful children that, by the time a year had passed, they were moved to organize a particularly grand *śrāddham* feast to atone for their neglect. Today, although Alphonsa's death anniversary celebration is officially considered to be her feast day, it is still done in the spirit of a *śrāddham* in which copious amounts of rice, two different curries, and the requisite *neyyapam* (a sweet rice pastry fried in oil) are prepared to feed to the crowds.[52] Also in the spirit of the first *śrāddham* performed in Alphonsa's honor, the local community still contributes the bulk of the ingredients for the feast themselves.[53]

Alphonsa's annual death anniversary celebration, a nine-day affair complete with overflowing crowds, speeches, liturgies, vendors, colorful processions, a feast, and a few requisite explosives, acts as both an instigation and confirmation of her reputation as an efficacious (almost) saint (see Figures 21 and 22). This yearly testimony to Alphonsa's posthumous powers, bolstered by continuous reports of miracles granted to people of different religions, regions, and economic backgrounds, indeed speaks louder than Vatican decrees. Although many of the Clarist Sisters would consider it an ultimate victory for their saint if she were to be fully canonized by Rome—and anxiously await the day—such foreign approval seems of little consequence to many of her devotees. As is true for Kerala's St. George, Alphonsa's ability to work miracles and conjure up a faithful following is not dependent upon Roman decree but, as Sr. Josephina puts it, because of her own effective self-promotion.

In spite of Alphonsa's resolute self-advocacy and the subsequent lofty position that she assumes among Kerala's pantheon of saints, the themes of weakness, pain, and self-effacement continue to be an integral part of her identity. Her posthumous victory does not overshadow or negate her earlier trials but, rather, the two strands are continuously interwoven in songs and stories performed in her honor. As a

Figure 21. Alphonsa's statue adorned with lights ready to bring up the rear of the festival procession from Clarist Chapel to Alphonsa Chapel across the street. Priest in the background displaying the relic will follow behind.

Christian from a Hindu culture who was a blissful sufferer, victorious through her defeat, Alphonsa's life is, for many, a celebration of a multilayered paradox rather than an attempt at its resolution.

And so, I hope, is this book.

> Oh Virgin, who has fulfilled the vow of chastity
> Through the trials of fire,
> Perpetual amazement is your life
> That is radiant with divine love.
>
> You were then a mark of honor, a mark of gold
> On the forehead of the Indian Church.
> With you the Jordan joined the Gangetic flow
> In the culture of ancient India.
>
> Oh Mother, your life that went unnoticed by any
> Has now become world famous.
> The Bharananganam that was fortunate to be your grave
> Has become sanctified—the Lisieux of India.
>
> Oh Virgin, who has renounced worldly life,
> You became blessed, embracing the cross.
> An insect in a burning furnace, yearning to be burned.
> You became a celestial daughter, you became Alphonsa.
>
>   Panachicken (n.d.), "From the Fire"
>   (*Agniyālē*)

Figure 22. Festival vendor displaying religious trinkets, St. Mary's Church grounds, Bharananganam.

Conclusion

Of U.S. Angels and Ethnographers

I began this book by warning the reader that its exploration of Kerala sainthood would stray, at times, from the subject of saints, and focus its attention on seemingly mundane issues such as identity formation, hybridization, and the complexity of power relations. This it has done and, moreover, when the discussion lingered more explicitly on saints and their cults, other themes invoked by cultural and ideological collisions and negotiations kept surfacing.

Although Alphonsa's religiously pluralistic context and her mediation of gendered expectations propels the fourth chapter's discussion of hybridity and ambivalence, the theme of identity formation is also implicit on two levels. Most immediately, it appears that Alphonsa's expressed desire to achieve sainthood, which led her to follow yet subtly defy expectations for women, meant fashioning an identity for herself according to available models of holiness. On another level, hagiographical formulae likewise provide a framework from which devotional writings, songs, and oral accounts further help to form and conform Alphonsa's identity within preset parameters for female sanctity. These attempts at forging a particular identity—expressions that are neither entirely historical nor entirely fabricated—stand for a collective effort, past and present, of people trying to make sense not just of saintliness but of their world. More specifically, this larger "making sense" points to the ways these identity formations help those creating them narrow (or obliterate) the gap between the divine and mundane realms. The fact that Alphonsa conformed herself to a certain model of holiness makes surer her path for identifying/uniting with Christ and, for many of her devotees, the formation of a particular saintly identity assures them of earthly access to heavenly powers.

Sainthood's role in the construction of identities, as described in earlier portions of this book, seemingly involves rather mundane matters but consistently underscores what I see to be one of sainthood's primary functions: that of earthly conduit to the sacred and its powers. For instance, through Malayali constructions of Sr. Alphonsa as pinnacle of Indian Christian identity, discussed in chapter 1, the divide between the holy and the profane within Kerala society—ruptured most dramatically by the influences of a hedonistic, technically oriented "West"—is somewhat mended.

Communal identity expressed metaphorically through the drama of saint-deity interactions, played out in chapter 2—often having tangible effects, both frightening and fruitful, upon constituent human communities—vividly communicates the meeting and melding of the earthly and heavenly spheres. Finally, although chapter 3 has less to do with human identity negotiations, perceptions of saints as ambivalent figures demanding material offerings from their devotees speak most directly to the blurring of boundaries between the sacred and the mundane.

Although the preceding chapters may, at times, have veered from a direct consideration of saints themselves, they thus return regularly, at a number of levels, to this central capacity of saint as the sacred go-between for his or her human devotees. This theme wherein sainthood blurs and rearranges two seemingly separate domains in turn offers a convenient setting from which to view the likewise destabilizing concepts of ambivalence, hybridity, and paradox. It seems fitting that such postmodern categories, diagnostics for disruptions of rigid boundaries and absolutes, find a forum for discussion thanks to saints and their cults: champions, themselves, of boundary breaking and bending.[1]

This book clearly does not impartially chronicle the presence of so-called hybridities and the tentative nature of total power as seen through constructions of saints and their cults. It is on the side of such dynamics, cheering on the ways in which they shatter preordained categories and divisions. I am on Sr. Josephina's side as she shrugs and laughs at rigid constructions of absolute imperial domination, even as I mock myself and the Belgian foreigner for our presumptuous blunders. I am clearly sympathetic with St. George's seemingly awkward yet expedient compliance with colonial authorities—performed in order that he might offer a heavenly tool for those wishing to divert the same. I applaud local sibling stories for their honest portrayal of communal ambivalence and thus I devalue opposing systems that either build contrived barriers between traditions or wish them away completely. I am even enthusiastic about St. George and the posthumous Sr. Alphonsa during their naughty moments, and argue that sacred powers of total benevolence are, ultimately, of no use to Keralite devotees.

My motive for questioning and complicating the prescriptions and constructions that lead to rigidity, as we have seen, is to reveal the ways in which such abstractions can often overlook the variegated nature of identities and histories, on both an individual and collective level. By pointing out the limitations of such perceptions—identified to different degrees with "Western" liberals and ethnographers, Indian nationalists, religious clergy, and feminist scholars—I furthermore critique the ways in which they, in spite of possible good intentions, underestimate the capacities of individuals and their communities to act and create. Chapters 1, 2, and 4 argue that, in spite of theoretical assertions to the contrary—scholarly, religious, and political—a crucial (although often limited) measure of creativity and autonomous power belongs to the lived experiences of the colonized, the pluralistic community and its members, and the female ascetic, respectively. Chapter 3 makes a similar argument about creative agency, but speaks of something slightly different; the agent to which it refers is not the corporea human, but an embodiment of the sacred in the form of a local saint or deity. Authoritative Christian abstractions of the totally benign saint in heaven limits his or her ability to act forcefully on earth. Conversely, the ambivalent saint—emerging from a lived relationship of immediacy and intimacy—becomes active and available through a system of tangible exchange.

It is this idea of materially accessible sacred power that especially intrigues me, after trekking to different shrines for nearly a year—sites of special access to such powers—and thinking and writing about these locations from where I sit now, in North America. From this position of hindsight, which offers a fresh array of cultural and ideological collisions, I find it revealing to compare Kerala saint cults to a somewhat analogous phenomenon within the United States: our recent fascination with angels. Marked by a proliferation of angel books, angel jewelry, angel newsletters, myriad movies about angels, specialized angel stores, and even an angel cover story in *Time* magazine (December 1993), the angel craze is, I believe, something to be reckoned with.[2] Among the multitudes of books recently written about angels, the majority appear to revel in modern-day encounters or else offer helpful hints designed to guide the reader in locating his or her very own guardian angel. Most generally, what this present angel phase seems to celebrate, often expressly, is the capacity for humanity to bridge the chasm between the spiritual and material realms. For this reason, one might suspect that this growing tradition of angelic interaction with mainstream North American humanity finds an expression parallel with Kerala's local saint cults.

What most strikingly separates this recent interest in angels from saint devotion in Kerala, however, is that angels, by and large, are looked upon as entirely benevolent entities. A few of the books I came across do mention fallen angels, or angels of darkness, but these "bad" angels were not to be confused with "good" angels. Robert Kirven makes a slightly different distinction between bad spirits and angels, but the schism between good and evil remains: "only good spirits are angels; but not all spirits are good" (1994: 24). Almost nowhere to be found among the many popular angel books I examined was an angel who acted, as many of the saints can, in a capricious manner. The one exception to this I discovered in a book by Rabbi Morris Margolies (1994), who discusses Jewish representations of angels. He includes a section on "argumentative angels" who have disputes with God, but are not entirely evil. In his discussion of North America's current angel craze, Harold Bloom (1996) expresses disappointment with what he considers to be today's saccharine, domesticated copies of the powerful angels of earlier centuries, who were often ambivalent or decidedly nasty. Instead of offering relationships of real substance, these late twentieth-century angels appear to Bloom to be like puppies in their aim to please as well as in their display of unconditional love.

In further contrast to many of the saints discussed above—who require tangible, reciprocal interactions with their devotees—access to the angels described in recent books and movies is merely a matter of praying, channeling, dreaming, or simply experiencing distress. Nothing seems to be expected in return for angelic favors, whether physical, emotional, psychic, or otherwise. Thus, in spite of the superficial similarities between Kerala's saint cults and contemporary North American angel lore, the perceived chasm between the spiritual and material worlds as well as between good and evil is bridged much more dramatically by saints (depicted locally) and their expectations.

Although Bloom expresses disappointment with New Age angels, I feel, on the other hand, that we have no choice but to live with mainstream creations that support the status quo—formulations that only slightly threaten or disrupt previously assigned categories. By this, I am not suggesting that local Indian or European saint traditions necessarily do challenge the norm but, rather, that the status quo for those engaged in vowed transactions with saints is, to some extent, different. Interactions between saints and devotees (or angels and their charges) reflect and confirm particular understandings of the cosmos. The angelic images that currently proliferate within parts of mainstream North American culture—saccharine, domesticated, and unintimidating—express a worldview in which the supernatural realm is divided neatly between good and evil and, furthermore, is not fully admitted into the (constructed) scientific realm. Angels cannot be materially accessible creatures who capriciously expect tangible offerings in return for favors, inasmuch as people's imaginings of the universe do not support such thinking.

Thus, even though I "cheer on" boundary-breaking dynamics such as ambivalence and hybridity and, along with these, the seemingly audacious and disruptive aspects of sainthood, a recommendation that mainstream segments of my culture adopt a similar approach to sacred power would have its limitations, at best.[3] Yet the extent to which the intensity of devotion Keralites expressed toward their saints occasionally challenged and altered my own worldview and emotions—in spite of apparent cultural limitations for such a shift—is worth mentioning.

Although this slight adjustment to my worldview was most probably part of a gradual and subtle process that affected me over a period of time without my noticing, it took me by surprise one evening during Alphonsa's feast-day celebration. Although the festival lasts, in its entirety, eight days, the event reaches a climax during the final two: on July 27 and on the death anniversary itself, the 28th. I had been traveling back and forth between our home and Bharananganam during the early days of the festival, but I arranged to stay in a room on the church grounds for the night of the 27th. Sr. Josephina and some of the other nuns had encouraged me to do so, as the evening of the 27th was, for them, the high point of the festival. We happened to have a family from Berlin visiting us in our Vadavathur home at the time, so my friend, Heike, joined me for my overnight stay in Bharananganam.

After a rather slow and rainy start to the day on the 27th (the next day was dry and much busier), buses loaded with pilgrims began arriving during the late afternoon. Although a number of liturgies had already been conducted in the morning and afternoon, both in the main St. Mary's Church and in Alphonsa's chapel up the hill from the church, the high mass performed at dusk in the main church, sung throughout, was packed and overflowing with devotees. An hour and a half later, after the mass finished, children lined themselves up with colorful festival umbrellas and candles and led the devotees in procession to the Clarist convent across the street and into their small chapel. Transformed by candlelight, colorful electric lights, and a variety of garlanded images of Sr. Alphonsa, the chapel came alive with the singing of devotional songs—the nuns in full voice in the front wings of the chapel and the devotees in the main seating area. After about thirty minutes of singing, the procession resumed with the children and their candles and umbrellas leading the way. They were followed by devotees, many of whom were also holding candles and, finally, a large garlanded statue of Alphonsa. The candlelit procession wound its way back across the street, past the main church, and up the hill to Alphonsa's chapel, where her white marble tomb is situated.

At this point, Heike admitted to being exhausted. We decided that since this final event of the evening was to be a sermon in Malayalam, she would not be missing much if she went back down the hill and to bed. Feeling tired as well, I huddled near the side doorway of the crowded and overflowing chapel, whirling tape recorder in hand, and listened to the priest's sermon.[4]

After the priest finished speaking to a somewhat attentive audience, I knew the scheduled events for the evening were finished, but thought I would stay a while longer in case anything unscheduled, yet noteworthy, happened. It was at this point that, in contrast to the evening's earlier din of liturgical and devotional singing and sermonizing, the chapel seemed to be filled with a startling, reverent silence. As soon as the priest stepped down from his podium, devotees gently swelled to the front of the chapel and toward Alphonsa's raised tomb. One by one, or in small groups, people knelt before the tomb or placed their hands or forehead upon it, often with tears, but always with what seemed to me facial and bodily expressions overflowing with devotion. Although for six months I had been coming regularly to Bharananganam and this chapel, I was particularly struck, at that moment, by the profound depth of feeling people had for their saint. Realizing that I would explode if I did not allow myself to cry, but feeling embarrassed at the thought that people might see me break down, I quickly left the chapel, found a dark, secluded, spot behind a bush, and sobbed as quietly as I could.

If Heike (a somewhat committed East German atheist) had not been waiting back at our room, I probably would have trudged quietly on home to bed, maybe sobbed some more, and slept. But she was still awake when I stumbled into the dark room and, as it turned out, it was not so easy for me to stop my tears. As a result, I was forced to step outside what seemed to me an ineffable experience to try to give it words. I described the scene as best I could and explained (by a rather lame analogy) that I felt as though I was watching a wonderful party from a distance but was not, in fact, invited to take part. My emotions were similar to the way I might feel—although in a heightened sense—if my very favorite people or loved ones were all sharing a wonderful experience but, for reasons beyond our control, I was not included. In other words, I was stranded outside of something I understood to be profoundly rich but did not know how I could, ultimately, enter into it.

Loring Danforth (1989) describes a similar disjunction between himself and a group of Greek Anastenarides during a dramatic healing ritual performed by Yavasis, a man whom Danforth had grown to respect greatly. In this particular situation, Yavasis, who attributes his powers to St. Constantine, performs a ritual involving icons, holy water, incense, singing, and tears on behalf of a woman who is unable to walk. In spite of this ritual performance as well as his insistent pleading with St. Constantine, Mary, and Jesus, however, no miracle occurs. Danforth then describes his place in the scene:

> All this time I had been watching from a distance, sitting on a chair by the door outside of the room where Yavasis and the young woman were waiting for a miracle. I was writing in a notebook on my lap. I was crying. I felt awkward, embarrassed, and

out of place. . . . But most of all I felt guilty. I felt guilty because I just didn't believe
Saint Constantine had the power to make her walk.

At the same time I found myself hoping that the miracle I didn't believe in would
actually happen. I wanted the incense and the holy water and the songs about young
Constantine to work, but I was afraid that my presence had interfered somehow. I
was afraid that a miracle might have happened if only I hadn't been there. (37)

The emotional responses that Danforth and I describe are a result, I believe, of
the fraught place occupied by the ethnographer in which the world of miracles and
intense devotion becomes familiar and perhaps even real, though we continue to
stand, in our own ways, on its perimeters. Although Danforth states that he does not
believe in the powers of St. Constantine to heal, he contradicts this by surmising
that he is the cause of the saint's inaction. Likewise, Jill Dubisch says she does not
believe in the efficacies of Greek saints, but finds herself making a vow one night—
and soon after, fulfilling it—while she was being driven down a treacherous mountain
road in Greece by a drunk driver (1995: 97–100). Although I chose to go to the
bushes to have my cry rather than join the devotees at Alphonsa's tomb, the tears
emerged from a sense of loss at being unable to partake in something I believed to be
beautiful and powerful. Being overwhelmed by the implications, I felt compelled to
distance myself from them rather than embrace them.

The fact that Danforth and I would be moved to tears and that Dubisch would
be moved to make a vow attests to the fact that although we may not share exactly
the same worldview as the people whom we have come to know and respect, neither
do we entirely reject it. It seems that by spending enough time and listening to
enough people within a universe where miracles exist, the strangeness of this idea
might, for some of us, begin to seem less strange.[5]

With this in mind, I return to the suggestion, mentioned above, that saints'
capacities for boundary bending and breaking are in the eyes—and culture—of the
devotee-beholder. From the point of view of someone whose world allows for miracles
and material access to the sacred, wonder-working saint cults are not such a radical
idea.[6] They are only truly radical and disruptive to those of us whose reality separates
us from these possibilities. In a sense, therefore, local saint cults do not really bridge
the gap between the sacred and the profane but, rather, they emerge from a realm
that presumes the possibility of this connection—or finds little use for such
categories—to begin with.

Moreover, after singing the praises of hybrid identities and the ambivalence of
power throughout this book I must push the point, suggested in the first chapter, that
their existence can be perspectival, as well. Although an outsider may label a
phenomenon as paradoxical or variegated, those who are most intimately involved
probably do not feel the kinds of tensions implied by such terminology. The insider
may identify, instead, a certain consistency that negates hybridity or an internal logic
that defies ambivalence.[7] For instance, as I have suggested, the "hybrid" cults of Sr.
Alphonsa and St. George may involve the appropriation of foreign ideologies and
traditions, but for many of their devotees there is no question that these saints are
indigenous. Along the same lines, although I may label mythic relations between
saints and deities as "ambivalent," people who are more closely tied into village
dynamics may instead see such interactions to be appropriate consequences of saintly

or divine character flaws. And, although saints' behavior toward devotees may be viewed as capricious, these stories can likewise be understood as part of a consistent system of sacred justice. It is true that, when viewed from afar and juxtaposed with totalizing constructs, these examples may indeed involve types of hybridization or ambivalence that are important to recognize and acknowledge. It is also important to acknowledge, however, the possibility that the complexity of what looks like hybridization and ambivalence can be complicated further by considering an array of perspectives—particularly of those most intimately involved with the phenomenon being discussed.

In sum, what may seem paradoxical to one person may seem perfectly natural to the next. My ethnographic tales, although they might sound strange and are somewhat embarrassing to recount due to their disjunction with "normative" scholarly thinking and (non)feeling, likewise show how spontaneous actions and reactions emerging from a particular time and place make sense to their performer in spite of discontinuities. In our postmodern view of the world we find, moreover, that such examples of colliding cultures and worldviews are not the exception but, rather, are the rule. This book has highlighted the ways in which competing hegemonies and clashing perspectives reflect and support individuals' and communities' abilities to act and create. But by acknowledging the perception of continuity and integrity that organizes such actions, we make room for the possibility that a fractured world does not necessarily create fractured people but, rather, whole people who continuously work their way through its many divides.

Notes

Acknowledgments

1. For further mention of this self-mirroring in hagiographical texts, see also Weinstein and Bell (1982: 6) and Mooney (1991: 1).

2. In Geertz's most recent book, *After the Fact*, he describes the process of ethnographic writing amid the layers of inevitable social and political shiftings, occurring over time within the "culture" one studies. Add to this the ever-changing philosophical and methodological approaches fashioned by the discipline, and the ethnographic endeavor becomes all the more slippery. He observes that "what we can construct, if we keep notes and survive, are hindsight accounts of the connectedness of things that seem to have happened: pieced-together patternings, after the fact" (1995: 2).

3. For a discussion of some all-too-human motivations potentially lying behind ethnographical endeavors—as "religious" quests for authenticity and authentic Otherness not found at "home"—see Dempsey (2000).

4. About her female interviewees in Banaras, Anne Pearson likewise contends that she has "'created' these women, even as they 'created' themselves to me as they talked about their lives and reflected on my questions. Whatever the 'reality' of their lives is, it is refracted through several lenses—their lens, my lens, and the lens of the reader." Pearson nonetheless asserts that something valid and important can be learned from such approximations (1996: 16). In a similar vein, Nandy's preface to *The Intimate Enemy* describes his work as "an alternate mythography of history" (1983: xv).

Introduction

1. When I talked to various Keralites about the motto, many said they thought it was invented by the tourist industry. Nonetheless, no one was unfamiliar with the phrase and most felt that it was quite commonly used among Malayalis themselves. It is perhaps significant that the saying seemed more familiar to people when rendered in English than in Malayalam, *Devattinde svantam naṭā.*

2. Although Kerala's religious pluralism embraces a number of Muslim communities as well (and a few communities of Jews), this study concerns itself primarily with Hindu-Christian relations. This is, in part, because my research took place in Kottayam district, a region predominantly inhabited by Christians and Hindus. I have also chosen to leave matters

of Muslim-Christian or Muslim-Hindu influence for another study, to prevent the topic at hand from becoming too unwieldy.

3. Delooz (1983); Mooney (1990: 1); and Weinstein and Bell (1982: 6) likewise assert that saints reflect the agendas and identities of their devotional society.

4. Gauri Viswanathan notes that scholars of subaltern studies, coming from their position of "postmodern skepticism," have focused their attention largely on issues of race, sex, class, ethnicity, and colonialism, but not—until recently—on religion (1998: xiv). She argues for scholarly analysis of religious belief and conversion, as such ideologies and actions provide a means for people to grapple with this-worldly concerns such as establishing political identities and resistances in a way that does not duplicate preestablished boundaries of community and ethnicity. Although religious negotiations of identity and community articulated through acts of conversion do not apply to the discussion in this book, resistances and appropriations voiced by local religious traditions tell, as I see it, an equally compelling story.

5. Ortner posits that in relationships of power imbalance and resultant expressions of resistance the dynamic of ambivalence is a pervasive element that has largely been overlooked by mainstream scholars (1995: 175–76). She notes, however, that the theme of ambivalence has become a key issue for colonial and postcolonial studies. See Bhabha (1985); Hanks (1986); Nandy (1983); Parry (1994); and Suleri (1990). For an historical overview of understandings of hybridity—biological/racial and cultural—see Young (1995).

As they are played out through the following chapters, the phenomena of ambivalence and hybridity are inextricably mixed. This mixture is also noted in William Hanks's study of Mayan correspondence to Spanish colonial powers. Here, he describes the ambivalence contained in the letters as "a corollary of the hybridization in colonial contexts" (1986: 740).

6. Gauri Viswanathan (1996) discusses the difficulties behind sometimes well-meaning inclinations to romanticize religious syncretism. Even as they mask a dominant culture's efforts to assimilate minority traditions, portrayals of utopian mixing of traditions potentially rob people of their particular histories and identities. Using examples from local stories of saints and deities, I make a similar case in Chapter 2.

7. When I compare practices or ideas that emerge from individual shrine or community-based traditions with institutionally authoritative prescriptions, I commonly use the term "local" in lieu of other possible terms such as "popular" or "folk." For a discussion of my reasoning behind this preference, see pp. below.

8. As discussed in Chapter 2 in particular, Mikhail Bakhtin (1968) is a compelling—and one of the earliest—proponents of this position.

9. Talal Asad (1996, 1993) argues for an analysis of religion—and an understanding of the category "religion"—in terms of power relations rather than belief. He furthermore encourages scholars to think about religion in terms of bodily enactments rather than ideological prescription. See my "Lessons in Miracles" for a discussion that uses Asad's arguments, and extends his notion of power to connote miraculous saintly power (1999). For a fuller discussion of the ways in which current shifts in scholarly understandings of religion—influenced by anthropologies of religion—parallels anthropologists' shifting understandings of culture, see Malory Nye (2000).

10. I do not necessarily disagree with theories of hybridity; I find them quite helpful. The largely historical work of postcolonial theorists who make use of colonial writings and interpretations, however, will necessarily frame their analyses differently from my work, which relies more on ethnographical methods. Although I also investigate colonial structures (that is, European saint cults in India), the interpretations I attempt to analyze are largely postcolonial and locally based. I agree that a white-skinned or Western-clad saint who represents Indian agendas is—from a bird's-eye view—a site of hybridity and ambivalence,

yet I resist emphasizing this aspect. In the eyes of many Keralites, there is nothing at all ambivalent—or even hybrid—about *their* saints. As the following demonstrates from a variety of angles, Kerala Christians rightly argue that they are no less Indian than their Hindu neighbors, and certainly no less Christian than the foreign powers who have come and gone over the centuries—leaving much of their cultural baggage behind.

11. For further and far more in-depth treatments of Kerala Christianity, see Neill's two-volume set (1984, 1985) and the Church History Association of India's five volumes entitled *History of Christianity in India* (1982–1992). For more nuanced studies of south Indian Christianity, see Bayly (1984, 1989); Gladstone (1984); John (1981); Karayil (1995); Koilparampil (1982); Kuriedath (1989); Mathew and Thomas (1967); and Visvanathan (1993).

12. Nestorian heresy originates from Nestorius, patriarch of Constantinople (428–431), and his followers, who understood Jesus as having two distinct natures—one human and one divine. Because Jesus' human dimension is reflected through his birth and death, Nestorians refused to refer to Mary as "Theotokos" (bearer of God), preferring instead "Christotokos." This insistence led to a rejection of Nestorian theology at the Council of Ephesus in 431, causing a near schism in the fifth–century Church. According to Koilparampil, Indian Nestorians probably hail from a Nestorian stronghold in east Syria rooted in the celebrated theological school of Edessa led by Ibas. Although it is uncertain when Syrian Nestorians arrived in Kerala, there appear to have been very few. Between 1599 and 1663, they united with the Catholic Church, but broke off again after Portuguese power faded. Currently, a few families of practicing Nestorians live in Thrissur (Moosa 1981: 370; Koilparampil 1982: 50–52).

13. This massive outdoor Coonan Cross (*Kūnan Kuriśu*) event is, by most accounts, the way Kerala's Syrian Christians describe their dramatic seventeenth-century break with Portuguese Jesuits. But Thekkadath notes that contemporary written accounts give more attention to a priestly oath taken inside the church, before the crucifix and lighted candles, and over an open Bible. Thekkadath asserts that the two events probably happened simultaneously (he reasons that there was probably not enough room in the church for everyone); the different tellings are merely a matter of emphasis (1982: 93). It is also interesting to note that the outdoor Coonan Cross event included the tying of ropes to a large cross, which allowed everyone present access to the cross while taking the oath. The Keralite practice of tying ropes to a holy object so that large crowds could touch it vicariously is common at church (and temple) festival events.

14. Although Chaldean and Antiochan Syrian Christianity differed slightly in their theology, this new Antiochan bishop helped to ease Kerala's shift in allegiance. By his constant emphasis upon the differences between Roman and Syrian traditions, potentially troubling discrepancies between the Chaldean and Antiochan traditions seemed to have dropped into the background (Mathew and Thomas 1967: 38).

The term "Jacobite," connected with Antiochan Syrian Christianity, originates from a sixth-century group that followed Jacob Baradai, a Church leader who organized a schism within the Syrian Church (Karayil 1995: 35).

15. The most recent available survey (1968) of religious communities in Kerala does not give separate percentage figures for Jacobites and Orthodox Syrians within the Kerala Christian community. Antony Karayil explains that both denominations officially claim 70 percent of the Jacobite-Orthodox population, making any kind of conclusive data difficult. On the basis of a number of conversations with different Keralites, Karayil estimates that both denominations constitute around 50 percent (39).

Keralites often refer to the Orthodox Syrian denomination as "Syrian Orthodox," as well. Although there seems to be little consensus about the correct usage of the term, Dr. Paulos

Mar Gregorios, one of the most eminent Church leaders with whom I spoke, insisted that the former term was the correct one. For this reason, I tend to favor the use of "Orthodox Syrian."

Another means for categorizing Kerala's Syrian Christians, not mentioned above, is through differentiation between Pazhencoor ("old") Syrians and Puthencoor ("new") Syrians. Somewhat ironically (and perhaps indicative of who created the labels), the Pazhencoor or "old" Syrian Christians refers to those affiliated with the Catholic Church, whereas the Puthencoor Syrians include the various groups who originated with the "new" tradition begun at the Coonan Cross Revolt.

16. Although significant differences in social standing between Syrian- and Latin-rite Catholics continue to exist in Kerala, these distinctions are currently becoming less rigid. As a sign of this shift, cases of intermarriage involving couples with the same socioeconomic status have significantly increased in the past several decades (Koilparampil 1982: 114–53).

I mention the discrepancy between the relatively privileged Syrian Catholics and the less affluent Latin Catholics in chapter 4, section 3, when referring to political clout in the Vatican. This is reflected in the fact that the Syrian rite presently has seven Malayali candidates vying for sainthood, while the Latin rite has none. Koilparampil and Dougal both discuss the abundant presence of Kerala's Syrian Catholics in Rome versus the dearth of Latin Catholics (Koilparampil 1982: 9–10; Dougal 1971: 59).

17. Changes in external practices for the Mar Thoma tradition include slight revisions in liturgical language as well as, more significantly, the discontinuation of devotion to saints and death anniversary events for deceased relatives.

18. For further mention of the creative ways Malayalis have garnered Britain's support through its missionary system, see pp. 43–44.

19. In addition to these indigenous Catholic (almost) saints, the Orthodox Syrians and Jacobites have fairly recently canonized bishop-saints of their own. In 1989, the Jacobite Church canonized Elias III and, during a 1947 Christian Orthodox Synod, the Jacobites and Orthodox Syrians jointly canonized Baselius Yeldo and Gregorius of Parumala. The former two bishops were originally from Syria, but St. Gregorius was born in Kerala. I briefly discuss this Malayali's cult—popular primarily among Orthodox Syrians in Kerala—in chapter 3.

20. I use the term "foreign" here reservedly, as St. George's cult, although imported by a number of non-Indian cultures, takes on a number of indigenous characteristics and is often thought of by his Malayali devotees as a Keralite; see chapter 1, section 2. A "saint" who rivals St. George's universal appeal among varieties of Christians as well as Hindus is Mary, the mother of Jesus.

21. Michael Carroll warns us—and rightly so—not to essentialize European popular devotion. He makes his point by briefly discussing idiosyncratic differences between particular countries' preferences for saints or Madonnas and in the variety of devotional styles (1996: 243–45). Carroll asserts, however, that there is much yet to be learned about such nuances and, in any case, they must not keep us from viewing broad patterns of similarity across national divides. Although I feel slightly uncomfortable about the unwieldy "local European Catholicism" as a category for comparison (using examples from a number of European locales), I am heartened by Carroll's perspective. In any case, my primary aim in making such broad comparisons is to challenge ideologically driven divides such as East/West. Thus attention to intra-European distinctions becomes secondary.

22. Sr. Josephina's name, like many of the names used in the book, is a pseudonym.

23. In her study of a Greek pilgrimage shrine, Jill Dubisch describes it as being simultaneously bounded and unbounded. Although they are centered around a specific place, pilgrimage sites nonetheless defy perceptions of stability in that they are a meeting place for strangers who later scatter and return to their separate homes, taking something of the holy place with them (1995: 38–39).

24. Ann Gold likewise writes about her preference for making conversation with familiar people in private rather than with strangers in public. Although her work also involves pilgrimage, her primary ethnographic setting is the village, so that contact with strangers is less necessary (1987: 18–22).

25. In spite of my observations, there are fears among clergy that pilgrimage and other religious activities are on the wane, particularly among the youth. I take up this matter and associated concerns that Western ways are seeping into Kerala society in chapter 1.

26. See also my article "The Religioning of Anthropology: New Directions for the Pilgrim-Ethnographer," which deals with some of the problematically "religious" (that is, falsely faith-filled) motivations that lie behind ethnographic misrepresentations (forthcoming).

27. See James Clifford (1997).

28. The fact that the field of religion has focused on textual rather than lived expressions is, as Jonathan Z. Smith points out, part of a Protestant bias foundational to the discipline (1987: 98–102).

29. Examples of some scholars of religion in South Asia who have recently published extensive studies on nontextual expressions of Hindu religiosity are: Eck (1981), Erndl (1993), Feldhaus (1995), Daniel Gold (1987), Haberman (1994), Harlan (1992), Hawley (1981), Hiltebeitel (1988), and McDaniel (1989). Smith's (1969–1970) films documenting Hindu household rituals marks one of the earliest studies of nontextual materials by a historian of religion.
A South Asian ethnography of religion that discusses local Christian Practice is R. L. Stirrat's (1992) study of Sri Lankan Catholicism. Here Stirrat explores themes also treated in this book such as colonial, Church, and interreligious power dynamics. Rather than focus on sainthood, however, Stirrat's analysis centers on possession and exorcism at a healing shrine.

30. William Christian (1981: 79) notes the emphasis placed upon the literary and the literate by scholars of Christianity in particular. See also Colleen McDannell's (1995) discussion of prevalent divisions between the sacred and the profane that limit scholars' ability to recognize material manifestations of religious sentiments. Also see pp. 92–93.

31. This understanding of the globe as being neatly split between an East and a West, largely a colonial construction adopted wholeheartedly by many Indians themselves, I discuss in greater detail in the first chapter. In Kerala a couple of twists are added to this dichotomy. First, because Kerala has been intermittently a Marxist state for over four decades, some associate "the West" with capitalism, thus adding political and economic dimensions to what are, minimally, social and religious distinctions. Second, Orthodox Christians, a significant portion of Kerala's population, often take care to distinguish themselves from Christianity in "the West"—lands of European-based Protestant and Roman traditions. Because Keralite associations of things Western are commonly negative, Orthodox Christians and eastern-rite Roman Catholics in Kerala are often quick to emphasize the ways in which they are not like their Christian counterparts in Europe and North America.

32. In a somewhat similar fashion, Wendy Doniger discusses different approaches to the study of myth as involving "microscopic" and "telescopic" perspectives—each with its own strengths and shortcomings. Whereas a microscopic view interprets myths in terms of personal insight, a telescopic study involves a cross-cultural comparison. The middle view, as Doniger configures it, studies myths within their cultural context (1996: 544–47).

Chapter 1

1. Sr. Alphonsa belonged to the order of Franciscan Clarists and spent most of her life as a nun at the Clarist convent in Bharananganam. The nuns to whom I presently refer, including my research collaborator, Sr. Josephina, are from the same convent.

2. A description of this hermitage—the Kurisumala Ashram—can be found in Bede Griffiths' book (1964: 41–47). Griffiths, a Benedictine priest from England who later became internationally known for his writings on spirituality, came to India in 1955 to explore how Christianity might be practiced and enlivened in an Indian context. Griffiths established Kurisumala Ashram in 1958 with Francis Acharya and, in 1968, moved to the neighboring state of Tamil Nadu to set up his own, separate Christian ashram. Griffiths died in Tamil Nadu in 1993 at the age of 87.

3. Fr. Acharya was wearing, at the time, European-style clothing although he commonly dons sannyasi robes.

4. Ahmad (1992), Clifford (1988). In chapter 4, section 2, I introduce a feminist perspective that similarly argues for the agency of the oppressed rather than for the totalizing effect of patriarchal systems. See also Raheja and Gold (1994) and Mohanty (1994).

5. By "Syrian Christian" or "St. Thomas Christian" (used interchangeably) I refer mainly to the non-Protestant Christian denominations that claim a Syrian liturgical heritage described above in the introduction.

6. Such constructions of the globe are played out practically, as well. During a train trip from Kochi to Kottayam, I spoke with a man from the Marar caste of Hindu temple musicians about this issue of stereotypes and romanticizations of East and West. He was bemoaning the fact that schools for Kerala folk art forms such as dance and drama seem to draw a good number of eager Europeans and Americans, although he has seen a reversal in this trend during recent years. Mr. Marar was interested in hearing about the converse situation in the United States, in which graduate students in the technical fields such as the sciences and engineering are overwhelmingly from Asian countries.

7. See also Nandy (1987: 128) and Bondurant (1958: 129). For discussions of the ways Gandhi's (and others') ecclectic religious ideologies laid the foundation, somewhat ironically, for Indian secularism, see M. M. Thomas, particularly his essay, "Religious Fundamentalism and Indian Secularism" (1996: 10–20).

8. Gandhi's ability to draw upon non-Indian texts as a means to criticize colonial rule had much to do, of course, with his education outside India. Whether they lived in India or abroad, many of those who were active in the Independence movement were products of non-Indian—mostly English—education systems. Likewise (and perhaps ironically), the most prominent teachers of the Hindu Renaissance movement of the late nineteenth and early twentieth centuries were English speaking and English educated (Bharati 1970).

9. Another pitfall of which Said is often accused is an "occidentalism" that involves overly simplistic and rigid notions of Western discourse and suggests that European and American thinkers, writers, and media are unable to view the Orient other than monolithically. With this in mind, I must clarify that this process of Kerala Christian "othering" of the West reflects a trend rather than an all-pervasive discourse within the Malayali community. For instance, my Vadavathur neighbor, an Anglican priest and an ex-Catholic, proclaimed that the categorization of the East as spiritual versus the West as material was "hogwash." Although he did not agree with the dichotomy, he did admit that such notions were powerfully prevalent.

10. A European center of power that represents a significant exception to Inden's formula is the Vatican. Here, papal discourse regularly upholds imperially constructed East/West dualisms but comes to the same conclusion as many Kerala Christians in terms of "Eastern" superiority. The recent rise to power of a number of Asian and African cardinals as well as the Vatican's commonly proclaimed anti-American rhetoric further underlines this tendency. In a 1985 address to Indian bishops, the pope declared that "holiness is a language India understands." A Jesuit, George Nedungatt, proudly calls attention to this proclamation in an article published in a 1986 special edition of *The Passion Flower* but tempers potential

self-congratulation with a warning that "shams, frauds, hoaxes, charlatans and quacks abound where holiness and spiritual values are highly priced [*sic*]." He ends his article with a final reservation/exhortation by saying, "Some people may be religious enough, but only to hate each other and fight each other, but not be religious enough to love each other; however genuine holiness can break the barriers and unite all as brothers and sisters."

More recently, Pope John Paul II's 1998 encyclical, *Fides et Ratio* (Faith and Reason), dramatically extols the spiritual virtues of the East, particularly India—this time to a much larger audience. Discussing the potentials and problems of different cultures' influences upon, or "inculturation" of, Christianity (which he admits has been an issue since the beginning, due to Greek influences), the pope muses, "My thoughts turn immediately to the lands of the East, so rich in religious and philosophical traditions of great antiquity. Among these lands, India has a special place. A great spiritual impulse leads Indian thought to seek an experience which would liberate the spirit from the shackles of time and space and would therefore acquire absolute value" (chapter 6: 75). (Thanks to Frank Clooney for bringing this to my attention.)

11. During a 1998 trip to India, I encountered an interesting expression of this perspective in the September 7 issue of the *Indian Express*. During the period when the Clinton-Lewinsky scandal broke as front-page news in India (and throughout the world), an editorial appeared in the Kerala edition of this paper arguing that people should not judge Clinton harshly, nor should they be particularly surprised at his behavior. On the basis of charitable ideas of cultural sensitivity and relativity, the author, a Malayali, reasoned authoritatively that in the United States it was quite common for two mutually attracted adults to strike up a sexual relationship: marriage in the United States is plainly not, as it is in India, about fidelity. Boldly outlined in black and positioned in the dead center of the page, the editorial staff of the *Express* seemed to give their own endorsement to this opinion.

12. There is a certain degree to which some European and American clergy and women religious (nuns) would agree with this dichotomous formula, which designates the "East" as superior—as would some lay people—particularly in more conservative circles. It is, in fact, a common subject in papal addresses. The significant difference here is that this essentialized split does not contribute in the same way to the positive formulation of corporate identity for Europeans and Americans.

13. Although North American news and movies transmit images and messages undesirable for many Malayalis (and delectable for others), the greatest disdain appears aimed at foreign television programs, possibly because they, unlike the cinema, are aired in people's homes. For instance, at the Syrian Catholic seminary near our house, the seminarians staged a protest against the Star television network during its first year in business in Kerala (1994). This station's debut programming included suggestive soap operas such as *The Bold and the Beautiful* and *Santa Barbara*.

14. In cases where threats to Indian spirituality are not identified as part of U.S. or European influences, the culprit is often more vaguely referred to as "modernity." But it is difficult to distinguish between characteristics given to Western culture from those attributed to modern culture. Along these lines, Talal Asad (1996) discusses the ways in which global understandings of secular modernity are connected with what he describes as a Western model. Arguing that we ought to call a spade a spade—identify Westernization for what it is—Asad encourages us to rethink the categories of tradition/modernity.

15. As suggested above, popular Indian conceptions of technology as a necessary evil extends beyond Christian circles. An interesting example of this, found in the Amar Chitra Katha comic book, *Dasha Avatar: The Ten Incarnations of Vishnu*, was brought to my attention by my sons, Sam and Jack. Here, a Hindu force similar to Alphonsa, functioning to save the world from technological oblivion, is Kalki, the final avatar of Lord Viṣṇu. The artist's

illustration of the troubled world into which Kalki will someday arrive, ushering humanity into a new era, focuses on a Western-looking man in a suit and tie. With a sinister grimace on his face he draws up technical plans of some sort while answering what appears to be a madly ringing phone. In the background are high-rise buildings and factories belching smoke, foregrounded by an array of complicated-looking machinery whirling and sparking. The caption below the picture reads: "Many good men walked the earth after Buddha [Viṣṇu's previous avatar] but insignificant was the effect they had against the growing supremacy of evil and evil ones on earth. With the advance of scientific knowledge the longevity of man has increased but with the advance in technology, man's life has become a nightmare of hypertensions and pollution. But not all hope is lost" (87).

16. For a slightly different approach to the use of Vatican canonizations to further national agendas, see Rollason's description of the cult of royal sainthood that served, in part, to unify Anglo-Saxon England (1989: 133, 163).

17. In spite of perceived threats from foreign influences, Kerala Christians of all denominations still boast a level of church participation and religious vocation unequaled in any European or American Christian community. For this reason, the claim of spiritual supremacy over the West is in some ways well supported, regardless of the perceived encroachment of "foreign values."

18. This concern that foreign missionaries are stealing flocks of (Hindu) believers is particularly felt in north India, where segments of tribal populations have historically—continuing up to the last several decades—converted in large numbers. Such concerns are particularly strident among Hindu revivalist groups, which have also been gaining in strength in recent years. Anti-Christian rhetoric, which has fueled a marked increase in violence against Christians since 1998, particularly in the northern states of Gujarat and Uttar Pradesh, expresses resentments not so much against the tradition itself as against its imposition by foreigners and their power structures, allurements against which many feel they have difficulty competing.

19. Reflecting a common tendency in Malayalam for adding "m" or "am" to the end of commonly used Indian words, Malayalis often refer to śrāddha as śrāddham; this same tendency emerges when prasād is rendered prasādam, and so on. See above, "Note on Transliteration."

20. It is precisely these practices, feasts for the dead and devotion to saints, that nineteenth- and twentieth-century Anglican missionaries tried to eliminate from the Syrian Christian tradition. As Bayly describes it, the British considered these traditions to be Portuguese contaminations of an earlier pristine Syrian faith when, in fact, they represent ancient rites. Not only had they been a part of Kerala's Syrian Christian traditions for centuries but the śrāddham (colloquially, cāttam) feast was used to establish status within the larger community, and devotion to saints was often related to maintaining ties with Middle Eastern ecclesial powers. As a result, there was little chance in the nineteenth century of their abandoning such practices which were (as similarly described by my Vadavathur neighbor) the "cornerstones of Syrian faith" (Bayly 1989: 297).

21. Mar Thomites, although among the Syrian Christian denominations, do not leave behind the practices of śrāddham feasts and saint devotion upon conversion to the Pentecostal movement, as they are not part of the tradition to begin with.

22. In the case of Mar Thomites and Syrian-rite Catholics, the fact that they were influenced and, at one point, managed by Western European colonizers does not seem to weaken significantly their own sense of belonging to the St. Thomas lineage of Kerala Christians. This perception of continuity, especially when applied to Syrian Catholics, is not always shared by other Syrian Christian denominations. Jacobites express pride in their tradition as being uniquely ancient in its unbroken connection with the Middle East, whereas Orthodox Syrians often claim that theirs is the only truly indigenous denomination.

23. European and American authors generally dismiss the possibility of St. Thomas's actual presence in India. Stephen Neill, in his exhaustive exploration of Christianity in India, concludes his lengthy discussion of the issue with a more moderate assessment: "Millions of Christians in South India are certain that the founder of their church was none other than the apostle Thomas himself. The historian cannot prove to them that they are mistaken in their belief. He [sic] may feel it right to warn them that historical research cannot pronounce on the matter with a confidence equal to that which they entertain by faith" (1984: 49).

24. The Jacobite Church has its patriarch in Antioch and therefore—in a matter of degrees—is also "westward" looking. Nonetheless, Church members consider their tradition to be "Eastern" and, although it is not completely indigenous, it does not claim the same kinds of fraught institutional allegiances and resulting ideological tensions as does the Syrian Catholic Church.

25. Since the Second Vatican Council, the Syrian Catholic community has been encouraged by the Vatican to reclaim many of their older liturgical practices in an effort to bring back to life some of their ancient traditions.

26. It is perhaps worth noting that many Hindu deities are likewise depicted as having very fair skin, no less fair than their counterparts among Christian saints. Yet light hair and eyes along with European clothing mark the latter group, particularly to the casual observer, as distinctly non-Indian, which cannot be said of India's gods and goddesses.

27. He is now retired; I spoke to Fr. Mootherdom during a visit he made to Bharananganam.

28. For many Syrian Catholic theologians, efforts to indigenize their tradition include a retrieval of their own Syrian tradition from its earlier, less Romanized, form. Because of its ancient heritage, many Syrian Catholics argue that Christianity was entirely acculturated into Indian society before the arrival of the Portuguese and, in the interests of indigenization, only needs to be re-Syrianized in order to be reassimilated (see pp. 73–74). When Latin Catholics work toward an indigenization of Catholic Christianity, however, they more often rely on an assimilation of Hindu symbols and practices than on Syrian ones.

29. During a week-long conference on Syrian Christianity attended by a number of foreigners (mostly Europeans and North Americans), a number of them expressed disappointment at the conspicuous absence of Eastern icons and the popularity of European images.

30. For a discussion of the impossibility of a pure religion—of the ways in which all religious traditions are in fact syncretic and continuously in flux—see Stewart and Shaw (1994).

31. Although an argument could be made that the Roman Catholic Church is not presently a colonizing force in Kerala, the fact that it acts as a foreign (Western) authority, along with its history as a colonizing power via the Portuguese, makes the perspectives offered by Bhabha and other postcolonial theorists applicable in many respects.

32. Efforts to indigenize Christian practices, although they occasionally represent contrived misinterpretations (especially by foreigners), can nonetheless involve a rich melding of traditions that "works" for its adherents. It can also be an important and positive part of institutional Christianity's (especially Roman Catholicism's) reconstitution of itself in postcolonial India. For a discussion of the aims and politics of the Christian ashram movement in India, see Raj (forthcoming).

33. Regarding the power of the hybrid to dismantle colonial imposition, the same could be said of the concurrent nationalist and Hindu Renaissance movements, led primarily by those who knew well—and made use of—the dichotomizing rhetoric of Britain.

34. The most elaborate St. George festival in my experience—in Aruvithura, not far from Bharananganam—was equipped with carnival rides and other amusements for children along with the usual festival features. Michael Carroll (1996) describes similar festivities, including "kiddie rides," at a festival he attended in 1993 in southern Italy.

35. Aside from St. George, Joseph, Mary, and Thomas the apostle, most other saints in Kerala have denominational affiliations. For instance, Alphonsa and other indigenous "new" saints are associated with the Syrian Catholic tradition, whereas St. Thérèse of Lisieux, St. Francis Xavier, and St. Anthony, although universally Catholic, are more a part of the Latin tradition. Jacobites and Orthodox Syrians, on the other hand, have a number of their own cult traditions, some of which are a part of an official canonization process. They have a long tradition of venerating foreign bishops who came to Kerala to provide Malayali Christians with an ecclesial link to the Middle East. After dying upon Indian soil, many of these bishops were considered to possess posthumous miracle-working powers, and cults developed in their honor.

36. Taussig also finds that Cuna healing figures are superficially foreign, "hiding their inner Cuna secret" (1993: 191). This does not, however, make him (or me) any less honor bound to examine these figures in light of the larger colonial context.

37. A phenomenon similar to the one Scott (1990) describes can be found in the writings of folklorists, who argue that forms of acceptable aesthetic expression provide a means for communicating issues that would otherwise be unspeakable. See Raheja and Gold (1994); Abu-Lugod (1993); and Narayan (1986).

38. For a more extensive critique of the limitations of Scott's theories, see Gal (1995: 407–24).

39. In her plea for more scholarly studies that consider the complexities of power relations between subordinate and dominant groups, Sherry Ortner likewise reasons, "In a relationship of power, the dominant often has something to offer, and sometimes a great deal (though always of course at the price of continuing in power). The subordinate thus has many grounds for ambivalence about resisting the relationship" (1995: 175).

40. Bayly considers the motif of the hero as wounded or dead yet triumphant to contain "unmistakable echoes of Muslim and Hindu devotional tradition," suggesting fertile ground from which creative additions to St. George's *Acts* could emerge (1989: 264). On the other hand, Brooks notes that such embellishments are a typical part of some of the early Syrian texts, suggesting the possibility that Keralite renditions originated elsewhere (1895: 70).

41. Although statues are not currently on display in Jacobite and Orthodox Syrian churches, paintings have become acceptable within the last century. Before this, a priest from St. George Jacobite Church in Karingachira told me, their ancestors had to conceal the painting of the saint presently hanging in the front of the church. For fifty years, according to tradition, it lay hidden at the bottom of a nearby pond. Parishioners consider the painting to have special powers, including the miracle of having remained intact despite its lengthy immersion.

42. Bayly argues that the current rigid distinction between Catholics (Syrian and Latin) who keep statues and non-Catholic Syrian Christians who prohibit them was not as well defined before the arrival of the British. Appalled by the discovery that some non-Catholic parishes were displaying statues in their churches, the British, in their post-Reformation zeal to rid these non-Catholics of such deplorable practices, were effective in putting an end to this "error" (1989: 296). According to Joseph Thekkadath, it appears that seventeenth-century Antiochan Syrian prelates nonetheless promoted similar kinds of reform. Although their level of success is unclear, these foreign clergy, in line with their Antiochan tradition, attempted to remove statues and crucifixes from the church buildings and encouraged priests to marry (103).

43. As suggested by Fr. Arayathinal's argument for the Syrian statue's "Oriental" origin, a perceived polarization exists between Portuguese and Syrian influences. In spite of the fact that most Kerala Christians, whether from Syrian, Latin, or Anglican traditions, consider themselves to be different from, or even in opposition to, the European and American culture,

this distinction is often more sharply drawn by the Syrian Christian denominations, who consider themselves more explicitly "Oriental."

44. In Tamil Nadu, the famous Fort St. George in Madras offers another link between the British and St. George. Srinivachary states that it is not clear why this "nucleus of the present city of Madras" was named St. George, as its construction cannot be proven to have been started or finished on the feast day of the saint (1939: 4). Nonetheless, as he surmises (and I would agree), the saint's status as patron of England was enough to name the fort in his honor (45–46; see also Ramaswami 1977: 42). In the beginning of the nineteenth century, to meet the needs of the growing numbers of Anglicans in Madras, the British also built St. George Church, currently known as St. George Cathedral (Ramaswami 223–24).

45. See also Bayly (1989: 285), and Neill (1984: 241–47).

46. According to Bayly, Col. John Munro's campaign to revitalize the Jacobite tradition during the early 1800s included grants of large sums of money for the repair and reconstruction of its churches (1989: 288). Offering a slightly different perspective from the one given by my Orthodox friend, Bayly notes that prior to the arrival of British missionaries, Jacobites were not particularly threatened by the encroachment of Syrian Catholicism but, rather, the two traditions enjoyed amiable relations. In fact, she argues that they were nearly indistinguishable in their practices and often shared church buildings (see also Neill 1985: 62). Bayly contends that tensions around issues of church ownership arose only when the British stepped in, offering the Jacobites "Munro's relief money to buy out their Romo-Syrian co-shares and take sole control of the region's mutually managed churches" (295–96).

47. During the 1930s the St. George Church in Puthupally was one of the Syrian churches that split with the Jacobite tradition, offering its allegiance to the indigenous Katholicos rather than the patriarch of Antioch. The decision to break away from the Jacobites was not unanimous, however, resulting in an intraparish feud (mainly between bishops) that has yet to be resolved. As a result, litigation fees continue to mount and the government has, since the 1970s, taken charge of the church's finances.

48. Ommen Chandy mentions that the construction of Puthupally's St. George Church was connected to the demolition of an earlier church located near the temple at Vazhakulam. He also describes the original church as having been gifted to the Christian community by the local Hindu king—a fairly typical motif of Hindu-Christian interdependence found in church origin stories (1961: 230–32).

Although the pronunciation of the pan-Indian goddess, Kālī, is rendered "Kāḷi" by Keralites, I have chosen to maintain the more common Sanskritic transliteration throughout the book (see Note on Transliteration).

49. In addition to St. George, another popular south Indian saint affected by a similar Vatican demotion is St. Philomena. A church in Mysore, Karnataka, continues its tradition as a major pilgrimage center for devotion to the saint but has had its name changed from St. Philomena's to St. Joseph's. In Europe, the best known saint to fall prey to Vatican Skepticism is St. Christopher. The popular uprising against (and general inattention to) this decree was significant, especially in Italy (see also Orsi 1996: 38).

50. Skepticism about the efficacy of saint cults is a fairly universal, cross-cultural phenomenon and certainly not always a result of foreign influences. William Christian makes note of Spanish "skepticism and incredulity" about the healing powers of saints, which he found "as much in small villages as large towns" (1981: 147).

51. Because Eastern Orthodoxy was little affected by the Reformation and Counter-Reformation and their rationalizing effects, the disdain for popular piety or "superstitions" held by the Roman Catholic Church since the sixteenth century has not been shared equally by the Eastern traditions (Kokosalakis 1987: 37–52; Ware 1964: 275–79). It may be for this

reason that Jacobites and Orthodox Syrians in Kerala tend to be quicker to defend St. George's cult, although this is not uniformly the case.

52. In Mediterranean medieval Catholicism, St. George was most commonly invoked for protection from hail (Christian 1981: 71). A sixteenth-century Syrian prayer book, *Proemeon Sedra*, also lists hail (or "ice rocks" when translated from Malayalam) as one of the major calamities from which St. George protects his devotees.

There are also particularly "Hindu" ways of dealing with snakes in Kerala. *Sarpa* stones (*sarpa kalla* in Malayalam), representative of serpents' sacred efficacy and located outside most temples, commonly receive offerings from devotees for protection from poisonous snakes (discussed in chapter 2). In spite of this Hindu means for managing the calamity of poisonous snakes in Kerala, St. George's protection is nearly as important among Hindus of Kottayam district as it is among Christians. Although Hindus are often well represented at St. George shrines and festivals, few Christians seem to visit *sarpa* stones or snake temples.

53. Local Keralite depictions of St. Sebastian likewise portray him as being a native of Kerala. As told by devotees near his church in Ettumanur, Sebastian was originally a Hindu Brahman who was converted to Christianity by St. Thomas the apostle. The convert did not let on about his new religion until after a war broke out in the land and he was arrested. At this point the martyr-to-be confessed his conversion, and his captors shot arrows at him. Thus the iconographical image, prevalent in Kerala, is of St. Sebastian tied to a tree and pierced with arrows.

Reflecting a similar phenomenon in which a saint literally becomes indigenized outside his or her home, the cult of St. Blaise, believed to be from Armenia, became very strong in sixteenth-century Spain. During this period and also during the seventeenth century, there arose in several towns traditions of their own Spanish St. Blaise (Christian 1981: 131).

54. Aside from annual festival occasions, pilgrimages to St. George shrines are commonly carried out on Fridays, particularly the first Friday of the month. Fridays are traditionally when parish priests conduct novenas to the church's patron saint, especially at pilgrimage sites. Within the Roman Catholic tradition St. George's official novena has recently been altered to deemphasize the saint in exchange for prayers reflecting more generic (and therefore more acceptable) Christian concerns. Masses officially said in St. George's honor are no longer allowed, although occasional brief mention of him is permissible during liturgies.

55. Although Keralite constructions of reverse Orientalism help form a positive corporate identity and give important distance between Keralites (and other Indians) and colonial and postcolonial powers, there are ways in which the rigid formulation pitting East against West holds the former nonetheless bound—through being an antithesis—to the "West." Near the end of chapter 2, I revisit this issue.

Chapter 2

1. Kumar (1988) also discusses violence at a Banaras Durga festival.

2. Also often ignored, especially by the international media, is the intercommunal cooperation regularly carried out in north India. In *Father, Son and Holy War*, Patwardhan tries to emphasize the ways in which the lower classes are especially hurt by communal violence. In this light, he depicts some of the ways the poor among Hindu and Muslim communities assist one another in their common plight. The lesson seems to be that the abstract issues of religious dispute do not "belong" to these people, whose concerns revolve around the challenges of daily life.

3. I have chosen European Catholicism as a source of examples of non-Indian saint cults partly because of its long-standing tradition of such practices. As argued in the introduction, I also feel it is important to provide a comparison of Indian and non-Indian practices that

will cut across the orientalist East/West divide. Although examples from Mexico, Central America, or South America may represent a similar geographical disjunction, their common association with the "third world" eases a more stark comparison, and potentially lessens the effect of the striking similarities that exist in spite of this distinction.

4. During the larger festival events I attended in Kerala, I commonly met Malayalis who had emigrated to the United States. Their visits to their home village were deliberately planned so they could take part in festivals of local patron saints or deities.

5. My use of the term "communal" to describe disputes between communities in Europe is a deliberate mixing of categories. Pandey discusses how the term "communalism" has been primarily reserved for references to volatile relations between Indian religious groups. He argues that although European history has had its fair share of intercommunity and interfaith aggression, the term "communalism" and its associations with irrationality is not utilized in this context (1990: 7). Rather than delete the word "communalism" from my writing I choose to question and extend its accepted meaning, thus using it "out of context." Further discussion of this issue will be taken up in the second section of this chapter.

6. For other descriptions of European festival tensions, see Keith Thomas (1971: 27, 28, 40) and Riegelhaupt (1973).

7. Given this perspective, it seems likely that St. Behanan's church bells outside Puthupally, so annoying to neighboring Kālī during the nineteenth century (as described in chapter 1), reflects this larger sense of Hindu-Christian discord.

8. Known for its grand procession of elephants from various temples around Thrissur, and the competition of colored umbrellas (*muttukuṭaṅgaḷ*) in the center of town, Thrissur Puram is typically flooded with people from all over south India and seems invariably to appear in tour-book photographs of Kerala.

9. Muslim support of Hindu and Christian festivals and religious structures, and vice versa, is certainly not unknown in Kerala, although such exchanges are sometimes less overt than Hindu-Christian ones.

10. When referring to present-day relations between Christians and Hindus, Bayly likewise seems to overestimate the long-term effects of British rule on Kerala's communal relations (1989: 463).

11. As mentioned in the previous chapter (note 47), Puthupally St. George Church is one of the several Kottayam district churches that are battlegrounds for Jacobite and Orthodox Syrian claims for ownership. Because of their inability to come to a settlement, the government, since 1972, has had to step in as a neutral party and manage its finances. With the advent of government control, rooster sacrifice was banned on the church premises. Although I never witnessed the event, a ritual slashing of one rooster's neck is said still to occur on the church grounds, and additional sacrifices take place at local residents' homes.

12. The benefits and esteem coming from touching a rope attached to a holy object is a common theme in south Indian traditions, as mentioned in the discussion of the Coonan Cross Oath in the introduction. As might be expected, Hindu festival practices in Kerala include opportunities for participants to touch the deity's chariot's *cāṭu*, as well. Furthermore, Kerala's Cochin Jewish community, before its mid-century exodus to Israel, used a chariot to process holy objects from the synagogue through the streets during special occasions. Old Cochin Jewish folk songs also describe the *cāṭu* pulling the chariot as having particular efficacies (Barbara Johnson, personal communication).

13. The theme of saint-deity travel to particular church and temple destinations is not uncommon among saint-deity sibling and friendship stories. A similar tale of traveling sisters is told about the Kurumba Bhagavati in Kodungaloor and Mary from nearby Chalakutty. According to legend, the two began their journey in Mukambika, southern Karnataka, and eventually made their way to their present locations, where the locals recognized them for

who they were. They were then installed in their respective places of worship. The story (cited below) of traveling companions Kṛṣṇa and St. Sebastian, bonded in friendship through their long boat trip, also serves as part of the church and temple origin stories; see section 2 of this chapter for more church origin stories.

14. The theme of Hindu Nair rescue is also a prevalent one, particularly in Kerala Christian church origin stories. For further examples of how a Nair man or woman helps Christian communities to establish themselves against obstacles commonly posed by Brahmans, see section 2 of this chapter.

15. Harman argues that the perseverance of the myth involving the Viṣṇu-Śiva-Pārvatī familial relationship is due to its resonance with south Indian kinship systems (1989: 83–99). Hudson likewise notes that Madurai's "mythic consciousness" has chosen this particular brother-in-law relationship as a symbol of unity and antagonism because of the particular nature of kinship in south India (1977: 115). Be this as it may, Keralite configurations of sacred siblings include a vast array of combinations (for example, Hindu sister and Christian brother, Hindu brother and Christian sister, interreligious brothers and sisters) and, in many cases, it is difficult to decipher the elder of the pair. It is for this reason that I do not attempt to make any claims about how Kerala's kinship patterns fuel particular interreligious associations between sacred figures but, rather, I view the sibling tie more generically as metaphor for an occasionally rivalrous but ultimately reliant communal relationship.

16. Here I refer to the first chapter's discussion of imported customs such as saint cults and orientalist epistemology, which are adopted and transformed, and thus hybridized if not indigenized (depending on one's perspective) through local reinterpretations.

17. Renuka counters these suggestions with the claim that she is just a "normal girl." She emphasized this by telling me that she would really like to be "modern" and crop her hair. She once told some of the nuns in Bharananganam about this, but they advised her not to. They reasoned, according to Renuka, that Alphonsa would never have done such things.

18. The rose Alphonsa gave Renuka is a symbol commonly associated with Mary as well as St. Thérèse of Lisieux. Roses are often included in iconographical depictions of Alphonsa, offering, for many, an association between the Keralite nun and the "Little Flower" of Lisieux. For many more comparisons between the Indian and French nuns, see chapter 4, section 1.

Renuka told me that after her miraculous cure, a neighborhood boy passed by their home and, upon hearing the commotion inside, peered into the room where Renuka had been sleeping. Inside, he reported seeing an unidentified woman who fit the description of Sr. Alphonsa. It is in this spot—the same place where Renuka saw the nun—that she keeps her flower.

19. To contextualize this ideology further, the idea that "all religions are one" stems from the pan-Indian Hindu Renaissance movement of the same time period, and is still extremely influential today (Bharati 1970: 285). Bharati criticizes the Hindu Renaissance movement, led by such thinkers as Dayananda, Vivekananda, Sivananda, and Aurobindo, for its highly selective use of Sanskrit phrases taken from ancient texts as a means to offer simplistic solutions to complex philosophical issues. As Bharati puts it, "any writing which does not offer total solutions is unpopular and tends to be ignored" (1970: 285). Nonetheless, the popularity of these "anti-Sanskritic" Renaissance teachers, as Bharati labels them—especially among the English-speaking Indian elite—is such that few dare to criticize them (269).

20. A similar disregard for the mingling of Hindu and Christian paraphernalia in spite of recognized alliances is expressed through the story of sacred animosity in Piravam between the three Magi and Śiva (above). As explained by the local tale, the three kings were angered by the "insulting" presence of *tuḷasi* and *cetti* flowers (typically used by Hindus) in

their church. This concern for the interreligious "mixing" of ritual items such as plants and lamps is rather curious, since *nilaviḷakkā* oil lamps are conspicuously present in non-Protestant churches and homes and, during occasions such as house blessings—both Christian and Hindu—*tuḷasi* leaves are often a necessary part of the ritual.

21. Perhaps ironically, this Orthodox priest's idea that all in India are Hindu—regardless of their professed religious tradition—echoes sentiments commonly espoused by members of the Hindu nationalist movement. Although the BJP party—the mainstream political manifestation of Hindu nationalism—has Christian and Muslim members and even leaders in Kerala (although it is not a strong party overall in the state), Fr. Varghese is not one of them.

22. One of the better-known early cases in which the Catholic hierarchy was moved to deliberate about proper boundaries between Hindu and Christian traditions occurred during the seventeenth-century missionary effort of Robert de Nobili. De Nobili, an Italian Jesuit missionary to Madurai, adopted the lifestyle and appearance of a Hindu sannyasi, appealing to upper-caste Hindus through his knowledge of Sanskrit and his strict observance of high-caste Hindu customs and restrictions. For thirteen of his fifty-one-year career as a missionary, de Nobili had to defend himself against Vatican claims that he was overstepping the divide between Christianity and Hinduism. In the end, the Vatican supported de Nobili's efforts, asking simply that he use caution in his adoption of traditional Indian symbols so that none of "the old superstitions [were] perpetuated with them" (Neill 1985: 292–93).

23. Although the umbrella is historically associated with the royal houses of south India and Sri Lanka, during the eighth century the use of an umbrella was designated as the most prominent of the seventy-two privileges granted to Jews and Christians by a local south Indian king (Younger forthcoming).

24. The most dramatic exception to this usage of some Indian-looking practices by Kerala Christians occurs among the Pentecostal or Evangelical denominations. These groups not only discourage *cāttam* feasts but they commonly consider them to be counter to the teachings of the Bible and therefore completely unacceptable.

25. Generically and more commonly referred to as *tāli* by most Malayalis, some Christians refer to it—when in a Christian context—as *minnu*. The weddings themselves may be quite different in form, but both Christian and Hindus consider the tying of the *tāli* (or *minnu*) to be the climax of the event. This has only recently come into vogue for the Hindu Nair caste, who traditionaly consider the offering of a sari by the groom to the bride the focal point of the ceremony.

26. Early Christians upheld restrictions against menstruating women receiving communion, a practice allegedly abolished in Pope Gregory the Great's papal bull of 597. Nonetheless, there are some conservative Eastern Orthodox communities that currently maintain such practices (Wood 1981: 713–14). It is therefore probable that early Syrian communities prescribed such restrictions in Kerala, apart from Hindu influence. As for astrology, it was a common feature throughout European society up through medieval times, thus probably practiced by foreign communities in Kerala, both Syrian and Portuguese. Because astrology and menstrual restrictions have not been a part of Western European culture in recent centuries, however, I portray their current practice in Kerala as being more a part of shared Hindu culture than a foreign importation.

27. I encountered only one exception to the Hindu restriction on menstruating women while in Kerala, in relation to a friend's mother who is a disciple of Sai Baba. She (unlike most other women in her family) regularly enters temples or her *pūjā* room while having her period, as Sai Baba insists that women are not polluting during this time and should be allowed to worship.

28. This is the same Sr. Rita who accompanied Sr. Josephina and me up to Fr. Acharya's ashram.

29. The fact that Keralites enjoy such a high standard of living in comparison with people in most other states in India is due, in part, to their comparatively low birth rate.

30. A recent papal encyclical, *Fides et Ratio*, typifies this Vatican ambivalence toward inculturation. On the one hand, the pope encourages Indian Christians to make the most of their unique spiritual legacy: "In India particularly, it is the duty of Christians now to draw from this rich [Indian] heritage the elements compatible with their faith, in order to enrich Christian thought." A word of caution is thrown in, not nearly as strident as the report quoted above, arguing that Christianity must not stray too far from its European roots, "in engaging great cultures for the first time, the Church cannot abandon what she has gained from her inculturation in the world of Greco-Latin thought. To reject this heritage would be to deny the providential plan of God who guides his Church down the paths of time and history." The pope finishes this particular segment by walking the fine line between arguing for the uniqueness of Indian and Christian traditions and supporting the benefits of intercultural exchange: "care will need to be taken lest, contrary to the very nature of the human spirit, the legitimate defense of the uniqueness and originality of Indian thought be confused with the idea that a particular cultural tradition should remain closed in its difference and affirm itself by opposing other tradition" (chapter 6: 75).

31. Nita Kumar (1988) discusses the different ways members of a Banaras Muslim community garner their identity outside of religious factors. This complication of communal identity helps her to argue against simplified understandings of communal conflict based solely on religious distinction.

32. Examples of ongoing animosity within a religious tradition are the current struggles between the Jacobites and Orthodox Syrians for control over certain churches. Not coincidentally, the churches in question are popular (that is, lucrative) pilgrimage sites, one of which is the Puthupally St. George Church, presently managed by the government lawyers. During a recent (1998) trip to Kerala, I found the famous Kadamattam Church locked up by the police due to recent—and often violent—disputes over ownership. For detailed descriptions of these Syrian Christian battles, see Visvanathan (1993).

33. The Census of India 1961 volume, *Fairs and Festivals of Kerala*, includes stories of ecumenical church constructions in its descriptions of a number of prominent churches.

34. Although I heard a number of variations of this story, told in Bharananganam by nuns, priests, and lay people, I found the specifics regarding the wedding gifts tagged onto the end of a similar story told in the *Fairs and Festivals* volume (Mathew 1961: 179).

35. In a different context, *ceṟiamma* can also be a term of endearment for one's mother's younger sister.

36. As described in the first section of this chapter, a Nair hero, Chalassery Panikkar, also plays a starring role in Piravam's local tale of the Three Magi and Śiva. Like the Bharananganam Nair family, the Panikkars are still remembered for their ancestor's good deed.

37. This also extends Scott's (1990) thesis about the subversive strategies of hidden transcripts meant to challenge a troubled existence. The production of this kind of coded "subversion," which can look more like dreamed resolution, is, I argue, not always the role of the folk but of the dominant order.

38. Like the Keralite Christians described in the previous chapter, these Ayurvedic physicians seem to maintain orientalist categories of a spiritual East versus a technological West. Their desire to give validity to Ayurveda through an association with "Western" science shows an absence, however, of a similar reversal of orientalist conclusions (that is, to portray the "East" as unequivocally superior).

39. Although I suggest here that the labeling of sacred sibling stories as "silly" was done for my benefit or as a way to appear right-thinking in the eyes of a judgmental foreigner, it is also entirely possible that some of these Keralites sincerely thought of these stories as

"silly." Nonetheless, I would have to argue that this genuine disdain is not necessarily a separate phenomenon from my reading of it as performative disdain. The forces of rationalism or modernism (largely perceived as a part of Euro-American ideology) that would make Keralites increasingly suspicious or unappreciative of sibling stories (as witnessed by the generational differences) probably affect the performance of these stories, particularly to an American ethnographer.

40. Dr. Paulos Mar Gregorios, although in good condition when I met him in 1994, died rather unexpectedly after suffering a stroke two years later.

41. Along these lines, Ashis Nandy identifies similar reverse orientalist rhetoric in India. He critiques such a stance, one which argues that the East is diametrically opposed to the West, as functioning to bind India's identity all the more securely to the colonial and postcolonial forces they are trying to negate (1983: 73).

42. For a description of how orientalist stereotypes of Tibet, although not directly responsible for a bloody mess, nonetheless sustain political deadlock, see Lopez (1998).

43. In this discussion of the repetition of colonial mistakes by ethnography, my reference to "ethnographer" refers explicitly to those, like myself, who are trained in North America or Europe. In the case of native ethnographers hailing from previously colonized countries who have likewise been educated in North America or Europe, a number of arguments have recently been made which posit that the privilege associated with this position makes them in some significant ways an "other" to those in the ethnographic "field" back "home." See Nita Kumar's (1992) introduction, pp. 1–21. For a lucid complication of the term "native," as well as the nature of relationships out in "the field," see Narayan (1993). See also Clifford 1997.

44. I expand upon this idea of ethnographic intimacies in a separate article (Dempsey 2000).

45. For a somewhat similar discussion of feminist ethnography as failure or of feminist ethnographer as "trickster" who "mediates between cognitive failure and its success," see Visweswaran (1994: 97–101).

46. Speaking of sibling metaphors and the related intimacy of communal dynamics, Cohen describes the significance of a metaphor's production and expression as being the construction and validation of an "intimacy" between those who understand and share its use (1979: 6). As such, community, according to Cohen, arises not only out of "the shared awareness that a special invitation has been given and accepted but also from the awareness that not everyone could make that offer or take it up" (7).

Chapter 3

1. Because I considered the possibility that Sr. Josephina's presence in these interviews influenced people's responses, I tried conducting them with a lay woman or by myself to see if the outcome would shift. As it happened, regardless of whether or not Sr. Josephina accompanied me, the gist of the interviews remained the same.

2. Although I do believe my perception of sainthood as model for behavior rather than source of miracles represents a dominant view currently held by North American Catholics, a notable exception is devotion to St. Jude. As described by Orsi (1996), devotion to the saint in the United States emerged and developed primarily during the Depression, a time of fervent devotionalism among the children of Catholic immigrants. What sets St. Jude apart from other saints today is the strength of his cult in spite of the general waning of miracle-working saint devotion in this country. According to the shrine in Chicago that receives and publishes written correspondence from the devout, about three thousand pieces of mail are received every day (32).

3. Tambiah describes a similar phenomenon in his study of Thai Buddhism's cult of amulets. The official interpretation of the amulet—held by a small minority—is that it stands as a "reminder" of the virtue of Buddha (that is, his victories over desire and ignorance) and is worn to give inspiration to follow a similar path. However, the prevailing understanding of the amulet is that it operates to give the wearer protection or special powers in accordance with his or her desires (1984: 201, 335). Whereas the former approach views the amulet as a means for release from desire, the latter considers it as serving virtually the opposite purpose.

In Kiekhefer and Bond's edited book, *Sainthood: Its Manifestations in World Religions*, the preface attempts a definition of sainthood to be applied across religious divides. Most simply put, the saint is described as someone who is worthy of both imitation and veneration. The tensions inherent in this formula are immediately apparent, however, since the veneration of another human makes them, in a sense, "other" and thus difficult to emulate: "the more the saint's distinctive powers dominate and the more it seems that the saintly virtues themselves are rooted in or supported by a distinctive calling, the harder it becomes to take the saint as a model for imitation" (1988: viii).

4. For discussion of this issue within Christianity, see Bretell (1990); Badone (1990a); Klaniczay (1990: 21–25); Peter Brown (1981: 13–22); Christian (1981: 147–180); Devlin (1987: 6–21); Burke (1994: 1–87); and Brooke and Brooke (1984: 46–62). For discussions that aim to complicate the traditional notion of the written great tradition versus the oral or folk little traditions within Hinduism, see Ramanujan (1989) and Bharati (1968).

5. See Christian (1981: 178) and Carroll (1996).

6. For an extended discussion of this use and extension of Asad's theories on religion and the pull of institutional versus sacred power, see Dempsey (1999). There I argue that these two types of authoritative powers work to define religion and its parameters in drastically different ways. The "lessons" we learn from local devotion to miracle-working saints have to do with reconfigurations of otherwise static notions of religious affiliation.

7. Nolan and Nolan (1989) note that, although it is becoming increasingly difficult for pilgrimage sites to be approved or even tolerated by the official Church, the local practice of Catholic pilgrimage and its trappings are currently on the rise. They offer the "conservative" estimate that the six thousand operating pilgrimage centers in Europe receive sixty to seventy million religiously motivated visits per year. According to Nolan and Nolan, total annual pilgrims per year (which include casual tourists, curiosity seekers, and "art history pilgrims") "almost certainly exceed one hundred million" (1–2).

8. For a discussion of tensions between the modernization agendas of clergy and local practice, see Badone (1990b).

9. St. Thomas is also, without doubt, one of the most important saints to Kerala Christians, if not *the* most important. Unlike St. George, St. Sebastian, and St. Gregorios, however, Thomas is currently not so much a cult saint as he is an emblematic patron saint. In this way his function is much like Alphonsa's in her capacity to carve and justify a unique Kerala Christian identity.

"Speciality" saints are also a common part of European cult traditions. For further discussion of this phenomenon, see Christian (1981: 42–47) and Devlin (1987). For north Indian Hindu shrines specializing in particular kinds of problems, see Ann Gold (1994: 90–101; 1987: 34) and Wadley (1975: 112).

10. The term *yakṣī*, used throughout India, is pronounced slightly differently in Kerala as *yakṣi*. In an effort to lessen confusion I have used the more conventional transliteration throughout the book.

11. Although it is true that Christian saints are "officially" understood as mediators who intercede with God on behalf of their devotees—rather than answering their prayers directly—the overwhelming majority of Kerala Christians and Hindus refer to saintly power or action as though it comes straight from the saint.

12. Temple *sarpa* stones seem slightly more prevalent than *yakṣī* stones. Although the former appear in a variety of temple types, the latter are commonly though not exclusively associated with goddess traditions.

13. For a discussion of the ways in which Māriyammān devotion was and still is affected by the World Health Council's successful efforts to eradicate smallpox in the 1960s, see Egnor (1984).

14. In contrast to Kerala, many north and south Indian traditions manage snakes through a particular deity rather than through snake symbolism such as the *sarpa* stone. And Keralites also visit snake or *nāgā* temples and give offerings to the live snakes residing there. The most famous of these temples is in Manarshala, near Kollam. Aside from the protection from and healing of snake bites, devotees commonly approach the *sarpa* stone and snake temple for the treatment of infertility.

15. As told in many official accounts of saints' lives in which the hero or heroine's faith in Jesus enables him or her to overcome a seemingly insurmountable evil, such notions of the sure power of (Christian) good over evil can even be deployed as a tool for calling non-Christians to conversion. This proselytizing function of Christian heroes, although not universally agreed upon, was expressed to me several times by nuns and clergy in Kottayam district.

The possible public relations "benefits" that come from attributing benign rather than ambivalent characteristics to sacred powers apparently have been of interest for some Hindus, particularly earlier in the century and during the height of the nationalist movement. Nandy describes Bankimchandra Chatterjee as trying to highlight in Hinduism some of the qualities he considered to have made Christianity strong. For example, he remodeled Kṛṣṇa into an historical figure who was moral according to "modern norms." Kṛṣṇa's most important attribute, in Chatterjee's eyes, was that he was a god of all-perfection, and, as Nandy puts it, "one that would not humiliate his devotees in front of progressive Westerners" (1983: 23–24).

16. It bears mentioning that Jewish scriptures, which depict God as potentially wrathful and punishing in response to human misdeeds, are not as indebted to divine benevolence as is Christianity. The saintly pranksters discussed in this chapter thus seem to challenge Jewish attributes of sacred power less than they do Christian ones.

17. As mentioned in chapter 2, although a number of fowl were originally sacrificed ritually in front of the Puthupally church, common practice today is a token slashing of one neck while the rest are auctioned off to be unceremoniously killed and cooked.

18. Although St. George's powers offer particularly useful examples of saintly ambivalence, a number of other Kerala saints demonstrate similar characteristics. For instance, although usually portrayed as benign, Mary at the Manarkad Church is described as curing devotees inflicted with insanity, yet—particularly during festival time—also causing madness in those who have not fasted appropriately.

19. Rooster offerings are not unusual within south Indian Hindu traditions. Among contemporary cults of Christian saints, however, St. George's current widespread association with such offerings is unique.

20. Bayly's apparent misunderstanding of this aspect of popular sainthood is reflected in the writings of other scholars, as well. In *Mama Lola: A Vodou Priestess in Brooklyn*, Karen McCarthy Brown regards the *sen-yo* (saints) of Haiti as not being "saintly types" due to their ambivalent nature (1991: 6).

21. For a wide-ranging and captivating study of the many ways Indian images are brought to life, see Davis (1997).

22. Nolan and Nolan found that although miraculous weeping, bleeding, moving, and speaking images are not uncommon in the twentieth century, few get official recognition from the Vatican (1989: 244).

23. A possible argument that the cult of saints in Europe is merely an extension of

pagan practice, similar to perceptions that Indian saint cults are strictly extensions of Hindu observances, needs to be addressed. There have, admittedly, been a number of scholars of local Christian devotions who focus on the ritual behavior that takes place in Mediterranean Europe, and who argue that such observances, particularly as carried out by women, represent a tenacious preservation of paganism. Peter Brown notes that the earlier Enlightenment mentality which considered such traditions (most pronounced in the cult of saints) to be "vulgar" has recently been replaced by a romantic nostalgia, expressed by scholars who consider these same practices to be positive "avatars of classical paganism" (1981: 20). Brown counters this position, however, by arguing that the cult of saints represents a decisive departure from pagan beliefs. According to Brown, the difference lies in the fact that saint cults represent "radically new forms of reverence, shown to new objects in new places . . . deriving its momentum from the need to play out the common preoccupation of all, the few and the 'vulgar' alike, with new forms of the exercise of power, new bonds of human dependence, new, intimate, hopes for protection and justice in a changing world" (22). Although I may not agree with Brown about the extent to which popular Christian practices represented a "radical" break from earlier systems, it seems important to acknowledge the complex differences arising from and responding to new frameworks of power, both sacred and temporal.

24. Christian argues that during the Catholic Reformation the institutional church in some ways affirmed the local side of religion but tried to make it subordinate to universal symbols and discourse. In spite of these ecclesial efforts, communities continued to domesticate these universal symbols in order to incorporate them into local votive use (1981: 178–81).

Demonstrating the political importance of indigenized saint cults, John Thornton's *The Kongolese Saint Anthony*, describes an indigenized early eighteenth-century African cult of St. Anthony, led by a bold and charismatic young woman who insisted she was possessed by the saint. In her preached messages to her followers, Dona Beatriz challenged the authority of European Capuchin priests in her midst by revising Christian history. She did this by asserting the "truth" about St. Anthony—that he was actually Kongolese, as was St. Francis, the founder of these missionary priests and friars. Furthermore, Mary, Jesus, and Joseph were likewise from different regions of the Kongo (1998: 113–14). Although Dona Beatriz's statements seem rather dramatic and extreme, her revision and subsequent indigenization of Christianity was part of and not much different from an already established revisionist tradition in the Kongo.

25. The regionalization of "new" saints such as Alphonsa and others who are awaiting canonization is much less noticeable than that of older saint cults. In the case of the new saints, a shrine containing the bodily remains of the newly deceased Keralite will act as the ultimate pilgrimage site or seat of power.

26. In spite of these interreligious similarities, more extreme acts of asceticism are typically reserved for Hindu temple festival rituals. As described in chapter 2, although Hindu and Christian practices often look similar, practitioners give them different interpretations. These differences commonly cut across religious lines, but not always. For instance, while Sr. Josephina may refer to bodily vows as "acts of humiliation" that translate into penance for sins committed, many Christians understand such actions strictly in terms of earning sacred favor in exchange for human hardship.

27. I have seen *milagros* (miracles), metal representations of body parts meant to be used for religious vows in Central and South America, put to secular use in the United States through their presence in make-it-yourself jewelry shops.

28. Nolan and Nolan argue that writings about local European saint cults, if they exist at all, largely neglect traditions that take place in the twentieth century. Studies of local religion in Europe have traditionally dealt with the medieval era although, more recently, the transition period between medieval and early modern times has been picked up by a few

scholars (1989: 3). This dearth of exploration of contemporary local religious practice appears to contribute to a false assumption that local saint devotion and its trappings are only a phenomenon of the past. Notable exceptions to this trend are studies of modern European saints and pilgrimage by anthropologists such as the Turners, Dubisch, Bretell, Christian, Riegelhaupt, and Vauchez. Nonetheless, although such anthropological studies, though limited, are available, they will probably not be a part of an Indian seminary's library collection and will thus not be available to influence clerical notions of the larger world of local Christian practices.

29. A published example of this phenomenon can be found in P. David's discussion of Indian Christian popular observances. Here, he views local Indian devotion to statues as a kind of idol worship to which non-Indians apparently do not fall prey. Distinguishing the perceived difference between Indian and non-Indian uses of religious art, David writes, "The Roman Catholic observance of this phenomenon in the West is more a mystic appreciation of the art (or the image) than an act of image-worship" (1980: 73).

30. Although European Catholic authorities have been fully aware of "superstitions" in their midst, it is interesting to note that the "errors" of these practices have, at times, been emphasized by equating them with non-European traditions. Carroll describes sixteenth-through eighteenth-century missionaries who preached not only to heathen in far-away lands but also in the European countryside. Southern Italy's Catholicism was apparently so far off the mark that these missionaries referred to the area as "our Italian Indies" (1996: 3).

In Ruby Daniel and Barbara Johnson's *Ruby of Cochin: An Indian Jewish Woman Remembers*, Ruby describes Indian Jews as having a propensity for superstition not found in non-Indian Jewish communities, due to influences of "the Hindus, who believe in reincarnation and ghosts and spirits" (1995: 36). In spite of this shortcoming, Ruby notes what she sees to be, more importantly, the superior moral codes of the Hindu community. She compares them with Christians—who hypocritically call themselves humanitarians—and Muslims, both of whom have a habit of killing Jews. "The Muslims and Christians as well as the Jews have stamped the Hindus as idolaters. But if you want to know what is humanitarianism you must go to them. You must look at a group of Jews who lived under the regime of these Hindu rajas for the last two thousand years without knowing discrimination. The Hindu rulers protected them when they came under attack by the Portuguese and Muslim rulers" (123).

31. At one time fowl was a common offering for a variety of saints, particularly at the more powerful shrines. In chapter 2, I mentioned the tradition of offering fowl to Manarkad Mary, the blood being shared with her Hindu sister's bodyguards. During the latter part of this century, however, the practice of fowl sacrifice to Christian saints has largely fallen into disfavor, with the notable exception of St. George.

32. In related fashion, the contemporary use of St. George's image as war propaganda—in which the enemy is depicted as a dehumanized dragon—is not impossible to find. Keen's *Faces of the Enemy* (1986) shows a Civil War-era sketch in which General Scott is poised to club a many-headed secessionist serpent. Also, more directly invoking the St. George image is a German pre-World War II drawing depicting a caped warrior on horseback, slaying a dragon. The warrior, who represents the Nazi party fighting off the reptilian menace, is surrounded by the caption, which translates, "Wake up! Look out. Vote the People's ticket." (Thanks to Don Fadden for introducing me to Keen's book.) On the other side of the political divide, a towering statue of St. George in Treptow Park in the former East Berlin celebrates victory in World War II. Erected by the former German Democratic Republic, this St. George holds a child in one arm and, with the other, thrusts his sword into a broken swastika. By reorganizing iconographical cues—replacing one menace for another (the dragon for the Nazis) and the vulnerable maiden for the child—St. George as protector of the meek and

victor over evil is still recognizable. (Thanks to Richard DeMaris for bringing this statue to my attention.)

33. The receiving of the holy leftovers from devotees' offerings to the deity is a pan-Indian practice. *Prasādam* (*prasād* in north India) or *nērcca* is considered to have curative powers and is often taken home for ailing family members or for those who are unable to carry out a pilgrimage. As described by Ann Gold in relation to north Indian Hindu traditions, "To bring home and redistribute a god's power-imbued leavings is integral if not defining to the act of shrine pilgrimage" (1987: 188).

Although this Kerala Christian practice of taking *prasādam* from a saint seems particularly Indian, Dubisch describes something similar to it as taking place in Greece. As observed by Dubisch, pilgrims maintain that anything which comes into close proximity to the icon is "imbued with therapeutic or protective power" (1990: 130). For this reason, dried remnants of flowers left as offerings, along with used incense or pieces of cloth rubbed on the icon, are sold in street stands.

34. As in the miracle story told in chapter 4, section 3, involving Alphonsa's healing of a Muslim boy, it is not normally expected that conversion to Christianity will accompany belief in Alphonsa. Except in the more unusual case of Renuka, Alphonsa's Hindu medium, I found that non-Christian acknowledgment of Alphonsa's efficacy was welcomed and encouraged—no strings attached.

35. When I returned for a visit in 1998, the convent parlor museum was being refurbished, and many of Alphonsa's belongings were scheduled for transfer to a different museum currently under construction. This new structure was expected to open shortly across the street and up the hill, near Alphonsa's shrine. Alphonsa's room, although purposefully left in its original state, was newly surrounded on all sides by a protective structure, adorned on its top windows with a large stained-glass portrait of the saintly Sister.

This practice of preserving the personal items of a holy person is not unlike the tradition of establishing secular museums for famous people of recent history. Other Malayali candidates for sainthood also have museums with personal artifacts available for public perusal. European Christian saints from recent history typically have museums erected in their name, as well (Nolan and Nolan 1989: 224–25). For Hindu holy figures such as Vivekananda, Shankaracharya, and Sri Narayana Guru, similar places of commemoration have been established throughout India.

36. Another argument could also be made, not without a few snags, that would construct Sr. Alphonsa as an embodiment of calamity for those who perceive her as an antidote against encroaching Western materialistic excesses. From this perspective, we could view Alphonsa, a nun in Roman habit, as one who simultaneously represents things Western while acting as their antidote. Nonetheless, the importance of her life of suffering or asceticism (not her "Westernness") remains central for those who accept her as an antidote to "Western" material excess. In this light, her identity is constructed as a symbolic embodiment or model of holy living to be emulated rather than calamity to be cured.

37. As noted by Farmer, an "unexpected" byproduct of Apollonia's cult is the naming of a dentist's quarterly out of Boston "The Apollonian" (1992: 28).

Another important manifestation of Christian suffering that stands as antidote to suffering emerges in the many contemporary Jesus-centered cult shrines found throughout Europe. As described by Nolan and Nolan, the healing relics established in these shrines are overwhelmingly represented by "Relics of the Passion," including "pieces of the True Cross, nails from the Cross, thorns from the Crown of Thorns, rods from the beating, garments worn during the Passion, earth soaked with Holy Blood spilled during the Crucifixion, and the famous shroud of Turin" (1989: 176). Furthermore, although early Christian crucifixes typically show a "triumphant" figure with no apparent signs of pain, the crucifixes that are given cult status are almost uniformly those dated from the Renaissance and the Catholic Reformation, which features Jesus in agony or dead upon the cross (188).

38. For a description and explanation of St. Jude's rise to fame in the United States from a position of virtual obscurity to towering strength, seemingly overnight, see Orsi (1996). Consistent with this discussion of the melding of calamity and cure, at different points in his book Orsi refers to Judas as Jude's mirror image, a polarity that sometimes loses its definition and infuses Jude with fearsome, unwieldy qualities. As benign as the officially constructed saint may be, his devotees seem to have a certain respect for the negative potential wrought by engagement with his tremendous yet vulnerable power (99–100, 114–18, 209).

39. Proponents of an ascetic life would undoubtedly argue that emulation of Alphonsa (for instance) through devotion likewise offers a transformation of sorts. The transformation occurring here, however, would be spiritual rather than material. In any case, Alphonsa as model of and for spiritual giftedness—as opposed to deprivation—does not apply to the present discussion of calamity management.

40. Taussig's reference to a Western "classical" tradition, I assume, infers the existence of a "nonclassical" tradition in Europe and North America—one not necessariy sharing the same yearning for harmony and so on.

41. Bakhtin makes a similar case when he describes the carnival atmosphere that surrounds popular religious events in which "blood is transformed into wine; ruthless slaughter and the martyr's death are transformed into a merry banquet. Bloodshed, dismemberment, burning, death, beatings, blows, curses and abuses all these elements are steeped in 'merry time'" (1968: 211). Furthermore, somewhat like Taussig and Schneider, Bakhtin argues that the dominant "new official culture" attempts to bring an end to this kind of ambivalent symbolism, as it contains "a tendency toward the stability and completion of being, toward one single meaning, one single tone of seriousness" (101).

Chapter 4

1. Kieckhefer and Bond's (1988) edited volume, *Sainthood: Its Manifestations in World Religions*, grapples with the category from a variety of religious perspectives. As such, most of the articles dealing with non-Christian traditions do not assume an easy transfer of the term "saint." A number of the essays, along with the preface to the book, work out conceptions of sainthood and then apply this to their respective traditions rather than simply imposing or assuming a preexisting label.

2. Although the process of canonizing Christian saints was once a local affair that reflected popular inclination and faith—similar to Hindu recognition of extraordinary holiness—it became increasingly formalized and formulaic and, by the year 1234, came entirely under the jurisdiction of the Vatican (Delooz 1983: 199). For a more detailed description of the twelfth-century period when the process of canonization definitively moved away from a secular, local process to one controlled by the papacy, see Kemp (1945).

3. For a description of these and other similar modes of female holiness, see Wadley (1993: 124); Ojha (1981); and Denton (1991).

4. Some recognized holy women within the Hindu tradition have been wives and even mothers who became renunciates in spite of their householder status. Anandamayi Ma of Bengal, for instance, was married but lived a celibate life with a husband who viewed her as his guru and the goddess incarnate. Those who depict Anandamayi Ma as living out the normative *pativratā* lifestyle (although this is difficult to argue, since her husband eventually had to feed her instead of vice versa) seem to do so in order that she appear less deviant in the face of traditional expectations.

5. The exception to this, of course, is the *satīmātā*, who remains faithful to her role as devoted wife by burning herself on her husband's funeral pyre. Representing, for some, the culmination of the *pativratā* role, she is singled out for achieving superhuman status and is thus worthy of devotion (see Harlan 1992).

6. In his study of gender and renunciation, Kinsley (1981) reasons that famous female *bhaktas'* abandonment of domesticity has to do with the incompatibility of a woman's *dharma*, or social duty as a *pativratā*, with this kind of fervent, world-denying religiosity. The former, socially acceptable, lifestyle must be forfeited—and with it often goes safety and comfort— in order that the latter religiosity can flourish. It is interesting, however, that a similar argument about the separation of householder *dharma* and extreme devotion does not always apply to male *bhaktas*. There are many cases in which famous male *bhakta* poets live out their fervent devotion while residing comfortably at home with their family. For instance, Jnanadev, the male *bhakta* and founder of the Warkari Panth, a Maharashtrian *bhakti* movement, wrote extensively in support of combining the lifestyles of the *bhakta* devotee and householder. Hagiography figures him to be the son of a Brahman sannyasi who dared to return to his position as householder and, as a result, altered the status of his family to that of outcast. In expiation for their sins, both of Jnanadev's parents committed suicide in the Ganges, leaving him, his brother, and his sister orphaned at an early age (Ranade 1983: 33; Kher 1979: 60; Zelliot 1987b: 41).

An example of a case in which the mixing of *bhakti* devotion and male *dharma* resulted, from the wife's perspective, in catastrophe, is in the life of Tukaram, one of the most beloved of Maharashtrian *bhakta* "saints" (Zelliot 1987a: 93). An understanding of Tukaram's home situation as catastrophic, the result of his devotional wanderings and consequent unemployment, is bolstered by the loss of his son to malnutrition and both his parents to poverty and disease. Rather than viewing these calamities in a negative light, however, Tukaram saw them as opportunities to grow closer to God through suffering and detachment to earthly ties. Skeptical of her husband's zeal for suffering, Tukaram's wife viewed the "good life" of male *bhaktas* who spend their days chattering about religion as akin to "saying good-bye to shame" (Ranade 1983: 272). R. D. Ranade, a present-day Warkari devotee and scholar, clearly does not sympathize with the complaints of the sole survivor of Tukaram's household. In reference to the *bhakta's* response (or lack thereof) to his wife's complaints, Ranade comments that he "suffered all these things in patience" (264).

7. Ojha argues that the renunciative life led by a widow should not be confused with the performance of renunciative asceticism per se. A widow does not give up her *strī dharma* but maintains it through her austerities, whereas a female renunciate necessarily abandons her *strī dharma* (Ojha 1981: 255).

8. I found, with a few exceptions, that events in Alphonsa's life as related by elderly nuns and family members who knew her did not differ consistently or widely from hagiographical accounts. It is difficult to gauge, of course, to what extent people altered their perceptions over time, in accordance with the written material. Professionally produced cassettes, which occasionally contain songs with hagiographical (as opposed to devotional) material, also include many of the same themes reiterated below.

9. The literacy rate in Kerala is around 90 percent, well above the rest of India. Those who do not take up a copy of Alphonsa's hagiography therefore do so more out of a sense of priority (that is, they believe that her power is more important than her story) than with their inability to read.

10. For the most part, Chacko's use of first-person quotes attributed to Alphonsa are surmises based on his interviews with people in whom she confided—primarily, her confessor, the Mother Superior, and a select few of the Clarist nuns—as well as borrowings from her own writings.

11. Although Chacko mentions Alphonsa's desire to become a saint as occurring during different periods in her life, this wish is also emphatically expressed in Alphonsa's own letters to her confessor. I discuss below the tension inherent in the life of a woman who simultaneously strives for nothingness yet, at the same time, for recognized sainthood.

12. Annamma, Alphonsa's stepmother-aunt, died shortly before this ceremony.

13. In this study of *bhakti* saints and the ways they challenge normative moral codes, Hawley concludes that these practitioners adhere to their own "ethical logic that demands more, rather than less, from those who come under their spell" (1987: 66). For this reason he considers these individuals as not discarding but supplementing religious and social expectation, or *dharma*, by adhering to a *bhakti dharma* of their own.

14. For further discussion of the distinction between Indian martial and sacrificial epics, see Blackburn and Flueckiger (1989).

15. Regarding the motif of supernatural birth, hinted at by Alphonsa's hagiography, Blackburn found that it often replaced the theme of deification-by-death in cases when a hero or heroine increased in supernatural status and whose localized cult became one with a wider appeal (1989: 21–22). From this perspective, the hero or heroine's divine status is established from the very beginning rather than at the end of his or her life.

16. There are, of course, exceptions to this trend. Catherine Newman, an early twentieth-century German mystic, is best known for her Friday episodes, when she would physically and mentally live through Jesus' Passion, receiving a fresh stigmata each week. The life of this German laywoman was brought to my attention by a retired priest who felt that Alphonsa's life story was "not particularly Indian," as it reminded him of Catherine Newman's (see also Dempsey forthcoming).

17. Mariam Thresia's story is a fascinating one, worthy of further study. This more dramatically lived life, however, does not seem to have the same kind of devotional appeal as that of the simple suffering Alphonsa. As a result—and perhaps for other reasons unknown to me—Mariam Thresia's cult following is not nearly as thriving as Alphonsa's.

18. Although she produces an argument different from Stace's, Evelyn Underhill draws a similar distinction between the European Christian mystical traditions and those of the "Oriental traditions." She contracts the Christian mystic's goal of union with God with the similar aims of Sufi mystics and Buddhist practitioners by arguing that the aim of the latter two is for the self to be completely absorbed in the Divine. Christian mysticism, she posits, stops short of this complete absorption and the resultant annihilation of self (1930: 170–71).

19. For the difference between the tantric ascetic whose aim is to become the deity and the *bhakti* devotee who worships the deity, see Coburn (1991: 171).

20. For further discussion of yoga as mystic union, see Chattopadhyay (1987: 249) and Katz (1978: 57–58).

21. For further discusson of *samādhi*, see Denton (1991: 225–31).

22. The fact that there are far more male saints than female has been attributed to the fact, among others, that accepted male roles earn them recognition through their public visibility. Female saints, on the other hand, traditionally live lives of relative seclusion and anonymity, which lessens their chances for recognition (Mooney 1990: 15; Schulenburg 1978). Mooney also notes that although women's religious roles have become increasingly public during the last century, the women who are considered by the Vatican for canonization continue to reflect antiquated notions of women and their role in society (1990: 25).

23. See also Goodich (1981: 23).

24. This reversal of worldly standards and the special place it carves out for women can be seen most expressly in the *bhakti* movement in India. For mention of this dynamic, see Ramanujan (1983) and Wadley (1993: 123). For a North American example of this

phenomenon, see Braude's (1989) description of women's roles during the Second Great Awakening, especially in the Spiritualist movement.

25. Nandy similarly discusses Western sexual stereotypes and their perceived relevance to the colonial-colonized dynamic in India. According to Nandy, it "produced a cultural consensus in which political and socio-economic dominance symbolized the dominance of men and masculinity over women and femininity" (1983: 4). For a more general discussion of the conflation of the nondominant "other" and the "feminine," see Doniger (1996: 538–42).

26. The fact that three out of the seven Malayali candidates for sainthood are women is somewhat representative of a larger trend. Historically, the ratio of female to male saints has been a little more than one for every five (22 per cent) (Weinstein and Bell 1982: 220). On the other hand, over half of the women who have been canonized between the years 1000 and 1987 were canonized during the twentieth century, which means that there have been approximately three women for every five men canonized this century. Mooney attributes this shift to the fact that there has been a growing number of nuns (likely candidates for sainthood) in comparison with priests and brothers during the last several decades (Mooney 1990: 15–16, 19). In Kerala, where there are approximately 30,000 nuns and only 7,000 priests and brothers, the ratio of female to male religious offers an extreme example of this Churchwide phenomenon and contributes to the significant portion of women being considered for canonization.

I also argue that the Catholic Church's heightened emphasis against modernism in the past century played an additional role in supporting the likelihood of female saints, especially those depicted in traditional roles. For a discussion of the feminization of the antimodernist Catholic Church in nineteenth-century France—displayed by such phenomena as an almost exclusively female churchgoing population and an increase in Marian devotion—and its associated valorization of female attributes displayed by Thérèse of Lisieux, see Pope (1988). See also Bruneau (1998: 16–17).

27. Mariam Thresia (1876–1926), known for her dramatic supernatural experiences, is also honored as the main foundress of the Holy Family Congregation. Compelled to work with the poor and the sick as a young woman, she broke with societal norms by venturing off alone into other people's homes to offer aid and consolation. A house was eventually built for her with the help of local priests and the Hindu raja. Like-minded women joined her and, from this small group, the new religious order was established.

Mother Euphrasia (1877–1952) also performed mortifications and took on her many sufferings and illnesses as a means to become closer to God. Aside from her strict ascetic discipline, Mother Euphrasia is known for being the Mother Superior of the Thrissur Carmelites.

28. Newman (1995) describes in more detail the ways in which the fourth-century promotion of virile womanhood was rearticulated in the thirteenth through fifteenth centuries.

29. Mukta, in her prologue, describes a very different reaction to Mira Bai among Rajasthanis. On the basis of interviews, she found that "the public humiliation that Mira had inflicted on collective honor meant that her name could not be evoked without rubbing salt on an old wound" (1994: 1). She does not mention, however, whether or not this humiliation was felt by men, women, or both. Mukta does offer a detailed description of the many ways—social, political, and otherwise—in which Mira Bai defied her expected *dharma* as a sixteenth-century Rajput woman (49–66).

30. A. K. Ramanujan notes that whereas male *bhakti* practitioners often take on the role of guru, women rarely do. Although their poetry may be well respected and widely recited, these women normally shun the public interaction typically required of *gurus* (1983: 324).

Moreover, the widely revered Anandamayi Ma, although commonly surrounded by disciples, tried to distance herself from the role of guru by insisting that she was not at all versed in scriptures. After founding twenty-eight ashrams, charitable hospitals, schools, and dispensaries, Anandamayi Ma still referred to herself, at the age of eighty-six, as "a small child" (Halstrom 1999: 185–86).

31. In a similar vein, the writings and activities of Christian female mystics, including Sr. Alphonsa, are typically mediated by male confessor priests.

32. From the perspective of Fredric Jameson (1981), as mentioned in chapter 3, such aphorisms of reversal would be typical of "folk" expressions of dreamed resolutions to perceived problems. Again, I would argue that these expressions of dreamed resolutions indeed act as a diagnostic for troubled relations, but they do not necessarily involve "the folk."

33. This is not to say that, within Christian cultures, the path of a good wife—or any "good" woman for that matter—does not include similar expectations for "ascetic" behavior such as silent suffering, restraint, and modesty. The differences between these expectations and those prescribed for the Hindu *pativratā* do emerge, however, in the associations normative Hinduism makes between the self-controlled *pativratā* and her *śakti* power. Institutionally recognized ascetic power—however informal—within Christian traditions, on the other hand, has not historically been associated with the married "householder" (as opposed to convent) woman.

34. For another example in which suffering is given particular value for the creation of women's self-identity, see Grima (1992) and her study of Paxtum women's performance of emotion in Pakistan.

35. Narayan (1986) also discusses north Indian women's resistance to patriarchal prescription through aesthetic genres such as song or poetry.

36. In Marie-Florine Bruneau's (1998) introduction to *Women Mystics Confront the Modern World*, she assumes a similar middle position. Although highly appreciative of Bynum's work, Bruneau is also critical of what she sees as Bynum's seemingly myopic glorification of women's agency and subversion through mysticism. Although she agrees that female mystics used their practices as a form of critique, Bruneau argues that one cannot ignore the larger misogynistic context from which the women understood themselves. She drives home her point by arguing that a suffering woman "mystic," living after the Protestant Reformation and on into the nineteenth century—when mysticism was no longer valued—was reconfigured as either sick or insane. As such, the modern woman, like her medieval counterpart, was understood through the eyes of misogyny, which dictated that she suffer and which gave meaning to that suffering. Her attempts to gain power and to mold her own image must be done within the constraints of the ubiquitous "contract between the suffering woman and the men having the power to name her" (31).

37. See chapter 1, section 1 above.

38. Rosaldo and Lamphere's (1974) edited volume includes a number of articles that argue for women's ability to influence, strategize, and maintain authority from a seemingly disadvantaged position. These studies include discussions of "third-world" women as well as "first-world" ones, and primarily refer to the agency wielded within the domestic realm. See especially articles by Collier, Lamphere, Stack, and Wolf.

39. For an example of an ethnographic study exploring how North American women negotiate their place within mainstream Christianity as ordained ministers, see Lawless (1993).

40. For studies suggesting that Vatican recognition of someone like Alphonsa is somewhat unlikely, see Schulenberg (1978) and Mooney (1990), both of whom draw a direct correlation between the visibility of a person within society and the likelihood of becoming a saint.

41. A priest and seminary professor who was, at the time of Alphonsa's death, a student in a Bharananganam school, recalls similar snide comments made by the boys in his class.

Upon seeing her funeral procession pass by their window, the boys who were closest to the windows (including himself) joked that the Clarist nuns, known for their poverty and simplicity, were beautifying their dead with makeup.

42. By all accounts, the members of Alphonsa's family who were able to attend the funeral only numbered three: her elderly father, sister, and niece, Thressiamma. The relatively small number of village community members who attended the funeral probably resulted from her convent-bound lifestyle, in contrast with that of most of the other nuns, who generally spent their careers in local schools or hospitals.

43. As mentioned above, cults of early Christian saints emerged based upon the strength of popular devotion, but by the year 1234 the canonization of saints was entirely in the hands of Rome. In his discussion of this gradual historical process, Pierre Delooz notes that, since the thirteenth century, the pressure and perseverance needed for Vatican recognition and canonization is most effectively provided by religious orders (1983: 199–200).

44. "Kunyachan" literally means "little priest," a name given him because of his diminutive size. His hagiography emphasizes this aspect of his character in much the same way that Alphonsa's hagiography highlights her self-abnegation. He is also depicted in a paradoxical manner, as a tiny, unremarkable man who achieved great things.

45. The fact that Chavara's cult is related to and in some ways dependent upon Alphonsa's is suggested by its origins. It was not until 1936 (he died in 1871) that the C.M.I. Fathers considered pursuing his canonization. This decision was apparently spurred on by Alphonsa's report of her vision of Fr. Chavara and the subsequent cure of her disease (see Chacko 1986).

46. A similar situation, in which a saint is so great in the eyes of his or her devotees that he or she becomes, in a sense, inaccessible, often occurs at churches dedicated to Mary. During my stay in Kerala, I noted that many St. Mary churches had strong cults to other saints as well, and attention to these "lesser" saints often took precedence among devotees. For instance, Kottayam district's biggest cult center for St. Sebastian takes place in a St. Mary's church. Likewise, I talked with a number of people who considered the power behind the Manarkad Mary Church to emanate from a Jewish woman "saint" named Marttaśmūni (for more on Marttaśmūni, see Dempsey 1999). The fact that Mary's lofty and therefore less accessible position is much like Jesus' or God's is substantiated by a common perception expressed by Hindus who do not view her as a Christian saint but rather as a goddess counterpart to Jesus.

47. This story of Alphonsa's youthful defiance of interreligious dining restrictions was enthusiastically related to me by the vice postulator, a priest who runs Alphonsa's canonization campaign from Bharananganam. The vice postulator, proud of the "Hindu culture" from which Kerala Christians live out their tradition, is a strong advocate of interfaith cooperation and understanding.

Lakshmikutty (Alphonsa's youthful partner in "crime"), eighty-four years old in 1994 and still living in Kudamalur, attests to the strong bond of friendship she and Alphonsa enjoyed as young girls. Lakshmikutty admitted to me that although she thought Alphonsa to be a wonderful friend and brilliant student, she does not understand why she is getting so much attention today. Although Alphonsa was a holy woman in Lakshmikutty's eyes, her elderly Hindu friend does not attribute to her the "divine" status of sainthood. Nevertheless, Lakshmikutty did pray to Alphonsa for some years before going to bed at night, as well as during a difficult period in her life. Once Alphonsa appeared to her in a lightning storm; Lakshmikutty said she could recognize her. At that point she became frightened, begged Alphonsa not to do it again, and ceased praying to her.

48. Sr. Josephina's favorite means for describing this retired bishop's devotion to Alphonsa is that he prematurely—and surreptitiously—lay the cornerstone and performed the dedicatory

rite for the first church built in her honor several years back. It was necessary for him to be "sneaky," according to Sr. Josephina, as no such church building for Alphonsa was acceptable until after her beatification, which had, at that time, not yet taken place. Now the bishop proudly maintains that he was responsible for the construction of the first church dedicated to Alphonsa in all the world.

49. The healing of the Muslim boy's clubbed feet as well as a similar healing recounted below are two among three of the official miracles recognized by the Vatican after approval by a team of medical experts.

50. Bishop Valopilly was made the first bishop of Thalassery in 1953, during the postwar period when Christians and Hindus were emigrating in great numbers from the south of Kerala in order to take advantage of the cheap land up north. Large communities of Muslims were already settled in the larger towns in the north, primarily in coastal trade centers. Infested with malaria and wild animals, the inland mountainous areas that the future agriculturists tried to manage created great difficulties for them. Bishop Valopilly is now famous for his many successful efforts at getting the government and other sources of financial assistance to help the new immigrants—Hindus and Christians as well as poor Muslims. The expansive oceanside grounds where the retired bishop presently lives (with the current bishop as well as a number of seminarians, nuns, and priests) was given to him by a Brahman politician as a token of his gratitude. This happened in 1957, when the politician left for Thiruvananthapuram, Kerala's capitol, as the Marxist Party first came into power.

51. As insisted upon by Sr. Josephina, healing clubbed feet is Alphonsa's "specialty."

52. Christian saints' feast days are traditionally celebrated on the anniversary of their death.

53. The difference between Alphonsa's feast-day food and a regular *śrāddam* feast is also that the former is considered a type of *prasādam* (Hindu) or *nērcca* (Christian). People consider the food to be like holy remains from the offerings given to Alphonsa, which contain the power to heal and bless those who eat it.

54. Although many major church festivals include a grand display of fireworks after dark, like major temple festivals, Alphonsa's festival kept to the basics. Located in the corner of the church compound was a canonlike contraption from which explosives intermittently sounded throughout the days and evenings of the festival, particularly during the last two days.

Conclusion

1. For an in-depth philosophical exploration of saintly ethics and their implications for postmodernism, see Wyschogrod (1990).

2. In a Syracuse Barnes and Noble bookstore, I recently found a special section dedicated to angel publications in which I counted eighty books on the subject, the vast majority of which have been published since 1990. Harold Bloom (1996) writes about current representations of angelic beings, attributing their popularity—along with an intensified interest in the meaning of dreams and near-death experiences—to the nearing of the millennium. Bloom is not surprised by this current belief in the mediation of angels and explains that it is a part of a larger tendency among North Americans—Protestants, Catholics, and Jews, alike—to approach religion in a pragmatic manner (76). Bloom compares this pragmatic tendency with what he considers to be a European emphasis upon doctrinal or orthodox religiosity. He thus ignores the increasing popularity of pilgrimage and the performance of vows throughout Catholic Europe—to name only two manifestations of a pragmatic approach. Unlike Bloom, I find it difficult to identify North American religiosity as significantly more or less practice-oriented than European religiosity, particularly in Catholic Europe.

3. The proliferation of angel experiences and appreciation in North America is paralleled to some extent by a similar interest in saints. Recently written books in appreciation of saints seem to give them characteristics more like benign angels than like the complex saints of popular devotion. For instance, Michael Finley, author of *Everybody Has a Guardian Angel*, recently wrote *Heavenly Helpers, St. Anthony and St. Jude: Amazing True Stories of Answered Prayers* (1996) in a format typical of many contemporary angel books, where he recounts the modern-day miracles of heavenly helpers.

4. This is the same sermon that was quoted in chapter 4, section 3, above.

5. Robert Orsi displays an in-between position somewhat like Dubisch's when he opens his book about St. Jude with his own story of an anxious plea and its answer. This time, the vehicle of concern is an airplane rather than a truck and the vow is (appropriately for this saint) public acknowledgment rather than shrine offering. Placing his anecdote of saintly rescue at the end of his 'Acknowledgments,' he writes, "I am not a devout, but I promised to tell this story at the time, and here it is" (1996: xxi). Stephanie Kane not only identifies her kind of fieldwork as requiring a leap of imagination between the known and unknown realms, but claims that the ensuing transformative process "lends authenticity to the ethnographer's voice" (1994: 18–19).

6. Dubisch likewise writes about the inseparability of the material and the spiritual realms within parts of Greek culture. From this perspective, she argues that it is therefore "reasonable to expect that one can call upon spiritual beings to help with the concerns of everyday life" (1995: 89–90).

7. In his introductory remarks about growing up in a culturally eclectic family, Kwame Appiah relates the "wholeness" of his hybridity: "If my sisters and I were 'children of two worlds,' no one bothered to tell us this; we lived in one world, in two 'extended' families divided by several thousand miles and an allegedly insuperable cultural distance that never, so far as I can recall, puzzled or perplexed us much. As I grew older, and went to an English boarding school, I learned that not everybody had a family in Africa and in Europe; not everyone had a Lebanese uncle, American and French and Kenyan and Thai cousins. And by now, now that my sisters have married a Norwegian and a Nigerian and a Ghanaian, now that I live in America, I am used to seeing the world as a network of points of affinity" (vii).

References

Abu-Lughod, Lila. 1993. *Writing Women's Worlds: Bedouin Stories*. Berkeley and Los Angeles: University of California Press.

Ahmad, Aijaz. 1992. "*Orientalism* and After: Ambivalence and Metropolitan Location in the Work of Edward Said." In *Theory: Classes, Nations, Literatures*, edited by Aijaz Ahmad. Delhi: Oxford University Press, 159–219.

Amritaswarupananda, Swami. 1993. *Mata Amritanandamayi: Life and Experiences of Devotees*. Kollam, Kerala: Mata Amritanandamayi Mission Trust.

Appiah, Kwame Anthony. 1992. *In My Father's House: Africa in the Philosophy of Culture*. New York: Oxford University Press.

Arayathinal, Thomas, M.O.L. 1953. *A Short History of Irapuzhai or Aruvithurai Church*. Erattupetta: St. Thomas Mission League, Aruvithurai.

Asad, Talal. 1993. *Genealogies of Religion: Discipline and Reasons of Power in Christianity and Islam*. Baltimore: Johns Hopkins University Press.

———. 1996. "Modern Power and the Reconfiguration of Religious Traditions." Interview by Saba Mahmood. *Stanford Electronic Humanities Review* 5/1: Contested Polities, n.p.

Badone, Ellen. 1990a. "Introduction." In *Religious Orthodoxy and Popular Faith in European Society*, edited by Ellen Badone. Princeton: Princeton University Press, 3–23.

———. 1990b. "Breton Folklore and Anticlericalism." In *Religious Orthodoxy and Popular Faith in European Society*, edited by Ellen Badone. Princeton: Princeton University Press, 140–163.

Bakhtin, M. M. 1968. *Rabalais and His World*. Translated by Helen Iswolsky. Cambridge: M.I.T. Press.

———. 1981. *The Dialogic Imagination: Four Essays by M. M. Bakhtin*. Edited by Michael Holquist; translated by Caryl Emerson and Michael Holquist. Austin: University of Texas Press.

Bauman, Richard. 1986. *Story, Performance and Event: Contextual Studies of Oral Narrative*. Cambridge: Cambridge University Press.

Bayly, Susan. 1984. "Hindu Kingship and the Origin of Community: Religion, State and Society in Kerala, 1750–1850." *Modern Asian Studies* 18: 177–213.

———. 1989. *Saints, Goddesses and Kings: Muslims and Christians in South Indian Society, 1700–1900*. Cambridge: Cambridge University Press.

Beck, Brenda. 1971. "Mariamman: The Vacillating Goddess." University of British Columbia. Manuscript.

Bhabha, Homi. 1985. "Signs Taken for Wonders: Questions of Ambivalence and Authority under a Tree outside Delhi." *Critical Inquiry* 12: 145–65.

Bharati, Agehananda. 1968. "Great Tradition and Little Tradition: An Anthropological Approach to the Study of Some Asian Cultures." In *Anthropology and Adult Education*, edited by Th. Cummings. Boston: Center for Continuing Education, 72–94.

———. 1970. "The Hindu Renaissance and Its Apologetic Patterns." *Journal of Asian Studies* 29: 267–88.

Blackburn, Stuart H. 1985. "Death and Deification: Folk Cults in Hinduism." *History of Religions* 24: 255–74.

———. 1989. "Patterns of Development for Indian Oral Epics." In *Oral Epics in India*, edited by Stuart H. Blackburn, Peter J. Claus, Joyce B. Flueckiger, and Susan S. Wadley. Berkeley and Los Angeles: University of California Press, 15–32.

Blackburn, Stuart H., and Joyce Flueckiger. 1989. "Introduction." In *Oral Epics in India*, edited by Stuart H. Blackburn, Peter J. Claus, Joyce B. Flueckiger, and Susan S. Wadley. Berkeley and Los Angeles: University of California Press, 1–11.

Bloom, Harold. 1996. *Omens of Millennium: The Gnosis of Angels, Dreams, and Resurrection.* New York: Riverhead Press.

Bolton, Brenda. 1978. "Vitae Matrum: A Further Aspect of Frauenfrage." In *Medieval Women*, edited by Derek Baker. Oxford: Basil Blackwell, 253–73.

Bondurant, Joan Valerie. 1958. *Conquest of Violence: The Gandhian Philosophy of Conflict.* Princeton: Princeton University Press.

Braude, Ann. 1989. *Radical Spirits: Spiritualism and Women's Rights in Nineteenth-Century America.* Boston: Beacon Press.

Brettell, Caroline. 1990. "The Priest and His People and the Contractual Basis for Religious Practice in Rural Portugal." In *Religious Orthodoxy and Popular Faith in European Society*, edited by Ellen Badone. Princeton: Princeton University Press, 55–75.

Brooke, Rosalind, and Christopher Brooke. 1984. *Popular Religion in the Middle Ages: Western Europe, 1000–1300.* London: Thames and Hudson.

Brooks, E. W. 1895. "Acts of St. George." *Le Museon*, 38: 67–115.

Brown, Karen McCarthy. 1991. *Mama Lola: A Vodou Priestess in Brooklyn.* Berkeley and Los Angeles: University of Calfornia Press.

Brown, Peter. 1981. *The Cult of Saints: Its Rise and Function in Late Christianity.* Chicago: University of Chicago Press.

Brubaker, Richard. 1979. "Barbers, Washermen and Other Priests: Servants of the South Indian Village and Its Goddess." *History of Religions* 19: 128–52.

Bruneau, Marie-Florine. 1998. *Women Mystics Confront the Modern World: Marie de l'Incaration (1599–1672) and Madame Guyon (1648–1717).* Albany: SUNY Press.

Bureau of Economics and Statistics, Government of Kerala. 1969. "Percentage Distribution of Christian Population in Kerala, 1968." *Report on the Socio-Economic Survey on Castes/Communities, Kerala, 1968.* Trivandrum, 6–10.

Burke, Peter. 1994. *Popular Culture in Early Modern Europe.* 2nd ed. Hants, England: Scholars Press.

Butler, Alban. 1985. *Butler's Lives of Saints.* Edited by Michael Walsh. San Francisco: Harper and Row.

Bynum, Caroline Walker. 1987. *Holy Feast and Holy Fast.* Berkeley and Los Angeles: University of California Press.

———. 1991. *Fragmentation and Redemption: Essays on Gender and the Body in Medieval Religion.* New York: Zone Books.

Campbell, Joseph. [1959] 1968. *The Masks of God: Oriental Mythology.* Volume 2. New York: Viking Press.

Carroll, Michael. 1992. *Madonnas that Maim: Popular Catholicism in Italy since the Fifteenth Century*. Baltimore: Johns Hopkins University Press.

———. 1996. *Veiled Threats: The Logic of Popular Catholicism in Italy*. Baltimore: Johns Hopkins University Press.

Chacko, K. C. [1948] 1990. *Sr. Alphonsa*. 6th ed. Bharananganam: Vice Postulator, Cause of Blessed Alphonsa.

———. [1959] 1986. *Blessed Kuriackos Elias Chavara*. 3rd ed. Mannanam, Kerala: Vice Postulator, Cause of Fr. Kuriackos Elias.

———. [1981] 1992. *Mother Mariam Thresia*. 2nd ed. Thrissur, Kerala: Rev. Mother Mary Benitia, C.H.F.

Chandy, Ommen. 1961. "Feast in St. George's Church, Puthupally." In *Fairs and Festivals of Kerala*, volume 7 of *Census of India*, edited by M. K. Devassy. Delhi: Manager of Publications, 230–231.

Chattopadhyay, Umandarayan. 1987. *Epic Anandamayee*. Haridwar: C. U. Chatterjee and N. K. Chatterjee.

Chengalam, Kavyan. N.d. *Alphōnsāmma Gītanga!* [Kerala]: Swaraśrī Audio Visions Audiocassette.

Christian, William. 1972. *Person and God in a Spanish Valley*. New York: Seminar Press.

———. 1981. *Local Religion in Sixteenth-Century Spain*. Princeton: Princeton University Press.

Church History Association of India. 1982–1992. *History of Christianity in India*. 5 volumes. Bangalore: Theological Publications in India.

Clifford, James. 1986. "Introduction: Partial Truths." In *Writing Culture: The Poetics and Politics of Ethnography*, edited by James Clifford and George Marcus. Berkeley and Los Angeles: University of California Press, 1–26.

———. 1988. *The Predicament of Culture: Twentieth-Century Ethnography, Literature and Art*. Cambridge: Harvard University Press, 266–76.

———. 1997. *Routes: Travel and Translation in the Late Twentieth Century*. Cambridge: Harvard University Press.

Coburn, Thomas. 1991. *Encountering the Goddess: A Translation of the Devī Māhātmya and a Study of Its Interpretation*. Albany: SUNY Press.

Cohen, Ted. 1979. "Metaphor and the Cultivation of Intimacy." In *On Metaphor*, edited by Sheldon Sacks. Chicago: University of Chicago Press, 1–10.

Collier, Jane Fishburne. 1974. "Women in Politics." In *Women, Culture and Society*, edited by Michelle Zimbalist Rosaldo and Louise Lamphere. Stanford: Stanford University Press, 89–96.

Danforth, Loring. 1989. *Firewalking and Religious Healing: The Anasternia of Greece and the American Firewalking Movement*. Princeton: Princeton University Press.

Daniel, Ruby, and Barbara Johnson. 1995. *Ruby of Cochin: An Indian Jewish Woman Remembers*. Philadelphia: Jewish Publication Society.

David, P. 1980. "Influence of Hinduism on Christianity on Mystical and Popular Level." In *Influence of Hinduism on Christianity*, edited by Gnana Robinson. Madurai: Publication Department Programme, Tamil Nadu Theological Seminary, 72–81.

Davis, Richard H. 1997. *Lives of Indian Images*. Princeton: Princeton University Press.

Delooz, Pierre. 1983. "Toward a Sociological Study of Canonized Sainthood in the Catholic Church." In *Saints and Their Cults: Studies in Religious Sociology, Folklore and History*, edited by Stephen Wilkins. Cambridge: Cambridge University Press, 189–216.

Dempsey, Corinne. 1999. "Lessons in Miracles from Kerala, South India: Stories of Three 'Christian' Saints. *History of Religions* 30: 150–176.

———. (2000). "The Religioning of Anthropology: New Directions for the Ethnographer-Pilgrim." *Culture and Religion*, 1.

Denton, Lynn Teskey. 1991. "Varieties of Hindu Female Asceticism." In *Roles and Rituals For Hindu Women*, edited by Julia Leslie. Rutherford, N.J.: Farleigh Dickenson University Press, 211–31.

Derrida, Jacques. 1981. *Dissemination*. Translated by Barbara Johnson. Chicago: University of Chicago Press.

Devlin, Judith. 1987. *The Superstitious Mind: French Peasants and the Supernatural in the Nineteenth Century*. New Haven: Yale University Press.

Doniger, Wendy. 1996. "Myths and Methods in the Dark." *Journal of Religion* 76: 531–47.

Dougal, Sonia. 1971. *The Nun Runners*. London: Hodder and Stoughton.

Dubisch, Jill. 1990. "Pilgrimage and Popular Religion at a Greek Holy Shrine." In *Religious Orthodoxy and Popular Faith in European Society*, edited by Ellen Badone. Princeton: Princeton University Press, 113–39.

———. 1995. *In a Different Place: Pilgrimage, Gender, and Politics at a Greek Island Shrine*. Princeton: Princeton University Press.

Eck, Diana L. 1981. *Darśan: Seeing the Divine Image in India*. Chambersburg, Pa.: Anima Books.

Egnor, Margaret. 1984. "The Changed Mother or What the Smallpox Goddess Did When There Was No More Smallpox." *Contributions to Asian Studies* 18: 24–45.

———. 1991. "On the Meaning of Śakti to Women in Tamil Nadu." In *The Powers of Tamil Women*, edited by Susan Snow Wadley. Foreign and Comparative Studies/South Asian Series 6. Syracuse, N.Y.: Maxwell School of Citizenship and Public Affairs, 1–34.

Elliot, Alison Goddard. 1987. *Roads to Paradise: Reading the Lives of Early Saints*. Hanover, N.H.: University Press of New England.

Erndl, Kathleen. 1993. *Victory to the Mother: The Hindu Goddess of Northwest India in Myth, Ritual, and Symbol*. New York: Oxford University Press.

Farmer, David Hugh. 1992. *The Oxford Dictionary of Saints*. Oxford: Oxford University Press.

Feldhaus, Anne. 1995. *Water and Womanhood: Religious Meaning of Water in Maharashtra*. New York: Oxford University Press.

Finley, Michael. 1996. *Heavenly Helpers, St. Anthony and St. Jude: Amazing True Stories of Answered Prayers*. New York: Crossroads.

Flannery, Austin, ed. 1981. *Vatican Council II*. Vol. 2. Collegeville, Minn.: Liturgical Press.

Flueckiger, Joyce Burkhalter. 1989. "Caste and Regional Variants in an Oral Epic Tradition." In *Oral Epics in India*, edited by Stuart H. Blackburn. Berkeley and Los Angeles: University of California Press, 33–54.

Gal, Susan. 1995. "Language and the 'Arts of Resistance.'" *Cultural Anthropology* 10: 407–24.

Geertz, Clifford. 1973a. "Religion as a Cultural System." In *The Interpretation of Cultures: Selected Essays by Clifford Geertz*. New York: Basic Books, 87–125.

———. 1973b. "Thick Description: Toward an Interpretive Theory of Culture." In *The Interpretation of Cultures*. New York: Basic Books, 3–30.

———. 1995. *After the Fact: Two Countries, Four Decades, One Anthropologist*. Cambridge: Harvard University Press.

Gerould, Gordon Hall. 1916. *Saints' Legends*. Boston: Houghton Mifflin.

Gladstone, J. W. 1984. *Protestant Christianity and People's Movements in Kerala: A Study of Christian Mass Movements in Relation to Neo-Hindu Socio-Religious Movements in Kerala, 1850–1936*. Thiruvananthapuram, Kerala: Seminary Publications.

Gold, Ann Grodzins. 1987. *Fruitful Journeys: The Ways of Rajasthani Pilgrims*. Berkeley and Los Angeles: University of California Press.

———. 1994. "Jātrā, Yātrā, and Pressing Down Pebbles: Pilgrimage within and beyond Rajasthan." In *The Idea of Rajasthan*, edited by Karine Schomer. Vol. 1. New Delhi: Manohar, 80–109.

Gold, Daniel. 1987. *The Lord as Guru: Hindi Sants in North Indian Tradition*. New York: Oxford University Press.

Goodich, Michael. 1981. "Contours of Female Piety in Later Medieval Hagiography." *Church History* 50: 20–32.

Griffiths, Bede. 1964. *Christ in India: Essays toward a Hindu-Christian Dialogue*. Springfield, Ill.: Templegate Publications.

Grima, Benedicte. 1992. *The Performance of Emotion among Paxtun Women: "The Misfortunes Which Have Befallen Me."* Austin: University of Texas Press.

Haberman, David. 1994. *Journey through the Twelve Forests: An Encounter with Krishna*. New York: Oxford University Press.

Hallstrom, Lisa Lassell. 1999. *Mother of Bliss: Ānandamayī Mā (1896–1982)*. New York: Oxford University Press.

Hanks, William F. 1986. "Authenticity and Ambivalence in the Text: A Colonial Maya Case."*American Ethnologist* 13: 721–44.

Harlan, Lindsey. 1992. *Religion and Rajput Women: The Ethic of Protection in Contemporary Narratives*. Berkeley and Los Angeles: University of California Press.

Harman, William. 1989. *The Sacred Marriage of a Hindu Goddess*. Bloomington: Indiana University Press.

Hart, George. 1973. "Woman and the Sacred in Ancient Tamilnad." *Journal of Asian Studies* 32: 233–50.

Hawley, John Stratton. 1981. *At Play with Krishna: Pilgrimage Dramas from Brindavan*. Princeton: Princeton University Press.

———. 1987. "Morality beyond Morality in the Lives of Three Hindu Saints." In *Saints and Virtues*, edited by John Stratton Hawley. Berkeley and Los Angeles: University of California Press, 52–72.

Hiltebeitel, Alf. 1988. *The Cult of Draupadi*. Vol. 1. Chicago: University of Chicago Press.

Hole, Christina. 1965. *Saints in Folklore*. New York: M. Barrows.

Hudson, D. Dennis. 1977. "Śiva, Mīnākṣi, Viṣṇu—Reflections on a Popular Myth in Madurai." *Indian Economic and Social History Review* 14: 107–18.

———. 1982. "Two Citrā Festivals in Madurai." In *Religious Festivals in South India and Sri Lanka*, edited by Guy Welborn and Glen Yocum. New Delhi: Manohar, 101–56.

———. 1996. "Trivikrama's Prasasti (c. 753–754)." Manuscript.

Inden, Ronald. 1986. "Orientalist Constructions of India." *Modern Asian Studies* 20: 401–46.

———. 1990. *Imagining India*. Oxford: Basil Blackwell.

Jameson, Fredric. 1981. *The Political Unconscious: Narrative as a Socially Symbolic Act*. Ithaca, N.Y.: Cornell University Press.

John, K. J. 1981. *Christian Heritage of Kerala*. Cochin: Xavier Press.

John Paul II. 1998. *Fides et Ratio (Faith and Reason)*. Encyclical Letter, 14 September.

Johnson, Elizabeth. 1998. *Friends of God and Prophets: A Feminist Theological Reading of the Communion of Saints*. New York: Continuum.

Joseph, Perumal. 1993. *Mār Gīvarugīs Sahadāyuṭe Jīvacaritram*. Pandalam, Kerala: K.V. Book Depot.

Kane, Stephanie C. 1994. *The Phantom Gringo Boat: Shamanic Discourse and Development in Panama*. Washington: Smithsonian Institute Press.

Karayil, Antony, C.M.I. 1995. *Church and Society in Kerala: A Sociological Study*. New Delhi: Intercultural Publications.

Katz, Stephen. 1978. "Language, Epistemology, and Mysticism." In *Mysticism and Philosophical Analysis*, edited by Stephen Katz. New York: Oxford University Press, 22–74.

Keen, Sam. 1986. *Faces of the Enemy: Reflections of the Hostile Imagination*. San Francisco: Harper and Row.

Kemp, Eric W. 1945. "Pope Alexander III and the Canonization of Saints." *Transactions of the Royal Historical Society* 4. Vol. 27. London: Offices of the Royal Historical Society, 13–28.

Khandelwal, Meena. 1996. "Walking a Tightrope: Saintliness, Gender and Power in an Ethnographic Encounter." *Anthropology and Humanism* 21: 111– 134.

Kher, B.G. 1979. "Maharashtrian Women Saints." In *Women Saints: East and West*, edited by Swami Ghananand and John Stewart-Wallace. Hollywood, Cal.: Vedanta Press, 58–63.

Kieckhefer, Richard. 1984. *Unquiet Souls: Fourteenth-Century Saints and Their Religious Milieux.* Chicago: University of Chicago Press.

Kieckhefer, Richard, and George D. Bond, eds. 1988. *Sainthood: Its Manifestations in World Religions.* Berkeley and Los Angeles: University of California Press.

Kinsley, David. 1981. "Devotion as an Alternative to Marriage in the Lives of Some Hindu Women Devotees." In *Tradition and Modernity and Bhakti Movements*, edited by Jayant Lele. Leiden: Brill, 83–93.

Kirven, Robert, H. 1994. *Angels in Action: What Swedenborg Saw and Heard.* West Chester, Pa.: Chrysalis Books.

Klaniczay, Gabor. 1990. *Uses of Supernatural Power: The Transformation of Popular Religion in Medieval and Early-Modern Europe.* Translated by Susan Singerman, edited by Karen Margolis. Princeton: Princeton University Press.

Koilparampil, George. 1982. *Caste in the Catholic Community in Kerala: A Study of Caste Elements in the Inter Rite Relationships of Syrians and Latins.* Ernakulam, Kerala: St. Francis De Sales Press.

Kokosalakis, Nikos. 1987. "The Political Significance of Popular Religion in Greece." *Archives de Sciences Sociales des Religions.* 64: 37–52.

Kothari, Komal. 1989. "Performers, Gods, and Heroes in the Oral Epics of Rajasthan." In *Oral Epics in India*, edited by Stuart Blackburn, Peter Claus, Joyce Flueckiger, and Susan Wadley. Berkeley and Los Angeles: University of California Press, 102–17.

Kumar, Nita. 1988. *The Artisans of Banaras: Popular Culture and Identity, 1880–1986.* Princeton: Princeton University Press.

———. 1992. *Friends, Brothers, and Informants: Fieldwork Memoirs of Banaras.* Berkeley and Los Angeles: University of California Press.

Kuriedath, Jose. 1989. *Authority in the Catholic Community in Kerala.* Bangalore: Dharmaram Publishers.

Lamphere, Louise. 1974. "Strategies, Cooperation, and Conflict among Women in Domestic Groups." In *Women, Culture, and Society*, edited by Michelle Zimbalist Rosaldo and Louise Lamphere. Stanford, Cal.: Stanford University Press, 97–112.

Langford, Jean. 1995. "Ayurvedic Interiors: Person, Space and Episteme in Three Medical Practices." *Cultural Anthropology* 10: 330–36.

Lawless, Elaine. 1993. *Holy Women, Wholly Women: Sharing Ministries through Life Stories and Reciprocal Ethnography.* Philadelphia: University of Pennsylvania Press.

Lisieux, Thérèse of. 1957. *The Story of a Soul: The Autobiography of St. Thérèse of Lisieux.* Translated by John Beevers. New York: Image Books.

Lopez, Donald S., Jr. 1998. *Prisoners of Shangri-La: Tibetan Buddhism and the West.* Chicago: University of Chicago Press.

McDaniel, June. 1989. *The Madness of the Saints: Ecstatic Religion in Bengal.* Chicago: University of Chicago Press.

McDannell, Colleen. 1995. *Material Christianity: Religion and Popular Culture in America.* New Haven: Yale University Press.

McGee, Mary. 1996. "Regimens of Domestic Asceticism in Hindu Traditions." Paper read at Ascetic Impulse in Religious Life and Culture Group and Comparative Studies in

"Hinduisms" and "Judaisms" Consultation, American Academy of Religion annual meeting, New Orleans, 24 November.

McNamara, JoAnne. 1991. "The Need to Give: Suffering and Female Sanctity in the Middle Ages." In *Images of Sainthood in Medieval Europe*, edited by Renate Blumfeld-Kosinski and Timea Szell. Ithaca, N.Y.: Cornell University Press.

Marcus, George E., and Michael M. J. Fischer. 1986. *Anthropology as Cultural Critique: An Experimental Moment in the Human Sciences.* Chicago: University of Chicago Press.

Marglin, Frederique Apffel. 1985. "Female Sexuality in the Hindu World." In *Immaculate and Powerful: The Female in Sacred Image and Social Reality*, edited by Clarissa Atkinson, Constance Buchanon, and Margaret Miles. Boston: Beacon, 9–60.

Margolies, Malcolm B. 1994. *A Gathering of Angels: Angels in Jewish Life and Literature.* New York: Ballantine.

Mathew, C. P., and M. M. Thomas. 1967. *The Indian Churches of St. Thomas.* Delhi: Indian Society Promoting Christian Knowledge.

Mathew, Thomas. 1961. "St. Mary's Forane Church, Bharananganam." In *Fairs and Festivals of Kerala.* Volume 7 of *Census of India*, edited by M. K. Devassy, 178–81.

Mitchell, Timothy. 1988. *Violence and Piety in Spanish Folklore.* Philadelphia: University of Pennsylvania Press.

Mohanty, Chandra Talpade. 1994. "Under Western Eyes." In *Colonial Discourse and Post-Colonial Theory: A Reader*, edited by Patrick Williams and Laura Chrisman. New York: Columbia University Press.

Mooney, Catherine. 1990. *Philippine Duchesne: A Woman with the Poor.* New York: Paulist Press.

Moosa, Matti. 1981. "Nestorian Church." In *The Encyclopedia of Religion*, edited by Mircea Eliade. New York: Macmillan, 369–72.

Mukerji, Bithika. 1989. "Sri Anandamayi Ma: Divine Play of the Spiritual Journey." In *Hindu Spirituality: Vedas through Vedanta*, edited by Krishna Sirraman. New York: Crossroads, 392–413.

Mukta, Parita. 1994. *Upholding the Common Life: The Community of Mirabai.* Delhi: Oxford University Press.

Nandy, Ashis. 1983. *The Intimate Enemy: Loss and Recovery of Self under Colonialism.* Delhi: Oxford University Press.

———. 1987. *Traditions, Tyranny and Utopias: Essays in the Politics of Awareness.* Delhi: Oxford University Press.

Narayan, Kirin. 1986. "Birds on a Branch: Girlfriends and Wedding Songs in Kangra." *Ethos* 14: 47–75.

———. 1993. "How Native is a 'Native' Anthropologist?" *American Anthropologist* 95: 671–86.

Narayana Rao, Velchuru. 1986. "Epics and Ideologies: Six Telugu Folk Epics." In *Another Harmony: New Essays on the Folklore of India*, edited by A. K. Ramanujan and Stuart Blackburn. Berkeley and Los Angeles: University of California Press, 131–64.

Nedungatt, George, S.J. 1986. "A Language India Understands." *The Passion Flower: Beatification Special.* Palai: St. Thomas Press.

Neill, Stephen. 1984. *A History of Christianity in India: The Beginnings to AD 1707.* Vol. 1. London: Cambridge University Press.

———. 1985. *A History of Christianity in India: 1707–1858.* Vol. 2. Cambridge: Cambridge University Press.

Newman, Barbara. 1990. "Flaws in the Golden Bowl: Gender and Spiritual Formation in the Twelfth Century." *Traditio: Studies in Ancient and Medieval History, Thought and Religion* 45: 111–46.

————. 1995. *From Virile Woman to WomanChrist: Studies in Medieval Religion and Literature*. Philadelphia: University of Pennsylvania Press.

Nolan, Mary Lee, and Sidney Nolan. 1989. *Christian Pilgrimage in Modern Western Europe*. Chapel Hill: University of North Carolina Press.

Nye, Malory. 1999. "Religion Is Religioning? Anthropology and the Cultural Study of Religion." *Scottish Journal of Religions Studies* 20: 193–234.

O'Flaherty, Wendy Doniger. 1976. *The Origins of Evil in Hindu Mythology*. Berkeley and Los Angeles: University of California Press.

Ojha, Catherine. 1981. "Feminine Asceticism in Hinduism." *Man in India* 61: 254–81.

Orsi, Robert. 1996. *Thank You St. Jude: Women's Devotion to the Patron Saint of Hopeless Causes*. New Haven: Yale University Press.

Ortner, Sherry B. 1995. "Resistance and the Problem of Ethnographic Refusal." *Comparative Study of Society and History* 37: 173–93.

P. L., Salomi. 1992. "Sister Alphonsa of Bharananganam." Masters thesis. University of Madras.

Pallickaparampil, Joseph. 1991. *V. Gīvarggīs Sahadāyuṭe Novēna*. Aruvithura: Cherupushpa Mission League.

Panachicken, Michael. (n.d.) *Alphōnsāmma: Kristīyabhakadigānaṅgaḷ*. [Bharananganam, Kerala]: The Alphonsa Centre, Audiocassette.

Pandey, Gyanendra. 1990. *The Construction of Communalism in Colonial North India*. Delhi: Oxford University Press.

Parry, Benita. 1994. "Resistance Theory/Theorising Resistance or Two Cheers for Nativism." In *Colonial Discourse/Postcolonial Theory*, edited by Francis Barker, Peter Hulme, and Margaret Iversen. Manchester: Manchester University Press, 172–96.

Pearson, Anne MacKenzie. 1996. *"Because It Gives Me Peace of Mind": Ritual Fasts in the Religious Lives of Hindu Women*. Albany: SUNY Press.

Pillai, A. N. R. n.d. *Sister Alphonsamma*. Ragini Audio Cassettes.

Pope, Barbara Corrado. 1988. "A Heroine without Heroics: The Little Flower of Jesus and Her Times." *Church History* 57: 47–60.

Porterfield, Amanda. 1990. Review of *Holy Feast and Holy Fast* by Carolyn Walker Bynum. *Religion* 20: 187–88.

Raheja, Gloria Goodwin, and Ann Grodzins Gold. 1994. *Listen to the Heron's Words: Reimagining Gender and Kinship in North India*. Berkeley and Los Angeles: University of California Press.

Raj, Selva. 1999. "Adapting Hindu Imagery: A Critical Look at Ritual Experiments in an Indian Catholic Ashram." Manuscript.

Ramanujan, A. K. 1983. "On Women Saints." In *The Divine Consort: Rādhā and the Goddesses of India*, edited by John Stratton Hawley and Donna Wulff. Berkeley: Berkeley Religious Studies Series, 316–24.

————. 1989. "Where Mirrors Are Windows: Toward an Anthology of Reflections." *History of Religions* 28: 188–216.

Ramaswami, N. S. 1977. *The Founding of Madras*. Bombay: Orient Longman.

Ranade, R. D. 1983. *Mysticism in India: The Poet-Saints of Maharashtra*. Albany: SUNY Press.

Ricoeur, Paul. 1969. *The Symbolism of Evil*. Translated by Emerson Buchanon. Boston: Harper and Row.

Riegelhaupt, Joyce F. 1973. "Festas and Padres: The Organization of Religious Practice in a Portuguese Parish." *American Anthropologist* 75: 835–52.

Robertson, Elizabeth. 1991. "The Corporeality of Female Sanctity in *The Life of St. Margaret*." In *Images of Sainthood in Medieval Europe*, edited by Renate Blumfeld-Kosinski and Timea Szell. Ithaca: Cornell University Press.

Rollason, David W. 1989. *Saints and Relics in Anglo-Saxon England*. Oxford: Basil Blackwell.

Rosaldo, Michelle Zimbalist, and Louise Lamphere, eds. 1974. *Woman, Culture and Society*. Stanford, Cal.: Stanford University Press.

Ruether, Rosemary Radford. 1974. *Religion and Sexism: Images of Woman in the Jewish and Christian Traditions*. New York: Simon and Schuster.

Said, Edward. 1978. *Orientalism*. New York: Vintage Books.

———. 1993. *Culture and Imperialism*. New York: Alfred A. Knopf.

Sanchiz, Pierre. 1983. "The Portuguese *Romarias*." Translated by J. Hodgin and Stephen Wilson in *Saints and Their Cults: Studies in Religious Sociology, Folklore, and History*, edited by Stephen Wilson. Cambridge: Cambridge University Press, 261–90.

Schneider, Jane. 1990. "Spirits and the Spirit of Capitalism." In *Religious Orthodoxy and Popular Faith in European Society*, edited by Ellen Badone. Princeton: Princeton University Press, 24–54.

Schulenberg, Jane Tibbetts. 1978. "Sexism and the Celestial Gynaeceum—from 500 to 1200." *Journal of Medieval History* 4: 117–33.

Scott, James. 1990. *Domination and the Art of Resistance: Hidden Transcripts*. New Haven: Yale University Press.

Siquiera, T. N. 1948. "Introduction to the Second Edition." In *Sister Alphonsa*, by K. C. Chacko 6th ed., 1990. Bharananganam, Kerala: Vice Postulator, Cause of Blessed Alphonsa, 19–21.

Smith, H. Daniel. 1969–1970. *Image India: The Hindu Way* (an eleven film series). American Institute of Indian Studies.

Smith, Jonathan Z. 1987. *To Take Place: Toward Theory in Ritual*. Chicago: University of Chicago Press.

Srinivasachary, Rao Sahib. 1939. *History of the City of Madras*. Madras: P. Vadachary.

Stace, W. T. 1961. *Mysticism and Philosophy*. London: Macmillan.

Stack, Carol B. 1974. "Sex Roles and Survival Strategies in an Urban Black Community." In *Women, Culture, and Society*, edited by Michelle Zimbalist Rosaldo and Louise Lamphere. Stanford, Cal. Stanford University Press, 113–28.

Stewart, Charles, and Rosalind Shaw, eds. 1994. *Syncretism/Anti-Syncretism: The Politics of Religious Synthesis*. London: Routledge.

Stirrat, R.L. 1994. *Power and Religiosity in a Post-Colonial Setting: Sinhala Catholics in Contemporary Sri Lanka*. Cambridge: Cambridge University Press.

Suleri, Sara. 1990. *The Rhetoric of English India*. Chicago: University of Chicago Press.

Sullivan, Lawrence E. 1990. "Seeking the End to the Primary Text or Putting an End to the Text as Primary." In *Beyond the Classics? Essays in Religious Studies and Liberal Education*. Atlanta: Scholars Press, 41–59.

Tambiah, Stanley Jeyaraja. 1984. *The Buddhist Saints of the Forest and the Cult of Amulets: A Study in Charism, Hagiography, Sectarianism and Millennial Buddhism*. Cambridge: Cambridge University Press.

Taussig, Michael. 1993. *Mimesis and Alterity: A Particular History of the Senses*. New York: Routledge.

Thekkadath, Joseph. 1982. *History of Christianity in India: From the Middle of the Sixteenth to the End of the Seventeenth Century (1542–1700)*. Bangalore: Theological Publications in India.

Thomas, Keith. 1971. *Religion and the Decline of Magic*. New York: Charles Schribner's Sons.

Thomas, M. M. 1996. *The Church's Mission and Post-Modern Humanism: Collection of Essays and Talks, 1992–1996*. Tiruvalla, Kerala: Christava Sahitya Samithi, and Delhi: Indian Society for Promoting Christian Knowledge.

Thornton, John K. 1998. *The Kongolese Saint Anthony: Dona Beatriz Kimpa Vita and the Antonian Movement, 1684–1706*. Cambridge: Cambridge University Press.

Turner, Victor, and Edith Turner. 1978. *Image and Pilgrimage in Christian Culture: Anthropological Perspectives*. New York: Columbia University Press.

Underhill, Evelyn. 1906. *The Miracles of Our Lady Saint Mary*. New York: E. P. Dutton.

———. 1930. *Mysticism: A Study in the Nature and Development of Man's Spiritual Consciousness*. New York: E. P. Dutton.

Vatican Sacred Congregation for the Oriental Churches. 1994. "Report on the State of Liturgical Reform in the Syro-Malabar Church." *Christian Orient: An Indian Journal of Eastern Christianity for Creative Theological Thinking* 15: 58–79.

Vauchez, André. 1991. "Lay People's Sanctity in Western Europe: Evolution of a Pattern (Twelfth and Thirteenth Centuries)." In *Images of Sainthood in Medieval Europe*, edited by Renate Blumenfeld-Kosinski and Timea Szell. Ithaca, N.Y.: Cornell University Press, 21–32.

Visvanathan, Susan. 1986. "Reconstructions of the Past among the Syrian Christians of Kerala." *Contributions to Indian Sociology* 20: 241–60.

———. 1993. *The Christians of Kerala: History, Belief, and Ritual among the Yakoba*. New York: Oxford University Press.

Viswanathan, Gauri. 1996. "Beyond Orientalism": Syncretism and the Politics of Knowledge." *Stanford Electronic Humanities Review* 5/1: Contested Polities.

———. 1998. *Outside the Fold: Conversion, Modernity, and Belief*. Princeton: Princeton University Press.

Visweswaran, Kamala. 1994. *Fictions of Feminist Ethnography*. Minneapolis: University of Minnesota Press.

Wadley, Susan Snow. 1975. *Shakti: Power in the Conceptual Structure of Karimpur Religion*. Series in Social, Cultural, and Linguistic Anthropology 2. Chicago: Department of Anthropology.

———. 1993. "Women in the Hindu Tradition." In *Women in India: Two Perspectives*, edited by Doranne Jacobson and Susan Wadley. Columbia, Mo.: South Asia Publications, 111–36.

Wagner, Roy. 1981. *The Invention of Culture*. Chicago: University of Chicago Press.

Ware, Kallistos. 1964. *The Orthodox Church*. Baltimore: Penguin Books.

Weber, Max. 1946. "The Social Psychology of World Religions." In *From Max Weber: Essays in Sociology*, translated and edited by H. H. Gerth and C. Wright Mills. New York: Oxford University Press, 267–301.

Weinstein, Donald, and Rudolph Bell. 1982. *Saints and Society: The Two Worlds of Western Christendom, 1000–1700*. Chicago: University of Chicago Press.

Wolf, Margery. 1974. "Chinese Women: Old Skills in a New Context." In *Women, Culture, and Society*, edited by Michelle Zimbalist Rosaldo and Louise Lamphere. Stanford, Cal.: Stanford University Press, 157–72.

Wood, Charles T. 1981. "The Doctor's Dilemma." *Speculum* 56: 710–27.

Woodward, Kenneth. 1990. *Making Saints: How the Catholic Church Determines Who Becomes a Saint, Who Doesn't, and Why*. New York: Simon and Schuster.

Wyschogrod, Edith. 1990. *Saints and Postmodernism: Revisioning Moral Philosophy*. Chicago: University of Chicago Press.

Young, Robert J. C. 1995. *Colonial Desire: Hybridity in Theory, Culture and Race*. London: Routledge.

Younger, Paul. (forthcoming). *Playing Host to Deity: Festival Religion in the South Indian Traditions*. New York: Oxford University Press.

Zelliot, Eleanor. 1987a. "Eknath's Bharuds: The Sant as Link Between Cultures." In *The Sants: Studies in a Devotional Tradition of India*, edited by Karine Schomer and W. H. McLeod. Berkeley: Berkeley Religious Studies Series, 91–100.

———. 1987b. "A Historical Introduction to the Warkari Movement." In *Palkhi: An Indian Pilgrimage*, edited by Digambar Balkrishna Mokashi. Albany: SUNY Press, 31–50.

Zimmer, Heinrich. 1946. *Myths and Symbols in Indian Art and Civilization*. New York: Pantheon Books.

Index

Portuguese, 42
saints and, 16, 92, 94, 99, 100, 101
secular, 130
spiritual, 132, 134
of Thomas, Saint, 98
See also sacred power
power relations, 172n. 39
prasādam, 106, 191n. 53
Presbyterians, 7
processions, 56, 67, 68, 83, 105, 106
prophecy
and Alphonsa, Sister, 120, 137–38
Protestants, 7–8, 13
Pūram festival, 55
Puthencoor Syrians, 166n. 15
Puthupally, 58

racism, 20
Raheja, Gloria, 142
Ramanujan, A.K., 122–23, 133
Rao, Narayana, 124
rationalism, 82, 84
reciprocity, 112, 113
Reformation, 42, 93, 112, 173n. 51, 189n. 36
Catholic, 182n. 24, 185n. 37
relics, 30, 100
religion, 5, 14–15, 92, 93, 164n. 4
local versus institutional, 90–94
Western, 27
religious art, 111, 183n. 29
religious exclusivity, 62–64
religious movements, 130, 133
religious music, 55, 67
religious pluralism, 3, 4
religious practices, 91, 92, 93
religious symbols, 112
religious traditions, 34, 66, 75, 106
cultural context and, 67
indigenous, 28, 31
terms and, 115
Western, 28
religious unity, 65–67
religious values, 92
Renaissance, 185n. 37
renunciation, 16
Ricoeur, Paul, 96
rites, 76, 79, 113
ritual items, 177n. 20
rituals, 68, 73, 76, 113, 114, 123
Roman Catholics. *See* Catholics; Roman

Romanization
of Alphonsa's cult, 19, 20, 27
of Indian Christianity, 20
of saint cults, 50
of Saint George Syrian Catholic Church, 41
romanticists, 22, 24
Rome, 7, 28, 31
rooster offerings. *See* offerings: rooster
roses, 176n. 18
R.S.S., 59–60
Ruby of Cochin: An Indian Jewish Woman Remembers (Daniel and Johnson), 183n. 30
Ruskin, John, 23

sacrality, 16, 93, 94
Sacred Heart Sisters, 150
sacred materiality, 98–101
sacred power, 44–45, 97, 156, 157, 159
ambivalent, 16, 98, 104
materially accessible, 88, 158
saints and, 94, 95, 100
symbols of, 112
women and, 134
sacred sibling stories, 15, 52–87, 157
and communal accord, 58–60
and festivals, 55–57
and George, Saint, 49
local, 80, 81, 82
rivalries in, 57–58
sacred versus profane, 79, 161
Sai Baba, 177n. 27
Said, Edward, 20, 21–22, 23, 84–85, 141
saint cults, 15, 176n. 16, 180n. 9
Hindu influence on, 88
Indian, 182n. 23
origins of, 29–30, 38, 142–55
Romanization of, 19, 20, 27, 50
traditions of, 45
saint-deity relationship, 157, 175n. 13
saint-devotee relationship, 60, 97, 101–4, 113, 159, 162
Saint George Cathedral (Madras), 173n. 44
Saint George Church (Aruvithura), 40, 41, 43, 48
Saint George Church (Madras), 173n. 44
Saint George Church (Puthupally), 43, 44, 55–56, 71, 76, 104, 105, 175n. 11, 178n. 32
sainthood, 9, 17, 42, 97, 116, 180n. 3